AN INTRODUCTION TO CATHOLIC ETHICS SINCE VATICAN II

This introduction provides a comprehensive overview of the development of Catholic ethics in the wake of the Second Vatican Council (1962–1965), an event widely considered crucial to the reconciliation of the Catholic Church and the modern world. Andrew Kim investigates Catholic responses to questions of moral theology in all four principal areas: Catholic social teaching, natural law, virtue ethics, and bioethics. In addition to discussing contemporary controversies surrounding abortion, contraception, labor rights, exploitation of the poor, and just war theory, he explores the historical sources of the Catholic worldview. Beginning with the moral vision revealed through the person of Jesus Christ and continuing with elaborations on this vision from figures such as Augustine and Aquinas, this volume elucidates the continuity of the Catholic moral tradition. Its balance of complexity and accessibility makes it an ideal resource for both students of theology and general readers.

ANDREW KIM is Assistant Professor of Theology at Walsh University. His articles have appeared in *Studies in Christian Ethics* and the *Journal of Moral Theology*.

D1475334

AN INTRODUCTION TO CATHOLIC ETHICS SINCE VATICAN II

ANDREW KIM

Walsh University

CAMBRIDGE
UNIVERSITY PRESS

CAMBRIDGE
UNIVERSITY PRESS

32 Avenue of the Americas, New York, NY 10013-2473, USA

Cambridge University Press is part of the University of Cambridge.

It furthers the University's mission by disseminating knowledge in the pursuit of
education, learning, and research at the highest international levels of excellence.

www.cambridge.org
Information on this title: www.cambridge.org/9781107446564

© Andrew Kim 2015

First published 2015

A catalog record for this publication is available from the British Library.

Library of Congress Cataloging in Publication Data
Kim, Andrew. 1980–
An introduction to Catholic ethics since Vatican II / Andrew Kim.
pages cm
Includes bibliographical references and index.
ISBN 978-1-107-08465-0 (hardback) – ISBN 978-1-107-44656-4 (pbk.)
1. Christian ethics–Catholic authors.   2. Christian sociology–Catholic Church.
3. Bioethics–Religious aspects–Catholic Church.   4. Catholic Church–Doctrines.   I. Title.
BJ1248.K53 2015
241′.042–dc23   2014043700

ISBN 978-1-107-08465-0 Hardback
ISBN 978-1-107-44656-4 Paperback

For Caitlin

"Behold, I make all things new."
Revelation 21:5

Contents

Foreword

With this book, *An Introduction to Catholic Ethics since Vatican II*, Andrew Kim explodes onto the scene of the discipline of moral theology with a wise, hospitable, and challenging overview of Catholic ethics. The book's title aptly names two contexts where Kim makes an important and successful contribution, and I'll allow these to structure my thoughts in this foreword.

"Catholic ethics since Vatican II": By all accounts, Catholic moral theology was in need of renewal at the time of the Second Vatican Council in the 1960s. The key figure in that post-conciliar renewal is Fr. Servais Pinckaers, O.P. In important ways the ongoing project of renewal is a further execution of the characteristic features of his work. With this book Kim joins the ranks of those of us who seek to join and advance that renewal. Allow me to identify four features of this book that make it exemplary of renewal in Catholic moral theology since Vatican II in the vein of Pinckaers's work.

First, as explicitly mentioned in the oft-quoted *Optatam totius* no. 16 call for the perfection of moral theology, and as particularly evident in the work of Pinckaers, Catholic ethics must be nourished by Scripture. This is no small task, as it is easy for moralists to merely proof text Scripture to adorn their predetermined conclusions. Not so for Kim. This book is replete with nourishment from Scripture. The chapter on justice, Chapter 7, relies nearly wholly on the Old and New Testaments. At key points in numerous chapters, Scriptural passages play formative roles in the presentation of the topic at hand. Examples include Genesis 18 on war, the Prodigal Son on justice, the Good Samaritan on universal human dignity, Job on suffering, the Magnificat on preferential option for the poor, and, by far my favorite, a reflection on the Annunciation in his treatment of commercial surrogacy. These passages are wonderfully integrated, doing true illuminative work in the analysis at hand. As we in

Catholic moral theology await a definitive post-conciliar methodological treatment of Scripture and moral theology, this book serves as an example of what such a method would look like in action.

Second, *Optatam totius* no. 16 mentions the faithful's vocation in Christ and their bearing fruit for the world. Balancing these two indicates another crucial theme in the renewal of moral theology, and again one prevalent in the work of Pinckaers and now Kim: attention to how Catholic ethics can account both for how morality is accessible to all in the tradition of natural law and for how it is elevated and supernaturally perfected in the light of revelation. This dual focus dominates Kim's book. It is methodologically explicit in each of the book's four parts. It is equally evident in the scattered test cases he treats, which contain conclusions accessible to all and yet further informed by Catholic theological commitments. Similar to Pinckaers, Kim succeeds in hospitably appealing to all, and yet doing so in a manner that refuses to suppress rigorously theological claims.

Third, Kim evidences the stereotypical Pinckaers insistence that rules are important for the moral life, yet they are not ends in themselves. They orient the person to happiness. Absent this orientation toward fullness of life, understood supernaturally yet also in a manner that includes natural flourishing, rules (especially pre–Vatican II) had come to resemble unintelligible taboos. Kim has no problem taking firm stands on matters such as the direct killing of the innocent or unjust labor practices. Yet rules, even the absolute ones, are always explained in a manner that makes them intelligibly oriented toward human flourishing. His readers may agree or disagree with the positions he presents, but they are hospitably invited into and equipped for debate over those rules by his manner of explicating his positions.

Fourth, in the post-conciliar period Catholic moral theologians have become increasingly aware that all ethics is social ethics. Despite a traditional separation of individual and social ethics, evident in how seminarian courses are taught and how faculty are commonly hired, we are increasingly aware of how this dichotomy is false. This point is famously presented in Benedict XVI's encyclical *Caritas in veritate*, widely regarded as part of Catholic social teaching and yet addressing "individual" issues such as contraception. Kim's book also evidences a refusal to perpetuate this dichotomy. Two of the book's four parts treat, in turn, a traditionally "social" topic (just war) and a traditionally "individual" topic (bioethics). Not only does his book contain both types of issues; Kim manages to treat each in a manner attentive to both refined action theory and more communal considerations.

For these four reasons, Kim's wonderfully lucid book is rightly understood as part of the ongoing tradition of renewal of "Catholic ethics since Vatican II." Before turning to the second way that Kim's book is especially timely, however, it should be noted that Kim does not simply evidence renewal in Catholic moral theology. He also contributes to the ongoing advancement of that project. Once again, Kim joins a cadre of students of Pinckaers who further develop trajectories named by the Belgian Dominican but that were left open for further development. This is particularly evident in Kim's work on the connection of the virtues. Readers of Pinckaers recall that famous diagram in *Sources of Christian Ethics* where the virtues (along with the gifts) are presented together and described as an organic whole. Kim's early career research has largely been a plumbing of the wisdom of this insight, especially the way the connectivity of the virtues illuminates how we understand moral development. It is because Kim not only evidences but also contributes to the renewal of moral theology since Vatican II that we will be hearing much more from him in the decades to come.

"An introduction to Catholic ethics": Kim's book is best understood not only in the context of renewal of Catholic moral theology in the universal Church since Vatican II; it is also fittingly understood as an introduction to moral theology that is perfectly fit for the context of American Catholic higher education fifty years after that council. In the previous discussion, I placed Kim's book in the tradition of Servais Pinckaers, O.P. Let me now do the same with one of Kim's favorite authors, C.S. Lewis. It is no small compliment to say that with his book, *An Introduction to Catholic Ethics since Vatican II*, Kim admirably follows in the footsteps of this twentieth-century giant with a lucid and accessible yet profound introduction to inquiry into the life of discipleship that is Catholic moral theology. Yet that is precisely what he does. Let me once again offer four reasons why Kim's book is a timely and wise introductory text in the vein of Lewis.

First, Kim's book joins a growing number of introductory theological texts that have appeared in the last decade. Whence the need for such texts? As any university teacher today knows, even at the collegiate level we find ourselves teaching students who are increasingly unformed in the Christian faith. Whereas a previous generation sought to distance academic theology from more basic catechesis, Kim's generation rightly recognizes that the former, while distinct from the latter, is also dependent on the latter. Absent a grasp of the basic teachings of Christian morality, any higher-level moral analysis proceeds as incoherently as the post-apocalyptic scientific inquiry in Alasdair MacIntyre's troubling *After Virtue* thought experiment. Therefore, Kim hospitably welcomes his readers into the tradition of Catholic moral theology in an accessible and engaging manner. He manages to introduce foundational topics such as the soul and the history of virtue in a few short paragraphs each. In Chapter 2 alone he successfully introduces students to topics as basic as natural law, grace perfecting nature, and the role of authority. What makes any introduction successful is not simply accurately describing core themes, but presenting them "coherently," fitting together as parts of a whole. This Kim achieves masterfully. He even includes helpful pedagogical aids such as a list of prominent figures in the history of moral thought, as well as summary questions and terms. Teachers and students alike will find this an invaluable introductory text in effectively supplying intellectual foundations for theological reflection, which are often missing today.

A second reason why Kim's text is successful as an introduction is its seamless integration of what I call "cases and bases." Any teacher knows the challenges of presenting both foundational material and practical examples. Do too much of foundations first and leave the concrete cases to the end, and the former is unclear and easily lost when attending to the latter. Yet without some grasp of the foundational material, examination of cases proceeds blindly. Kim manages to face this challenge by seamless integration of foundational material with test cases, from the start of the book until the end. Cases range from sweatshop labor, to female genital mutilation, to use of drones, to abortion and contraception, to commercial surrogacy. There are a plethora of concrete cases through which to explore the lucid foundational material presented by Kim.

Third, Kim is representative of many in his generation by refusing to rest content in a predictable left-leaning or right-leaning political agenda. The final part on bioethics addresses contraception, abortion, and surrogacy in a manner that would please those on the right. His positions, however, would as frequently please those on the left, as in his treatments of the use of drones, sweatshop labor, and female genital mutilation. It is not merely the positions Kim takes, however, that make him unable to be easily placed on the right or left. It is also his willingness to engage and appeal to the kernels of truth in rival positions. Although firmly positioned, he is not ideological in the sense of predictably standing on one side while unable to see any truth in the other side. This quality makes his introductory text very appealing to his target audience.

Finally, Kim's book is an effective introduction because it is thoroughly "postmodern." There are of course many ways to be "postmodern," but what they all have in common is a rejection of the axiomatic claim of modernity that moral truths are not only accessible to reason without the aid of authority but can also be presented in a manner that compels assent on the basis of the evidence of the claims themselves. As thinkers ranging from MacIntyre to Stout to Rorty have shown, this Enlightenment project has failed and thus we are "postmodernity." Of course, different thinkers draw different conclusions from that failure. To some, "postmodern" means that there is no truth. To others, such as Kim who exemplifies a MacIntyrian method of tradition-constituted inquiry, the rightful recognition that modern Enlightenment foundationalism has failed to secure moral truth does not mean there is no truth, but only that it cannot be "secured" in such a manner. Instead, different traditions of thought need to be taken on their own terms and placed in conversation with one another. In such a method people do not comprehend moral truths by inexorable deduction from compelling foundations; rather, people are persuaded of such truths by appealing to the best insights of their own traditions. This approach frees one to be positioned and requires him or her to more humbly engage others on terms accessible to them. This is exactly the method of Kim in his book, accounting for his firmly positioned and yet humbly engaging tone as described in the previous observation.

Kim's stated task is to "provide a comprehensive introduction to the discipline of moral theology in the post-conciliar period." In the tradition of Fr. Servais Pinckaers, O.P., Kim exemplifies and advances the project that is the renewal of Catholic moral theology after Vatican II. Similar to his mentor C.S. Lewis, Kim succeeds in providing an effective introduction largely because of his accurate grasp of what readers in his context are yearning for and his uncanny ability to deliver it to them. As I write this week of the Easter celebration of Jesus the Good Shepherd, it fills me with joy and pride to see my former student follow in the footsteps of the Master, Christ the Teacher, and lovingly guide his readers toward the fullness of life to which we are all called.

William C. Mattison III
The Catholic University of America
May 2014

Preface

All this is said simply in order to make clear what kind of book I was trying to write.

C.S. Lewis, *Mere Christianity*

Throughout this book, I frequently refer to the "Catholic moral tradition," "Catholic moral theology," and "Catholic ethics." However, at no point do I offer a sustained analysis regarding the meanings of these terms or how they relate to each other. Allow me, therefore, to use this preface as an opportunity to address these omissions for the sake of adding clarity to what is contained in the following pages.

With the term "Catholic moral tradition" I have in mind the authoritative moral teachings of the hierarchical Magisterium. These teachings are what they are independent of whether one agrees with them. For example, the Catholic moral tradition holds that one has a moral duty to help the poor. Someone may disagree with this claim, but it remains a Catholic teaching just the same. "Catholic moral theology," on the other hand, refers to continuous reflection on the contents of the Catholic moral tradition. The job of the Catholic moral theologian is to examine the contents of the tradition in the light of reason and revelation in order to assist in bringing out its interior meaning, beauty, intelligibility, and coherence for the sake of communicating it to a wider audience and applying its insights to particular contexts and cases. Thus, the discipline of Catholic moral theology is deeply rooted in the resources of the Catholic moral tradition. Put negatively, Catholic moral theology divorced from the Catholic moral tradition ceases to be Catholic moral theology.

Finally, "Catholic ethics" refers to the formal academic discipline that puts both the tradition and the reflection on the tradition into sincere and prudent conversation with rival theories and alternative points of view, thus exposing both to external critique. To subject Catholic moral theology to academic scrutiny outside of the tradition, however, does not mean that the moral theologian must bracket or ignore his or her own faith commitments. To the contrary, these commitments can nourish intellectually rigorous pursuits of truth and robust dialogue; the view that faith is for some reason hazardous to intellectual discourse stems only from a peculiarly modern prejudice against the supernatural.

Hopefully these definitions help explain why in the following pages I refer much more to the "Catholic moral tradition" than to "Catholic moral theology" or "Catholic ethics." The reason why I do so is because Catholic moral theology and ethics are what the book is doing. I am attempting to articulate key features in the development of the Catholic moral tradition in the post-conciliar period by reflecting on these features in a manner that responds constructively to rival points of view. The term "Catholic ethics" is employed in the title of this book because, as I am defining it, Catholic ethics already entails a grounding in the Catholic moral tradition as approached through the medium of moral theology.

A problem here arises, however, insofar as Catholic moral theologians are not all in agreement with each other relative to the contents or even, in some cases, the authority of the Catholic moral tradition. In response to this problem, I have attempted to cast as wide a net as possible without becoming entangled in the kind of minutiae and technical debates among moral theologians that would detract from the broad strokes presentation a comprehensive introduction requires. Such diversions would also not be of much benefit to the average reader.

At the same time, I do not veil my own positions on disputed matters. I wrote this book out of a desire to introduce the reader to the development of the Catholic moral tradition in the post-conciliar period in a manner informed by the continuity in sanctity that runs through all of the tradition as a kind of golden chord weaving throughout the whole of the Church's life and binding it all together. It is a golden chord woven by Christ with strands of patience and mercy. I hope this is communicated in the following pages.

Acknowledgments

"What has Athens to do with Jerusalem?" Tertullian's problem vexes me still, for the fault lines of common sense do seem to demarcate them as rival cities. Athens is the city of questions. Jerusalem is the city of answers. Athens is the city of searching. Jerusalem is the city of finding.

Let us, for the moment, accept the hypothesis that one cannot attain dual citizenship in both cities. If this were true, then I suppose I would need to begin by acknowledging those who helped me learn how to be a citizen of Jerusalem. These are, first and foremost, my parents and first teachers of the faith, Jhin and Becky Kim. My mother taught me the common doctrines of Christianity. My father taught me by his example. During my childhood, neither one of them was Catholic. Indeed, someday I should like to inquire further as to how the children of Baptist ministers and theologians should find and marry each other as Evangelicals and later have an only child who, as an adult, became a Roman Catholic. At any rate, it is from my parents that I received my first catechism, and for this I am grateful.

It was at the age of twenty-seven that I became Roman Catholic. In *The Seven Storey Mountain*, Thomas Merton wrote of his first experience visiting Corpus Christi Church on 121st Street in New York City. My first experience was similar. For it was at Corpus Christi that I underwent the adult confirmation process while I was an MA student at Union Theological Seminary across the street. My education at Corpus Christi was, in many ways, my first formal introduction to the Catholic faith and the formal study of Catholic theology. The late Fr. William Wizeman introduced me to Catholic spirituality. Msgr. Kevin Sullivan first explained Catholic social teaching to me. Fr. Raymond Rafferty taught my R.C.I.A. class, and he oversaw my confirmation and marriage, and the baptism of my son. I am grateful to these individuals for presenting the faith to me in an accurate and compelling fashion, in both word and deed.

At this point, I should like to acknowledge those who helped form me as a citizen of Athens. When I was an undergraduate, Dr. Ian Lising, Dr. Jason Niedleman, and Dr. Stephen Sayles taught me the skills of rhetoric, critical thinking, and research. When I was an MA student, Dr. Paul Knitter and Dr. John McGuckin helped me learn how to apply these skills to the discipline of theology. The professors at the Catholic University of America, who facilitated my doctoral studies, further developed these skills. In particular, I would like to thank Dr. Joseph Benson, Dr. Joseph Capizzi, Dr. John Grabowski, Fr. Brian Johnstone, Fr. Joseph Komonchak, and Dr. Tarmo Toom. Finally, I wish to thank my colleagues at Walsh University who continue to challenge me and help me grow as a scholar. In particular, I extend my thanks to Dr. Brad Beach, Dr. Koop Berry, Dr. Ann Caplea, Dr. Chad Gerber, Dr. Ty Hawkins, Dr. Ute Lahaie, Fr. Patrick Manning, Dr. Chris Seeman, Rabbi John Spitzer, Dr. Joseph Torma, and Dr. Donald Wallenfang. I would also like to offer my gratitude to Dr. Laurence Bove for his dedication to *Gaudium et spes* as a cornerstone of the university curriculum. Finally, thanks to Richard and Terry Jusseaume and to the Brothers of Christian Instruction for their commitment to Walsh University and the principles on which it was founded.

I suggested earlier that we accept the hypothesis that one cannot have dual citizenship in both Athens and Jerusalem. Happily, this hypothesis is false. Indeed, all of the people I just listed who instructed me in faith also taught me to think; all those who helped teach me to think also had an impact on my beliefs. This is preeminently true of my doctoral director, advisor, and friend, Dr. William C. Mattison III. By his example I was given a model of how to be a Catholic moral theologian. For this, and for much else, I owe him a tremendous debt of gratitude.

Without the kinds of training and mentoring I received from the people mentioned heretofore, I would not have been able to write this book. Additionally, there are several people whom I should like to thank for contributing to the development of this project. Lt. Col. Donald Bletz, and Uwe and SunHee Gertz have always shown me enormous personal support and have helped form me as a writer and as a scholar; to them I extend my love and gratitude. While on the subject of my writing, this book benefited greatly from the observations of my graduate research assistant, Mallory Slocum. The book also profited from my Theology 203 course at Walsh University who, in Spring 2014, read through the manuscript and offered me feedback. In particular, I would like to thank Ryan Bagley, Thomas Betzler, Sara Bickett, Brook Clark, Jen Harig, Jessica Jewett, Isabelle Lahaie, Morgan McDermott,

Mary Modena, Vicki Pierce, Abby Robertson, Jared Topp, and Taylor Warner for their contributions. This book also benefited from the observations of the external readers for Cambridge University Press to whom I offer thanks. Finally, I wish to express my deepest appreciation to Laura Morris and Alexandra Poreda for the support they have given to me as an author and to this project throughout the publication process.

While all of the people recognized heretofore are worthy of my gratitude, there is none more so than my wife, Caitlin, to whom this book is dedicated. Although I am somewhat ashamed to admit it, I suspect that were it not for her presence in my life, the delight I take in writing books, teaching classes, and everything else would quickly vanish. For Aquinas, the virtuous person is capable of discerning the right ways to act across the various domains relevant to the moral life with ease and consistency. This describes Caitlin, who is both my wife and the love of my life; thanks also to our children – Theo, Lucy, Zoë, and Phoebe – who fill our lives with joy.

In closing, while Tertullian's query still beleaguers me, I have come to think that not only is it possible to have dual citizenship in both Athens and Jerusalem; it actually makes one a better citizen of both. Athens can learn from Jerusalem's faith; Jerusalem grows by attending to the questions posed by Athens. This book was written with the citizens of both cities in mind. Thank you to the people mentioned earlier for helping me write it.

Abbreviations

AN	Pope John Paul I, *Angelus, September 10* (Vatican City: Libreria Editrice Vaticana, 1978).
CA	Augustine, *Contra Academicos* (Against the Academics), Johannes Quasten and Joseph C. Plumpe, eds., tr. John J. O'Meara (Westminster, MD: The Newman Press, 1950).
CCC	*The Catechism of the Catholic Church*, 2nd ed. (Vatican City, Libreria Editrice Vaticana, 1997).
CIV	Pope Benedict XVI, *Caritas in veritate*, Encyclical Letter addressed by the Supreme Pontiff Pope Benedict XVI to the Bishops, Priests, and Deacons, Men and Women Religious, the Lay Faithful, and All People of Good Will on Integral Human Development in Charity and Truth (Vatican City: Libreria Editrice Vaticana, 2009).
CONF	Augustine, *Confessions*, tr. Henry Chadwick (Oxford: Oxford University Press, 1991).
DCE	Pope Benedict XVI, *Deus caritas est*, Encyclical Letter addressed by the Supreme Pontiff Pope Benedict XVI to the Bishops, Priests, and Deacons, Men and Women Religious, and All the Lay Faithful on Christian Love (Vatican City: Libreria Editrice Vaticana, 2005).
DDC	Augustine, *De doctrina Christiana* (On Christian Teaching), tr. R.P.H. Green (Oxford: Oxford University Press, 2008).
DF	Thomas Aquinas, *De fraternis correctionis* (On Brotherly Correction), E.M. Atkins and Thomas Williams, eds., tr. E.M. Atkins (Cambridge: Cambridge University Press, 2005).
DM	Augustine, *De moribus ecclesiae catholicae et de moribus Manichaeorum* (On the Morals of the Catholic Church

	Against the Manicheans), CSEL 90. J.B. Bauer, ed. (Vienna, 1992).
DP	Ambrose, *De Paradiso* (On Paradise).
DPer	Congregation for the Doctrine of the Faith, *Dignitas Personae,* Instruction on Certain Bioethical Questions (Vatican City: Libreria Editrice Vaticana, 2008).
DV	Congregation for the Doctrine of the Faith, *Donum veritatis* (Vatican City: Libreria Editrice Vaticana, 1990).
DVCard	Thomas Aquinas, *De virtutibus cardinalibus* (On the Cardinal Virtues), E.M. Atkins and Thomas Williams, eds., tr. E.M. Atkins (Cambridge: Cambridge University Press, 2005).
DVComm	Thomas Aquinas, *De virtutibus communis* (On the General Virtues), E.M. Atkins and Thomas Williams, eds., tr. E.M. Atkins (Cambridge: Cambridge University Press, 2005).
DVer	Vatican II, *Dei Verbum,* Dogmatic Constitution on Divine Revelation, tr. Austin Flannery (Dublin: Dominican Publications, 1996).
EG	Pope Francis, *Evangelii gaudium*, Apostolic Exhortation of the Holy Father Francis to the Bishops, Clergy, Consecrated Persons, and the Lay Faithful on the Proclamation of the Gospel in Today's Word (Vatican City: Libreria Editrice Vaticana, 2013).
EN	Augustine, *Enchiridion* (CCEL 78).
EP167	Augustine, Letter 167 to Jerome (CSEL 44).
ERD	United States Conference of Catholic Bishops, *Ethical and Religious Directives for Catholic Health Care Services*, 5th ed. (Washington, DC: United States Conference of Catholic Bishops, 2009).
EV	Pope John Paul II, *Evangelium vitae*, Encyclical Letter addressed by the Supreme Pontiff Pope John Paul II to the Bishops, Priests, and Deacons, Men and Women Religious, Lay Faithful, and All People of Good Will on the Value and Inviolability of Human Life (Vatican City: Libreria Editrice Vaticana, 1995).
FR	Pope John Paul II, *Fides et ratio*, Encyclical Letter of the Supreme Pontiff John Paul II to the Bishops of the Catholic Church on the Relationship between Faith and Reason (Vatican City: Libreria Editrice Vaticana, 1998).

GS	Vatican II, *Gaudium et spes*, Pastoral Constitution on the Church in the Modern World, tr. Austin Flannery (Dublin: Dominican Publications, 1996).
HS	Pope John XXIII, *Humanae salutis* (Vatican City: Libreria Editrice Vaticana, 1961).
HV	Pope Paul VI, *Humanae vitae*, Encyclical Letter addressed by the Supreme Pontiff Pope Paul VI to His Venerable Brothers, the Patriarch, Archbishops, Bishops, and Other Local Ordinaries in Peace and Communion with the Apostolic See, to the Clergy and Faithful of the Whole Catholic World, and to All Men of Good Will on the Regulation of Birth (Vatican City: Libreria Editrice Vaticana, 1968).
LF	Pope Francis, *Lumen fidei*, Encyclical Letter addressed by the Supreme Pontiff Pope Francis to All the Bishops, Priests, and Deacons, Consecrated Persons, and the Lay Faithful on Faith (Vatican City: Libreria Editrice Vaticana, 2013).
LUC	Ambrose, *Expositio evangelii secundum Lucam* (Commentary on the Gospel according to Luke).
MC	Pope Paul VI, *Marialis cultus*, Apostolic Exhortation of the Holy Father Paul VI to the Bishops, Clergy, Consecrated Persons, and the Lay Faithful on the Right Ordering and Development of Devotion to the Blessed Virgin Mary (Vatican City: Libreria Editrice Vaticana, 1974).
MD	Pope John Paul II, *Mulieris dignitatem*, Apostolic Letter of the Supreme Pontiff on the Dignity and Vocation of Women on the Occasion of the Marian Year (Vatican City: Libreria Editrice Vaticana, 1998).
NA	Vatican II, *Nostra aetate*, Declaration on the Relation of the Church to Non-Christian Religions, tr. Austin Flannery (Dublin: Dominican Publications, 1996).
NAB	*The Catholic Bible New American Bible Revised Edition* (Oxford: Oxford University Press, 2007).
NE	Aristotle, *Nicomachean Ethics*, 2nd ed., tr. Terence Irwin (Indianapolis: Hackett Publishing Company, 1999).
SENT	Thomas Aquinas, *Commentary on the Sentences* in *St. Thomas Aquinas on Love and Charity: Readings from the Commentary on the Sentences of Peter Lombard*, tr. Peter A. Kwasniewski (Washington, DC: CUA Press, 2008).

SS   Pope Benedict XVI, *Spe salvi*, Encyclical Letter addressed
             by the Supreme Pontiff Pope Benedict XVI to the Bishops,
             Priests, and Deacons, Men and Women Religious, and All
             the Lay Faithful on Christian Hope (Vatican City: Libreria
             Editrice Vaticana, 2007).

ST   Thomas Aquinas, *Summa Theologiae,* tr. Fathers of the
             English Dominican Province (New York: Benziger, 1948).

VS   Pope John Paul II, *Veritatis splendor*, Encyclical Letter
             addressed by the Supreme Pontiff Pope John Paul II to All
             the Bishops of the Catholic Church Regarding Certain
             Fundamental Questions of the Church's Moral Teaching
             (Vatican City: Libreria Editrice Vaticana, 1993).

Introduction

> While distrustful souls see nothing but darkness falling upon the face
> of the earth, we prefer to restate our confidence in our Savior, who
> has not left the world he redeemed.
>
> St. John XXIII, *Humanae salutis* no. 4

On December 25, 1961, John XXIII solemnly convoked the Second
Vatican Ecumenical Council by promulgating the Apostolic Constitution,
Humanae salutis (Of Human Salvation). In this document, the Pope calls
attention to "a crisis happening within society."[1] It is, in several important
respects, an ethical crisis, in response to which the Church is to discern
"the signs of the times" with a view toward elucidating Christian hope
to a world that has grown forlorn in the face of so much despair.[2] Fifty
years after the conclusion of the council, therefore, it is worth reexamin-
ing the ethical dimensions of the crisis itself as well as responses to it,
which have both emerged from, and contributed to, the development of
the Catholic moral tradition in the post-conciliar period. The purpose
of this introduction is to situate the chapters of this book in the context of
the aforementioned task.

This introduction unfolds over four sections. The first section attempts
to provide a general definition of the crisis of contemporary ethics as
understood from the standpoint of the Catholic moral tradition. The next
section examines key features of the Catholic response to this crisis. The
third section draws from the preceding sections in order to explicate the
preliminary goals and governing objectives of this book and to explain
the correlation between them and its respective chapters. The final section
clarifies the relationship of the structure of this book to the aforesaid goals
and objectives.

---

[1] *HS* no. 2.
[2] *HS* no. 4; the "signs of the times" reference is to Matthew 16:4.

THE CRISIS

The term "crisis" refers to an unstable or dangerous state of affairs. So understood, the crisis of contemporary ethics is the result of the convergence of three distinct influences: postmodernism, liberalism, and secularism.[3] This section examines the manner in which these forces have helped bring about the universe of howling moral confusion in which we currently find ourselves. At bottom, ethics is concerned with the following three questions: What is true? What is good? And who is my neighbor? Postmodernism problematizes the first question, liberalism the second, and secularism the third. I begin with postmodernism.

The French literary theorist and philosopher, Jean-François Lyotard, understood postmodernism as demolishing the assumption that reason can arrive at truths beyond one's own making.[4] Absent such truths, humanity is left only with rival narratives from which we derive meaning. Now, if there is no truth, then, as John Paul II stated, "all positions are equally valid."[5] Do you see the problem? Suppose that one day a very good friend of yours suddenly and inexplicably began to treat you as his or her worst enemy and you had no idea why. The first thing you would do is search your memory for an explanation. If that failed, then you'd likely start asking your mutual friends if they knew why this was happening. One friend tells you not to worry, that it has nothing to do with you or anything you did. However, another friend tells you that the original friend is indeed very upset with something you did, but he or she won't say what. The problem is that each of those positions cannot simultaneously be true. Either you did something to upset your friend or you did not. The fact that your other friends have rival points of view on the matter is quite beside the point. You just want to know the truth so you can set things right with your friend.

Another problem with postmodernism is that is creates a "lack of confidence in truth."[6] If all of your friends offer you different explanations of why your other friend has abruptly turned on you, then you'll come to distrust all of them. Even if one of their explanations is the right one, it will be drowned out in the conflicting sea of opinions. I have used a

---

[3] See Nicanor Pier Giorgio Austriaco, O.P., *Biomedicine and Beatitude: An Introduction to Catholic Bioethics* (Washington, DC: CUA Press, 2011), 247–76.

[4] See Jean-François Lyotard, *The Postmodern Condition: A Report on Knowledge* (Minneapolis: University of Minnesota Press, 1984).

[5] *FR* no. 5.

[6] *FR* no. 5.

simple example, but something like this has been taking place with respect to ethical questions for quite some time and on a much larger scale. Ultimately, a true worldview is a prerequisite for an authentic morality. Yet, people today seem resigned to give up the quest for truth, accepting as true the disappointing claim that there is no truth. This leaves us forlorn. As Augustine cautioned, the denial of the possibility of truth causes us to give up on the diligent search for truth and even to "turn away from the desire for searching."[7] Thus, the epistemological crisis of the present age: it is no use asking "what is true?" in a world without truth.

The second factor contributing to the present crisis of ethics is liberalism. By "liberalism," I mean an understanding of freedom divorced from the pursuit of moral goodness.[8] According to this view, moral goodness is reduced to what a given society, or even a given individual, happens to find worthwhile and admirable. Freedom, then, is reduced to the uninterrupted pursuit of that which one finds pleasing. The problem is that this conception of freedom is false; it is the freedom of a man lost in the wilderness without a compass. He is free to go in whatever direction he pleases, but he would much prefer the freedom to find his way home. We all know what it is like to think that something is good only to find out later that we were deceived. Thus, we try to discern between that which is really good and that which is only apparently good, but liberalism paralyzes this discernment. It reduces moral goodness to a private opinion and leaves us in a state of wandering. We lack confidence as to whether moral goodness exists and, even if it does, whether it is attainable.

Finally, contemporary society is secular; faith is regarded as a kind of private sentimentality that one is to keep to oneself.[9] It does not have a constructive role to play with respect to informing social and political life. Whereas liberalism was supposed to give us greater freedom, secularism was supposed to be a unifying force. The idea was that traditional religious worldviews are divisive and lead only to conflict.[10] The authors of secularism, therefore, thought that we ought to construct a society built solely on secular foundations. By leaving our faith out of our public lives, we would get along better as a society and be able to recognize a wider scope of human dignity. In a world without God, we would gain a greater appreciation of our neighbor. At the same time secularism was

---

[7] *CA* 2.1.1.9–14.
[8] See Servais Pinckaers, O.P., *The Sources of Christian Ethics* (Washington, DC: Catholic University of America Press, 1995), 327–78.
[9] See Charles Taylor, *A Secular Age* (Cambridge, MA: Harvard University Press, 2007).
[10] See William Cavanaugh, *The Myth of Religious Violence* (Oxford: Oxford University Press, 2009).

promoting unity and dignity, however, it was seeking to diminish the relation between creature and Creator, which is the very source of unity and
dignity. Consequently, the neighbor is reduced to the status of a thing
that may be used "as if it had no relation to its Creator."[11]

In sum, the crisis of contemporary ethics is not the result of a particular set of responses to questions of the true, the good, and the neighbor.
Rather, the crisis of contemporary ethics is born from the obliteration of
the conditions needed to even engage the questions in a manner that does
not presuppose that one may never move beyond the arbitrary whims and
caprices of the person asking them. This crisis was already well under-
way when John XXIII evoked the Second Vatican Council. Subsequent
decades have witnessed the worsening of the crisis as the assumptions
of postmodernism, liberalism, and secularism have become more firmly
embedded. This is not without irony, for the brave new world has broken
all of its promises. The claim that there are no ultimate truths has itself
become an ultimate truth, an infallible dogma. Liberalism's elevation of
freedom of conscience has come to negate that very freedom. Finally, the
world's emancipation from God has exacerbated the systematic violations
of human dignity that define the present age. The universal dignity that
was supposed to follow the eclipse of belief turned out to be reserved for
the engineers of the new society and their disciples. Such are the factors
that make up the ethical crisis of our times.

THE RESPONSE

Having analyzed the crisis of contemporary ethics, we may now consider
the Catholic response to it. In response to postmodernism and liberalism, Catholic ethics reminds us that it is natural for "the human mind to
look for and to love what is true and good."[12] In response to secularism,
Catholic ethics reiterates that "human dignity rests above all on the fact
that humanity is called to communion with God."[13] This enjoins us "to
make ourselves the neighbor of every individual," and our neighbor is to
be regarded not as a means to some selfish end, but "as another self."[14]
Most of all, the Catholic response to the crisis of contemporary ethics is
to proclaim Christ; for it is Christ who "fully reveals humanity to itself

---

[11]   *GS* no. 26.
[12]   *GS* no. 15.
[13]   *GS* no. 19.
[14]   *GS* no. 27.

and brings to light its very high calling."[15] This statement is integral to the development of the Catholic moral tradition in the post-conciliar period.[16]

While the current work presents the Catholic moral tradition in the post-conciliar period as developing in response to the crisis detailed earlier and seeks to show the distinctiveness of this tradition by contrasting it with alternative ethical outlooks and approaches, this method is not to demean what is true and good in other systems of ethics, nor is it to embrace a fortress mentality, which regards Catholic ethics as necessarily and perpetually at war with rival traditions. Nor is it to suggest that the Church is somehow quarantined from modern society and therefore not susceptible to the same challenges. To the contrary, the Church is in the world, and the world is in the Church. The crisis of the modern age is one facing all of humanity. The role of the Church in the modern world is to address our common problems in the way that only the Church can, by "throwing the light of the Gospel on them and supplying humanity with the saving resources which the Church has received from its founder under the promptings of the Holy Spirit."[17] Keeping these things in mind, we are now in a position to summarize the preliminary goals and governing objectives of this book.

THE GOALS OF THIS BOOK

As stated earlier, the intention of this introduction is to position the chapters of this book in the context of the crisis of contemporary ethics and Catholic responses to it, which have both arisen from, and added to, the development of the Catholic moral tradition in the post-conciliar period. That being said, this book has four preliminary goals and three governing objectives. I begin with the former.

In conducting the research for this project, I routinely encountered four major areas of fecundity within the discipline of Catholic moral theology in the post-conciliar period. These areas make up the four parts of this book – foundations, virtue, Catholic social teaching, and bioethics.

---

[15] *GS* no. 22.

[16] Although the primary focus of this book is on the development of the Catholic moral tradition since the conclusion of the Second Vatican Council, this does not mean that the accumulation of history leading up to, informing, and contextualizing the Council is neglected. Instead, I use the method historians refer to as "arc" in order to connect contemporary issues to the thought of previous ages, allowing, as it were, for the chronology to be uneven for the sake of systematic presentation and clarity. In this way, we are able to arrive at a greater coherence than pure history allows without resorting to mere historiography.

[17] *GS* no. 3.

Obviously, these four domains are interrelated in important ways, but they also remain distinct. Indeed, there is a tendency on the part of Catholic moral theologians to allow one of the four areas to crowd out the other three, like a great oak tree in a forest of shrubs. I myself am not immune to this tendency. However, I have tried my best to treat all four domains as mutually illuminating, like four apple trees cross-pollinating each other and bearing more fruit as a result. At any rate, these four major areas inform the four preliminary goals pursued in these pages.

The first preliminary goal of this book is to make clear how the Catholic moral tradition understands the possession and pursuit of ethical truths. The chapters of Part I are ordered to this goal; in them, we treat what moral theologians and ethicists alike refer to as the "foundations problem." That is, whatever we say about right and wrong, fair and unfair, good and bad must be grounded in something. When sixth graders challenge the rule that says, "Gum may not be chewed in class," they are, without knowing it, coming up against the foundations problem. The teacher generally replies with an appeal to authority, "Because I said so," the legitimacy of which the students rightly question. Surely the arbitrary judgments of Ms. Smith do not form the bedrock for all ethics and morals. So then what does? Is there a universal law accessible to all rational agents that makes clear both that it is wrong to chew gum in class and also why it is so? Or is not chewing gum in class just a cultural convention, like wearing your hat backwards? Or is the mere appeal to power, "Because I said so," a sufficient foundation for moral norms? This in a nutshell is the foundations problem. Chapter 1 investigates five possible foundations for morality: historicism, cultural relativism, emotivism, social contract theory, and utilitarianism. I argue that these potential foundations for moral judgments turn out to be different variants of moral relativism. Chapter 2 examines the Catholic response to the foundations question, which involves the coming together of human reason and divine revelation. Chapter 3 draws from Ngũgĩ wa Thiong'o's classic novel, *A River Between*, to form a "test case" for the fundamental claims of Part I.

The second preliminary goal of this book is to demonstrate how the Catholic moral tradition understands the good of the individual. Thus, the chapters of Part II treat virtue in its classical form as well as issues arising from the resurgence of virtue ethics in the decades since Vatican II. Several factors account for this resurgence, such as the priority virtue ethics gives to the formation of character and the attainment of true happiness, which surprisingly can be easily put to the side, forgotten, neglected, or even vilified in several forms of modern ethics. The key to Catholic virtue ethics is the claim that morality is ultimately about more than duty and obligation. It is about the fulfillment of our deepest desire as human beings to live in friendship with God. Virtues are names for the good habits that accompany this kind of friendship. Another way of saying the same thing is that virtue is about living the good life, a life, that is, in which true happiness is achieved. In Chapter 4, we analyze the cardinal virtues of prudence, justice, temperance, and fortitude. Chapter 5 explores the virtues that come from grace. These include the theological virtues of faith, hope, and love, as well as graced versions of the cardinal virtues. Chapter 6 treats an essential belief supported by ancient and medieval virtue ethicists, the unity thesis, which holds that one must possess all of the virtues to possess even one of them. Here we consider more fully what it means to possess a virtue and to progress in the good life.

The third preliminary goal of this book is to elucidate how the Catholic moral tradition understands the good of society. Accordingly, the chapters of Part III introduce, investigate, and analyze the social doctrines of the Catholic Church. U.S. bishops have not infrequently lamented the fact that several Catholics remain uninformed regarding these important doctrines. However, Catholic social teaching is not relevant only to Catholics, rather it has to do with the overall course of humanity and is firmly grounded in scriptural themes of justice. These themes are examined in Chapter 7. The principles of Catholic social teaching, particularly as presented in the Pastoral Constitution of the Second Vatican Council, *Gaudium et spes*, form the subject matter for Chapter 8. The Catholic just war tradition is examined and assessed in Chapter 9. These chapters make clear the relevance of Catholic social teaching for the modern world.

The fourth and final preliminary goal of this book is to gain an appreciation of the Catholic moral tradition's commitment to the principle of universal human dignity and the implications of this commitment as it pertains to bioethics. Therefore, the chapters of Part IV focus on a select set of issues having to do with bioethical decisions pertaining respectively to the beginning and end of life. Chapter 10 builds on previous chapters in order to make clear the Catholic commitment to the principle of universal human dignity. This chapter includes an examination of the "capacities approach" and the human person/human nonperson distinction. Chapter 11 treats beginning of life decisions: contraception, abortion, and commercial surrogacy, or "contract pregnancy" as feminist ethicist Debra Satz calls it. Chapter 12 addresses the issue of euthanasia from the standpoint of a theology of providence. We examine ordinary kinds of euthanasia as well as the emerging "peaceful exit pill." The goal of these chapters is to make clear what the Catholic teaching holds with respect to select bioethical issues as well as to examine the link between these teachings and the essence of human dignity as understood from within the Catholic moral tradition.

The four preliminary goals of this book are ordered to the following governing objectives:

1. This book provides a comprehensive introduction to the Catholic moral tradition.
2. This book enables the reader to make preliminary observations regarding the interconnection of the four principle areas of Catholic moral theology in the post-conciliar period.
3. This book seeks to uncover the essence of Catholic ethics, its animating spirit.

This book, as a whole, is ordered to these objectives. Any other aims I may have had in writing it would come under the scope of these. To analyze the development of the Catholic moral tradition in the post-conciliar period is to analyze the Catholic response to the contemporary crisis of ethics detailed earlier. In response to postmodernism's leveling of truth claims, Catholic ethics offers natural law perfected by revelation. In response to liberalism's exaltation of freedom of indifference, Catholic ethics offers the freedom for excellence afforded by growth in the virtues. In response to secularism's assumption of selective human dignity, Catholic ethics offers a principle of universal human dignity rooted in the interpersonal communion of creature and Creator. It is this communion that also informs the principles of Catholic social teaching and the account of justice in which those principles are grounded. Above all, the Church proclaims Christ.

THE STRUCTURE OF THIS BOOK

Before concluding, I should like to make one further clarification regarding the structure of this book. As stated prior, this fourfold structure is intrinsically linked to the previously referenced goals. However, my ordering is chiefly for pedagogical reasons; it is not meant to suggest that the Catholic moral tradition begins ethical analysis with uncritical acceptance of the starting points for debate that are standard in ethical discourse since the Enlightenment. Rather, Catholic ethics begins with the encounter between God and the human person. With that being said, I wish to make clear that I have attempted to arrange the material such that as we progress through the text we draw nearer to the larger objectives by which this book is governed. Thus, as you move through these chapters, it would be wise not to lose sight of a few overarching questions: To what is the Catholic moral tradition ultimately ordered? To what end does it exist? By what means is it sustained and renewed?

PART I

Foundations of Catholic Ethics

CHAPTER I

Moral Relativism

> We must therefore pay careful attention to the conduct appropriate to different places, times, and persons, in case we make rash imputations of wickedness.
>
> St. Augustine, *On Christian Teaching*

Did the sun rise this morning? Think carefully about the wording of the question. I did not ask whether it appeared to rise or whether you perceived it as rising. Indeed, what takes place in our perceptions and what occurs in reality do not always coincide. If you are at a stoplight facing frontward and in your peripheral vision you sense the car next to you moving forward, you may for a moment feel as though you are moving backward. That is, to your perception, you are moving backward; in reality, you are not. In reality, the earth rotates around the sun; in our perceptions, the sun appears to rise, transverse the sky, and set. One way philosophers distinguish between reality as it is and reality as we experience it is with the terms "objective" and "subjective." Objectively, the sun did not rise this morning. Subjectively, it did.

At least since the time of Socrates, philosophers have disagreed as to whether there exists an objective reality beyond the subjective perceptions of various individuals or communities. On the one hand, the objectivist would say that for however many thousands of years human beings believed the sun to be actually rising, crossing the sky, and setting, before Copernicus set everyone straight; this error in the perception of prescientific peoples simply had nothing to do with the objective reality of what was really occurring. Everyone was equally mistaken. If, at some point in the future, all scientific knowledge is lost and human beings invent a myth that the sun is pulled across the sky every day by an invisible unicorn, even if everyone in the whole world subscribes to this belief, it will not change the objective reality one bit. It will only mean that humanity is suffering from a collective delusion. Meanwhile, the earth will go on rotating around the sun just as it did before.

The subjectivist, on the other hand, says that there is no reality beyond perception, because reality itself is a subjective concept. It is true that the earth would go on rotating around the sun even if the entire human race were no longer able to perceive it, but if no one knew about it, then it would be inaccurate to speak of this natural phenomena as an objective reality. It would rather be no one's reality. And that which is no one's reality is nothing, because "reality" already implies perception. Phenomena that have not entered into human perception on some level are beyond the words, concepts, images, and experiences that make up our reality. Moreover, who says there has to be only one reality? Subjectively, there can be several realities, and who is to say one is more true or real than any other?

Whether reality is objective or subjective is a question of particular importance for ethicists. Put simply, at issue is whether there is an objective moral law. Is "it is wrong to murder" simply a fact about the kind of universe in which we live, similar to the fact that the earth rotates around the sun? Or is morality subjective? After all, the subjectivist could ask, "Who defines murder? Is the death penalty murder? Is abortion murder? Is killing an enemy soldier in combat murder? Does it not all depend, subjectively, on the understanding of murder as held by particular individuals and communities?" This raises a further point. If murder were objectively wrong, then one would expect a fairly broad consensus attesting to this fact. But is there one? If everyone agrees that murder is wrong but disagrees as to what constitutes murder, then this turns out not to be much of an agreement.

In ethics, the view that moral laws and norms are only subjective matters of perception is referred to as moral relativism. In other words, moral relativism is the view that moral laws only exist relative to the perceptions of particular groups or individuals. In the 1950s, for example, the majority of parents in the United States believed that spanking one's children was not only morally acceptable but a positive moral duty. If we lived back then, it would not have been out of the ordinary to see a mother spanking her child in the grocery store or at the park. Today, if someone were to spank his or her child in public, everyone would give disapproving looks and someone may even attempt to intervene on the child's behalf. Society has changed, and today most people believe that spanking is wrong. Now, the relativist says that one view is not really better than the other. Spanking was morally legitimate for parents in the 1950s but not for parents nowadays, and this is because the society of the 1950s is very different from the society of today. In contrast, the objectivist says that spanking is either morally acceptable or it is not. If it is, then the people of today are simply mistaken. If it is not, then parents in the 1950s were mistaken. If spanking is really wrong, then the change from the 1950s to now is progress. If spanking is morally right, then the change is rather a regress. In any event, for the relativist, it is merely change.

HISTORICAL AND CULTURAL RELATIVISM

The technical term for the kind of moral relativism I have been describing is "historical relativism." It is the view that moral norms are relative to particular historical periods. This view, sometimes referred to as historicism, was espoused by the German philosopher Georg Wilhelm Friedrich Hegel. According to Hegel, one is no more able to know what is true and good in an absolute sense than one is able to live in every epoch of history at the same time. Similar to the developmental understanding of the natural world put forward by Charles Darwin around the same time, Hegel understood morality as being in constant flux. In Hegel's view, everyone is "a child of his time" and no one can "overleap his own age."[1] What people take as moral absolutes, therefore, turn out to be historically conditioned opinions.

Another common form of relativism is cultural relativism. This is the view that moral norms are relative to different cultures. For example, in the United States our law says that it is wrong for a person less than twenty-one years of age to drink alcohol. Just up north, in Canada, the limit is nineteen, and in France it is eighteen but not strictly enforced. According to cultural relativism, there is not a right answer as to when it becomes morally appropriate for a person to drink alcohol. There are only the different kinds of rules different cultures invent. For the objectivist, however, if drinking age limits reflect nothing more than the private ideas of different cultures, then they have no basis in reality. They are just conventions, similar to on which side of the road to drive. Of course, it is both possible and common to be a historical and a cultural relativist at the same time.

---

[1] G.W.F. Hegel, *Philosophy of Right*, Preface, in *Hegel's Philosophy of Right*, tr. T.M. Knox (Oxford: Clarendon Press, 1952), 11. This chapter is indebted to the thesis advanced in Montague Brown's excellent book, *The Quest for Moral Foundations: An Introduction to Ethics* (Washington, DC: Georgetown University Press, 1996).

There are at least three things about which moral relativists (I mean the historical and cultural kinds) are right. First, moral norms and laws do differ from culture to culture and age to age. Second, human beings never experience morality in the abstract. Morality is always mediated to us through historical and cultural frameworks. Finally, it is unreasonable to expect people living in other times and cultures to know and follow the exact moral code peculiar to our own time and place. To excoriate the ancient Hebrews for practicing polygamy or people in India who still believe in arranged marriage may just be a kind of prejudice. Indeed, as I just described the objectivist point of view, you may have been imagining a kind of absolutist, narrow-minded type of person with whom normal people have very little in common. And some objectivists do fit this description. In fact, it was Augustine who warned that we must "pay careful attention to the conduct appropriate to different places, times, and persons, in case we make rash imputations of wickedness."[2]

Nevertheless, Augustine knew that neither historical nor cultural relativism, nor a combination of the two, could, in and of themselves, serve as a sufficient foundation for morality. There are several problems with moral relativism (the historical and cultural kinds). In the first place, moral relativists often exaggerate the nature of the differences between different cultures and time periods to the neglect of greater areas of commonality. For instance, consider the earlier example of spanking. It is true that parents in the 1950s believed in spanking, whereas parents of today mostly do not, but both sets of parents agree in disciplining their children to better their behavior. Or consider the example of the ancient Hebrews and polygamy. There is a real difference between polygamy and monogamy, but both views have more in common with each other than either of them does with hedonism. Hence, those things touted by relativists as total differences in morality turn out not to be. It was C.S. Lewis who said that trying to imagine a culture with a totally different morality is like trying to imagine a country "where two and two made five."[3]

Furthermore, even when significant moral differences do appear, whether among historical periods, cultures, or both, we tend to want to describe these as progress or regress. For example, attitudes toward slavery are quite different today from attitudes in the early nineteenth

---

[2] *DDC* III.45.
[3] C.S. Lewis, *Mere Christianity* (San Francisco: Harper Collins, 1952), 6.

century. Most people, however, view this change as a positive one, as progress. Do you see the problem? To admit progress implies that one morality is truer than another, in which case there must be some objective standard against which the two can be judged (unless you are prepared to say that "slavery is wrong" is nothing more than the opinion of the current era).

Another problem with moral relativism is that even its proponents tend to shy away from it at several points. No one really wants to say that Nazi morality was perfectly fine for Germans in the 1940s, even if the peculiar moral outlook of contemporary Americans happens to find it disagreeable. And if you met someone who thought that Nazi morality was upstanding and commendable, would you think that a legitimate opinion to which that person was entitled, or would you rather feel compelled to disabuse them of this wrong view? If one wishes to be a strict relativist, then one must regard Nazi morality as just another way of being that is neither better nor worse than other ways of being. And the same is true for things we want to admire. Do you think that the struggle of Martin Luther King Jr. for civil rights was a good thing or a bad thing? Do you think the change he helped bring about was in the right direction? Was it progress? If you are a moral relativist you can't really think so, because there is no objective standard in the light of which progress can be measured. The moral views of the civil rights movement and those of the Ku Klux Klan are different, but one set of views is not morally superior to the other. In the absence of objective moral standards there can only be difference and opinion. Nothing can be true or good, not even relativism itself, which brings me to one further critique.

Moral relativism cannot even commend itself as a better ethical outlook than any other. It is absurd to claim that moral relativism is superior to any other ethical theory, because moral relativism denies the very foundation needed to make judgments of this kind. You can say that you believe there is no such thing as good and evil without contradicting yourself, but you cannot say that you think it good that there is no such thing as good and evil. Indeed, if there is no such thing as good and evil, then this absence must be, by definition, neither. One could say that he or she likes moral relativism because it helps one be more tolerant of other views, but he or she cannot say that being tolerant is morally superior to being intolerant. To say that tolerance is good and intolerance is bad is to reject moral relativism. At this point, then, we may advance beyond historical and cultural relativism and move on to a more difficult kind of relativism called "emotivism."

EMOTIVISM

The previous section treated two prominent kinds of moral relativism: historical and cultural. The current section deals with another form of moral relativism called emotivism. First, we explore what emotivism entails. Second, we see why it turns out to be a form of relativism. As should be becoming clear by this point, the common element in all the different kinds of relativism is an inability to secure a foundation for moral judgments and moral responsibility because of an assumption that an objective foundation for morality does not exist.

Similar to nearly all ethical theories, emotivism emerges in the thought world of ancient Greece. This particular theory is most prominent in the works of Epicurus. The modern version of emotivism, however, comes from the Scottish Enlightenment philosopher David Hume.[4] Emotivism refers to the theory that emotions-feelings-intuitions-sentiments are the source of moral judgments. Philosophers sometimes refer to this as "the Romantic ideal" or "Romantic Idealism," because it places the seat of morality in the heart rather than the head.

At first glance, emotivism makes a great deal of sense. Think about the last time you felt morally offended by something. Even the fact that I say "felt morally offended" rather than "thought something was morally offensive" speaks to the sensibility of emotivism. Say, for instance, that you saw a story in the news about a wealthy businessman who took advantage of a poor widow with some investment scheme and left her broke. There may have been several things that upset you about this. First, it is an example of the powerful preying on the weak. Second, there is the unfairness of it all, the Robin Hood–in-reverse nature of the case: some wealthy person gets wealthier by taking from someone who already has little. Empathy may come easily when we imagine a person who lacks basic necessities taking from someone who abounds in superfluities, but when someone who abounds in superfluities steals from those who already are lacking, most react with disgust and disdain. Why? Is it the outcome of a series of rational deductions or because of some theory as to what is best for society? Generally, this is not the case. Rather, it is simply moral emotions-feelings-intuitions-sentiments that tell us that this thing that took place was wrong. We may not be able to articulate why we feel this way or express it in terms of a rational formula any more than we can

---

4   See David Hume, An Enquiry Concerning the Principles of Morals, Section IX, Part I, in *Enquiries*, L.A. Selby-Bigge ed. (Oxford: Clarendon Press, 1975).

explain why we fell in love with this person rather than that one. Sure we can come up with theories that explain why, but all this rational theorizing will never be anything more than second-tier speculation about what are really matters of the heart differing from person to person.

Now, what emotivism says is that moral emotions-feelings-intuitions-sentiments are the only basis for moral judgments that we as human beings have available to us. Therefore, they are, indeed they must be, a worthy foundation for all moral judgments and responsibility. Whereas classical thinkers thought that reason was the seat of morality, emotivists say that the rational faculty of human beings does not play a significant role in morality at all.

According to Hume, reason performs only two operations: "relations of ideas" and "matters of fact."[5] The first operation has to do chiefly with mathematical functions. For instance, the fact that your mind is capable of determining that a right triangle with legs of three and four must have a hypotenuse of five has nothing to with your feelings about triangles. Determining and applying formulaic and spatial relations such as these is simply what the mind does.

The second operation, matters of fact, refers to the capacity to deduce from true premises a true conclusion. If it is true that all human beings are mortal, and if it is true that Jane is a human being, then it must be true that Jane is mortal. The conclusion is contained in and follows from the major premise (all humans are mortal) and the minor premise (Jane is human). In logic, however, it is possible for a conclusion to be valid but false. For example, if the major premise is that all dogs are green, and the minor premise is that Woofy is a dog, then "Woofy is green" is a valid conclusion (it follows from the premises). However, since the major premise is false, the conclusion is false. It has derived the error from the major premise. Or if the major premise is that all dogs bark, and the minor that Woofy is a dog, then the conclusion "Woofy barks" is valid. However, if in reality Woofy is a cat, then the conclusion fails because of the factual error in the minor premise. Even both of the premises could be wrong. If the major premise says all dogs are green and the minor that Woofy (who is in actuality a cat) is a dog, then the conclusion that Woofy (who happens to be an orange cat) is a green dog is doubly wrong. Notice that these are not reasoning errors but errors about facts. All dogs are not green, and Woofy, despite the misleading name, is not a dog.

---

[5] David Hume, *An Enquiry Concerning Human Understanding*, Section IV, Part I.

According to Hume, the kinds of things I have been describing are all that reason really does or can do. It deals with "relations of ideas," such as the right triangle, or "matters of fact," such as premises and conclusions. So how, in Hume's view, does all of this apply to moral questions? Well, clearly morality does not work like mathematical formulas. No one ever said, "$a^2 + b^2 = c^2$; therefore, lying is wrong." But also, in Hume's estimation, morality is not about matters of fact either. Consider, for example, the following syllogism: stealing is morally wrong (major premise); tricking widows with fraudulent investment schemes is stealing (minor premise); therefore, tricking widows with fraudulent investment schemes is morally wrong. The emotivist, however, asks you from whence you got these premises. Are these merely self-evident facts, such as all dogs bark or humans are mortal? Who says stealing is wrong (major premise) and who is to say that fraudulent investment schemes are a form of it (minor premise)? Perhaps, someone wants to say that this is just the nature of investment and it is the widow's own fault for not doing more research. You can't establish or prove with reason that tricking the widow was wrong; all you can do is appeal to your moral intuition or emotion that it was so.

Given that emotivists disconnect reason from moral judgments, they also deny that "ought claims" have any basis in rationality. If the major premise is "lying is wrong" and the minor premise "telling Suzy I like her new hairstyle is a lie," then the conclusion "I ought not to tell Suzy I like her new hairstyle" seems to follow. But Hume says that it does not. Look carefully at the premises. The only valid conclusion we could draw is that telling Suzy you like her new hairstyle is wrong, and this is if and only if we assume the accuracy and universality of the major premise. Hume wants to know where the "ought" in the conclusion came from, given that it was not in either of the premises. And this is really the main point of Hume and the emotivists: there are no self-evident "oughts" to be found in the universe resembling other self-evident facts or principles. The foundation of "ought" claims is always and can only be in moral emotions-feelings-intuitions-sentiments. Thus, when I say, or perhaps even shout, that tricking that widow was morally wrong, I am not describing a fact about the universe; rather I am describing how a particular occurrence made me feel, the kinds of sentiments it evoked in me. All moral claims, in Hume's view, turn out to be descriptive of nothing more than the subjective emotions-feelings-intuitions-sentiments of the person making them.

Do you see now why emotivism turns out to be a form of relativism? The mere fact that I feel a particular way about something does not mean

I am right. I may, for example, feel very strongly that tricking the widow was wrong, but the person next to me may feel differently or may not care at all. Who is to say which feeling is the right one? Now, Hume did think there was such a thing as benevolent impulses, which could lead us to moral intuitions such as "tricking the widow is bad." Still, emotivism cannot tell me that my benevolent impulses ought to be encouraged or that my domineering or selfish impulses ought to be suppressed. Morality is made relative to subjective emotions-feelings-intuitions-sentiments. Emotivism, then, like all forms of relativism, fails to provide a foundation for moral judgments and moral responsibility. It is true that emotions-feelings-intuitions-sentiments, just like historical and cultural variables, are significant ethical factors, but, again, in and of themselves, they are not a legitimate source for moral authority. By the way, to say this is not for one second to dismiss the importance of conscience, which people sometimes equate with emotions-feelings-intuitions-sentiments. In subsequent chapters, we see that conscience cannot be reduced to emotion; it also involves reason. I move on now to a fourth version of relativism.

SOCIAL CONTRACT THEORY

Thus far, we have discussed three kinds of moral relativism – historical, cultural, and emotivism. The purpose of this section is to discuss social contract theory, which turns out to be another type of relativism. First, we examine the nature of this theory. Second, we see why it also is relativistic. Whereas the distinguishing feature of emotivism is the relativizing of morality to emotions, social contract theory relativizes morality to power.

The roots of social contract theory can be found in Plato's *Republic*; it is embraced by interlocutors of Socrates such as Glaucon and Thrasymachus. In the famous *Ring of Gyges* story, for example, Plato narrates a great dispute between his teacher, Socrates, and Glaucon; the debate concerns the foundation of morality.[6] Both Socrates and Glaucon agree that morality has a foundation, but they disagree with respect to what it is. Glaucon thinks that human nature is rather nasty. We are mean, scared little creatures who care a great deal about our own survival and well-being, and who turn out to be surprisingly indifferent to the well-being of others,

---

[6] Plato, The Republic, II.359–60, in *Plato: Complete Works*, John Cooper, ed. (Indianapolis, IN: Hackett Publishing Company, 1997). See William C. Mattison III's discussion in *Introducing Moral Theology: True Happiness and the Virtues* (Grand Rapids, MI: Brazos Press, 2008), 19–36.

particularly those whose flourishing we do not regard as connected to our own in some way. So, sure, I may care a great deal about the well-being of my family, friends, and co-workers, but this is not selflessness; it is only an extension of selfishness. I realize that my doing well is linked to their doing well. More than this, however, what human beings ultimately want, what we are all at bottom really after is power. We want, more than anything, the power to do what we want without consequence. The thing we least desire is to be under the power of others. Humans, according to Glaucon, fear nothing more than being subject to the arbitrary whims and caprices of other humans who happen, for whatever reason, to hold greater power. Whether it is the mean kid in sixth grade who twisted your arm until you said "Uncle" or the government forcing you to jump through hoops to apply for a loan, we humans can't stand being under the power of others. We'd much rather have the power ourselves. According to Glaucon, there is nothing we want more.

But what does any of this have to do with morality? In Glaucon's view, human beings invented morality in order to avoid coming under the power of others. That is, even though what we really wanted was power for ourselves, we were so afraid of coming under the power of others that we all got together and agreed to make up a bunch of rules to follow, which would limit our abilities to infringe on the freedom of others. Hence, do not kill, do not steal, do not covet, these are only rules made up (by the weak, scared people) to keep those with more power in check. Morality and ethics, for Glaucon, is nothing more than a grand bargain struck in the infancy of the human race by a collection of the weak and scared who always make up the majority.

Before examining how Socrates responds to the argument of Glaucon, let us consider the development of the Glauconian view in its modern form. Thomas Hobbes developed the Glauconian view into what ethicists today refer to as social contract theory. Hobbes imagines a "state of nature," by which he means a condition of the human race before the emergence of patriarchal monarchy. In this state of nature, human beings are nasty, ruthless, cruel, violent, and lacking anything like a moral system. Because no king or sovereign exists to invent and enforce moral rules, there are none. We live as animals. Again, however, the weak come together out of fear and choose to hand over the pure freedom afforded them by nature to the king. In exchange, the king gives protections from the chaos and disorder of the state of nature, where the strong prey on the weak at will. This, then, is the social contract. I hand over my rights to the king in exchange for protection. Morality, then, becomes the invention of the will of the king. It is an invention to appease the self-interest of the feeble and frightened masses, just as it was in the Glauconian system.

Now, a key point on which both Glaucon and Hobbes are agreed is that morality is an invention of the weak, agreed to out of fear. To illustrate this point, Glaucon narrates the *Ring of Gyges* story. He asks us to imagine a poor shepherd who finds a magic ring that makes him invisible. Being invisible here is a symbol for power just as it is in J.R.R. Tolkien's *Lord of the Rings* saga. Having the ring makes one above the consequences of his or her actions. Glaucon submits that this poor shepherd certainly would not go on following all the moral norms that ordinary people have to follow. Why? Because he no longer has to; indeed, if he did, according to Glaucon, we'd all think him a fool. To bring the story up-to-date, imagine that you were given a magic license plate, the license plate of Gyges let's call it. When the police ran the plate in their computers it came back that you have full immunity from the rules of the road, rules that everyone else has to follow. Would you go on stopping at traffic lights, even when you can see that it is safe to go? Would you come to a total stop at the stop signs? How closely would you observe that speed limit? Because you enjoy the license plate of Gyges, would not the speed limit become rather more of a cute bit of advice than a law? And now imagine that your friend has the license plate of Gyges, but goes on observing the rules of the road just as rigidly as he or she did before. Would you not think him or her rather a fool? One can see Glaucon's point; self-interest and fear of consequences do influence one's moral compass.

According to Socrates, however, morality is not just about obligations and rule keeping. It is rather a description of what it means to live well. Returning to the license plate of Gyges, maybe you would speed or California-stop at stop signs and so forth, but you wouldn't drive head on into an oncoming diesel truck just because you could, in the legal sense, get away with it. Moreover, if you did crash into the diesel truck and were severely injured, this would not be because of the fact that the government sent out a decree that those who crash into diesel trucks must be injured. Rather, the fact that you were injured simply has to do with a law that stems from the nature of driving. Again, it is not a rule because someone made it up; it is a law in the sense that it is descriptive of reality, similar to the law of gravity.

We discuss this natural law of morality at length in the next chapter, but for now all that needs to be stated is that social contract theory fails to serve as a foundation for morality. It is true that there are some conventions that human beings arbitrarily invent, which probably do not have anything to do with natural morality. This does not make them immoral, even though they may be. Usually, they are neither moral nor immoral. It is also true that self-interest, fear of consequences, civil law, and governmental powers do play a role in shaping the morality of individuals. However, social contract theory is still but another form of relativism. It makes morality relative to the arbitrary judgments of a sovereign; that is, it relativizes morality to power. But morality must be about more than that. The fact that some unstable individual can legally spew hatred all day long, and make a good living doing it, certainly does not make it moral or ethical. We may turn now to a fifth version of moral relativism.

UTILITARIANISM

Utilitarianism, in its modern form, originates with the thought of the great British jurist, philosopher, and social reformer, Jeremy Bentham. According to Bentham, all of those philosophers (whether ancient, or more recent such as Hobbes and Hume) who sought to ground ethical judgments in something subjective (emotions, self-interest, etc.) were off the mark. Rather, in Bentham's view, the only thing that makes a moral act just or unjust, good or bad, right or wrong, is its consequences. If an act has positive consequences, then it is a good act. If it has negative consequences, then it is a bad one. Unlike sentiments (Hume) and self-interest (Hobbes), which are subjective (you can't observe sentiments and self-interest), consequences are objectively verifiable.

The first question that arises, then, is how to determine whether the consequences of an act or series of acts are good or bad. Bentham decides that good consequences are those that maximize pleasure and minimize pain; bad consequences are the reverse. Thus, "the principle of utility" states that good actions are those likely to bring about greater happiness (in the sense of pleasure) for a greater number:

By the principle of utility is meant that principle which approves or disapproves of every action whatsoever, according to the tendency which it appears to have to augment or diminish the happiness of the party whose interest is in question; or what is the same thing in other words, to promote or to oppose that happiness. I say of every action whatsoever; and therefore not only of every action of a private individual, but of every measure of government.[7]

It is worth pointing out here that much of what Bentham is saying seems to be self-evidently true and good. Of course, one should take the

---

[7] Jeremy Bentham, *The Principles of Morals and Legislation* (New York: Hafner Press, 1948), Ch. I, 2.

consequences of his or her action into account before doing it. Of course, one should consider the common good, not just one's own happiness, in the actions one commits. It is for reasons such as these that utilitarianism has been, and continues to be, the metaethical theory of choice for a great many fine minds.

At the same time, utilitarianism suffers from a few major weaknesses. In the first place, it reduces good and bad, in the moral sense, to pleasure and pain. However, we know that sometimes doing the right thing can involve pain. If Martin Luther King Jr. had employed the utilitarian calculus to sum up the pleasures and pains that would come from the series of acts in which he engaged in his pursuit of desegregation, then surely this would have pushed him down a different path. Pursuing desegregation brought him much reproach, imprisonment, and finally an early death by assassination – not much pleasure or happiness there. On the other hand, doing the wrong thing can often bring pleasure and even a kind of perverse happiness. As C.S. Lewis explained, a man "who has risen to wealth or power by a continued course of treachery and cruelty, by exploiting for purely selfish ends the noble motions of his victims, laughing the while at their simplicity; who, having thus attained success, uses it for the gratification of lust and hatred" may not have done all of this, as we tend to imagine, "tormented by remorse or even misgiving." Rather, strange and enraging as it is, he may have done this while "eating like a schoolboy and sleeping like a healthy infant – a jolly, ruddy-cheeked man, without a care in the world."[8] Thus, the retort to the "if it makes you happy it can't be that bad" mentality: it can when one's definition of happiness is false.

Furthermore, and more fundamentally, even if the aforementioned problem did not exist, it is questionable whether or not the whole procedure of objectively tabulating the pains and pleasures (consequences) that may follow from a given act is even possible in the first place. Suppose that a woman decided to leave her husband for another man. Obviously, she thinks this will make her happier. She may even say that it will make "everyone" happier in the long run. Children know that when parents get divorced they often use this utilitarian justification. And now suppose that because of her decision her children decide they want nothing more to do with her, which causes both her and the children great and irrevocable pain in the long term. These, then, are all, in some sense, the consequences of her choice. But is she responsible for not having foreseen them? Moreover, suppose that she ends up miserable with the man for whom she left her first husband. Is

---

[8] C.S. Lewis, *The Problem of Pain* (San Francisco: Harper Collins, 1940), 122.

that her fault too? No one ever marries someone because they think it will make them miserable, decreasing their pleasure and increasing their pain, as it were. Rather, in life not everything can be probabilistically measured, predicted, and predetermined. Not all the consequences of our choices can be foreseen at the time in which we are making them. Twenty-twenty hindsight comes easier than twenty-twenty foresight. Utilitarian ethics seems to presume and demand a capacity that ordinary human beings, who are neither psychics nor savants, simply do not have.

Finally, as already stated, utilitarianism is yet another version of relativism. Hume's emotivism tells me that I may in some cases care about the happiness of others because of a sentiment humans tend to have to do so, but it can't tell me why or whether I ought to care for others. The social contract theory of Hobbes says I should care for the well-being of others because in the long term it will be in my own self-interest to do so. If it turns out not to be in my self-interest, however, Hobbes can give me no other motive for caring about another's happiness. Utilitarianism offers me a questionable and problematic calculus, dressing guesswork up as a mathematical formula, in order to determine whether the consequences of my action will bring about greater pleasure or pain and, therefore, whether the action should be done. It has no way to tell me why I should be interested in promoting pleasure and decreasing pain. Of course, we should think long and hard about the consequences our actions are likely to have, but to make morality relative to probabilistic guesswork is not to secure an adequate foundation for moral choices and responsibility.[9]

An attempt to improve on the deficiencies of Bentham's utilitarianism can be found in the work of his disciple, J.S. Mill. The primary concern of Mill had to do with the nature of the utilitarian calculus itself and issues having to do with applying it to others. Mill makes clear both where he accepts the principles of Bentham and where he thinks further development, which he will provide, is needed:

The creed which accepts as the foundations of morals "utility" or the "greatest happiness principle" holds that actions are right in proportion as they tend to promote happiness; wrong as they tend to produce the reverse of happiness. By happiness is intended pleasure and the absence of pain, by unhappiness, pain and the privation of pleasure. To give a clear view of the moral standard set up by the theory, much more requires to be said; in particular, what things it includes in the ideas of pain and pleasure, and to what extent this is left an open question. But

---

[9] It is for similar reasons that the important Catholic moral philosopher, G.E.M. Anscombe decries contemporary forms of utilitarianism, which she refers to pejoratively as "consequentialism" in her famous essay, "Modern Moral Philosophy," *Philosophy* 33:124 (1958): 1–19.

these supplementary explanations do not affect the theory of life on which this theory of morality is grounded – namely, that pleasure and freedom from pain are the only things desirable as ends.[10]

As with Bentham, only consequences defined in the context of pleasure and pain determine the morality or immorality of a given act. However, Mill departs from Bentham by expanding pleasure and pain to include pleasures of intellect, sentiment, and imagination – pleasures, that is, which are not merely physical. However, this expansion of the utilitarian calculus into the subjective domain only further muddles a theory that was muddled at the outset. It is unhelpful in solving the problem of providing objective criteria for moral decision making.

With respect to the problem of grounding the utilitarian claim that I should care for the happiness of others, Mill draws from Hume's emotivist theory. We should be benevolent and care about the happiness of others, the common good, or the general well-being of society, because we find within ourselves a moral emotion-feeling-intuition-sentiment that says we should. However, similar to Hume, Mill cannot say why we ought to follow this feeling rather than any other, nor can he account for the wrongness of the man who is made happy by exploiting others and laughing while he does it. Thus, Mill cannot eliminate the problems of Bentham's utilitarianism.

In the interest of completeness, I should also mention the rule-utilitarianism (as distinct from the act-utilitarianism of Bentham and Mill) of Richard Brandt. In order to discern what makes rule-utilitarianism distinct from act-utilitarianism, it is helpful to review the categorical imperative of the Prussian enlightenment philosopher Immanuel Kant, who was not a utilitarian. Kant's categorical imperative refers to a formula that Kant believed could be deduced from and employed by one's practical reason in order to determine one's moral duty to others. It is stated in three different ways. The first way says, "Act as if the maxim of your action were to become through your will a universal law of nature." The second way says, "Act in such a way that you treat humanity, whether in your own person or in the person of another, always at the same time as an end and never simply as a means." The third way, which combines the first two, states, "According to this principle [autonomy] all maxims are rejected which are not consistent with the will's own legislation of universal law."[11] I know these

---

[10] J.S. Mill, *Utilitarianism*, Ch. 2, Oskar Piest, ed. (Indianapolis, IN: Bobbs-Merrill, 1957), 10.

[11] Immanuel Kant, *Grounding for the Metaphysics of Morals*, in *Kant's Ethical Philosophy*, tr. James W. Ellington (Indianapolis, IN: Hackett, 1983), First Section.

can sound complicated, and in some cases they are, but for the most part they are just plain common sense stated in an analytical and formal way. Remember our imaginary wealthy person from earlier in the chapter who tricked the poor widow with the investment scheme? And remember how we could not find a convincing way to condemn his action even though we felt compelled to do so? Well, Kant offers us a way. Tricking the poor widow was wrong, because if everyone behaved this way then society would collapse (first formulation of the categorical imperative). It is wrong because he uses her as a means for his own selfish benefit rather than as a human being worthy of respect (second formulation). Thus, the maxim of his action must be rejected if you want to be a decent person (third formulation).

In Kant's view, an individual must do his or her moral duty even when it does not feel good, may have negative consequences, goes against his or her own self-interest, and so forth. Kant grounds moral duty in the capacity of human reason to distinguish right from wrong. Kant's moral theory, the technical name for which is deontology or duty-based ethics, has much in common with the natural law tradition treated in the next chapter. Brandt's theory was an attempt to ground the act-utilitarianism of Bentham and Mill more firmly in a concern for the well-being of the community. Brandt does this by drawing from the first formulation of Kant's categorical imperative. Thus, whereas in the act-utilitarian model I may in particular instances be justified in breaking promises, if I can show it will increase happiness for the greater number, in rule-utilitarianism I keep the promise anyway because if everyone followed the bad maxim of breaking promises it would have bad general consequences for the community. However, like Bentham and Mill, and unlike Kant, Brandt still cannot tell me why I should have a concern for the well-being of the community or adhere to whatever rules may follow from such a concern.

In brief, utilitarianism, in the various forms it has taken throughout history, is another version of moral relativism. It cannot ground moral judgments in anything substantive, only calculated guesswork and questionable interpretations of what true happiness entails, a subject we discuss much further in subsequent chapters. A further problem, however, is that at bottom utilitarianism promotes an "ends justify the means" approach to morality. On the whole, Catholic ethicists have always rejected such an approach as dangerous and inherently immoral.

SUMMARY

To be clear, the point of this chapter is not that moral relativism has nothing to commend. It does. Cultural relativism teaches us to be more understanding and tolerant of moral codes that differ from our own. Historical relativism helps us to recognize and appreciate the vast differences between the moralities and systems of ethics found in different historical epochs. As Augustine says, this helps us to avoid making "rash imputations of wickedness" to others. Emotivism draws attention to the key role played by moral emotions-feelings-intuitions-sentiments in ethical decision making. Social contract theory helps us to recognize the importance that civil institutions and law play in shaping our moral outlooks. Utilitarianism emphasizes the significance of the consequences of one's choices with respect to both the individual and to the larger society. This chapter does not advocate for a wholesale dismissal of these important ethical theories. The point is rather that, whatever good things they have to commend, they are not equipped to provide firm foundations for moral judgments and responsibility. Culture, history, sentiment, civil law, and tabulations of pleasure and pain can all contribute to moral judgments; when set up as a foundation for morality, however, the result in each case is a different kind of relativism, the governing assumption of which, again, is the claim that objective moral foundations do not exist.

Let me close by restating the significance of this point. That the earth rotates around the sun is simply a fact about the universe. If the cultural norms of some group do not attest to this fact, it remains just the same. If a whole historical era fails to recognize that this is so, it remains just the same. If everyone simultaneously has a strong emotion-feeling-intuition-sentiment that this is not so, it remains so nonetheless. If the Supreme Court or the United Nations illegalizes the law of heliocentric motion, it will go on just as it did before. If denying heliocentric motion makes people feel nice, it does not matter. At issue is whether laws of morality are similar to the laws of nature in this respect. Just as laws of nature are only laws in the sense of being accurate facts or descriptions about the universe, so too the laws of morality may only be laws in the sense of being accurate facts or descriptions about what it means to live well as a human being. As we see in the next chapter, the Catholic moral tradition understands the moral law in just such a way and opposes those views that suggest that morality is merely something we have invented for ourselves.

CHAPTER 2

The Natural Law and Revelation

The Church's moral reflection, always conducted in the light of Christ, the "Good Teacher," has also developed in the specific form of the theological science called "moral theology," a science which accepts and examines Divine Revelation while at the same time responding to the demands of human reason.

St. John Paul II, *Veritatis splendor* no. 29

Thus far we have analyzed different forms of moral relativism. While recognizing their strengths and that which they have to commend, we have seen that they do not align with the Catholic moral tradition because they are incapable of providing a suitable foundation for moral judgments and responsibility. What, then, is the foundation for Catholic ethics?[1] The answer is twofold. On the one hand is revealed morality, accessible through faith. On the other hand is natural law morality, accessible through human reason. It is pivotal that one understands from the outset that the Catholic moral tradition has never understood faith and reason to be in competition with each other, nor has it regarded faith and reason as mutually exclusive.

There is a way of thinking called fideism, which holds that faith is inherently and inalterably irrational. In this view, faith propositions are necessarily absurd, and to try to make sense of them is to transmogrify them and waste one's time. There is another way of thinking called rationalism. According to this view, faith is all just make-believe and fairy tales and is, therefore, an obstacle to arriving at objective truth. Catholic teaching has never accepted either of these epistemological perspectives, but regards faith and reason as mutually informing and perfecting one another. Faith and reason are not like enemy soldiers on a battlefield. In the Catholic view, they are more like "two wings on which the human spirit rises to

---

[1] My use of the term "foundation" here is not meant to imply indisputable rational foundations in the Enlightenment sense. Addressing this topic directly is beyond the scope of the current chapter.

the contemplation of truth," as stated by John Paul II in his encyclical letter *Fides et ratio* (faith and reason).[2] The classical way of expressing this timeless Catholic truth is with St. Anselm's famous maxim: faith seeking understanding.

In this chapter, we examine the natural law tradition, predominantly as expressed by Thomas Aquinas. Next, we analyze the manner in which revealed morality, particularly as found in Christ's moral teachings, elevates our natural sense of morality to a higher level. We consider what this means through investigations of the Beatitudes and Catholic teachings on marriage. As a result, we find that it is in the coming together of revealed and natural morality that a suitable foundation for moral judgments and responsibility is finally found. A third section deals with the interrelated issue of how authority is understood in the context of the Catholic moral tradition. Here we analyze basic goods theory, proportionalism, and John Paul II's response to the latter in his encyclical letter, *Veritatis splendor*.

THE NATURAL LAW

In the previous chapter, I began by mentioning the possibility of an objective moral law – that is, a moral law that is similar to a fact about the universe, such as the law of gravity, rather than a mere human invention, such as which side of the road to drive on. Now, there are three possibilities with respect to a law such as this: it does not exist, in which case we may turn to some version of relativism; it exists, but is not accessible to us, in which case again we may turn to relativism, given that unknowable truths cannot help us in making ethical determinations; or the objective moral law may both exist and be accessible to us, which is what the Catholic moral tradition has always maintained. The name Aquinas gave to this moral law is "the eternal law," and in order to understand what he meant by "natural law," we must first understand the eternal law.

According to Aquinas, the eternal law has four main features, two of which require examination here.[3] First, the eternal law is the measure of all

---

[2] *FR* preface. An encyclical is a letter that a pope writes to the other bishops addressing some issue having to do with faith or morals.
[3] *ST* Ia IIae q. 93 aa. 1–6. The *Summa Theologiae* is Aquinas's masterpiece written near the end of his career as a theologian. It is divided into three parts. The first part (*prima pars*; Aquinas wrote in Latin) treats of God and the creation. The second part (*secunda pars*) treats of the moral life, and the third part (*terita pars*) treats of Christ. The second part is so massive that it is further divided into two sub-parts referred to respectively as the first part of the second (*prima secundae*) and the second part of the second (*secunda secundae*). The abbreviation for the *prima pars* is Roman numeral I followed by the letter "a" from the word prima (Ia). Following the same pattern, the abbreviation for the first of

truth. Second, it is known to all. Let us examine more closely what these features entail. To begin with, when Aquinas says that the eternal law is the measure of all things, he means that it is the objective reality by which perceptions can be measured. To understand this, it is helpful to distinguish the divine intellect from the human intellect.

In order for our human intellects to possess truth, we must think, deduce, or believe something that accords with reality. Think of it this way: if I was watching a baseball game and the man on second base goes sliding into third, I can believe that he was out. That is, my perception may tell me that the third baseman tagged his foot before it hit the base. If the umpire shares my perception, then he will call the base runner out. Now, to take it a step further, if both of our perceptions were right and indeed the third baseman did tag him out before his foot hit third base, then our intellects, as well as all those who saw the play and thought he was out, possess true opinions. Our opinions are true; the opinions of those who thought he was safe are false. If he was really safe, however, and the umpire calls him out, then the objective truth is that he was safe. The umpire just missed the call. In that situation, all of those who believe it was a blown call possess true opinions, while the rest of us are in error.

Now, the point of all this is that the mere fact that we human beings happen to think something is true does not make it so. Our intellects form judgments that either do or do not accord with reality. As Aquinas explains, "a human concept is not true by reason of itself, but by reason of its being consonant with things, since an opinion is true or false according as it answers to reality."[4] However, the eternal law, which resides in the divine intellect, is not just a divine opinion about reality that may be true or false; it is the reality itself. This is what Aquinas means when he says that the eternal law "is the measure of things" because it is "true in itself."[5] With respect to ethical questions, then, the eternal law is not just God's subjective point of view; it is the standard by which all competing systems of ethics and morality are finally to be judged. Without a standard,

the second part is Ia IIae, and the abbreviation for the second part of the second part is IIa IIae. The abbreviation for the third part is IIIa. Since the whole of the text is divided into questions and articles, "q" refers to the number question and "a" or "aa" to the article or articles. Thus, when I reference Ia IIae q. 93 aa. 1–6, I am referencing the first of the second part, question number 93, articles 1–6.

4 *ST* Ia IIae q. 93 a. 1 ad. 3. Aquinas's articles are in the form of an *utrum*, which means a "whether it is the case that" statement. He always begins with objections to the view that he is ultimately going to defend and ends by replying to those objections. In Latin, *ad*, is the word for the replies to the objections, so ad. 3 means the reply to the third objection.

5 Ibid.

competing moralities cannot be compared; one cannot be said to be superior to the other. There is only difference. But if there is a standard – an objective moral reality – then the one more consonant with this reality possesses a greater share of moral truth than the other.

An objective measure of morality would not be of much help to us if it was unknowable, but Aquinas maintained that the eternal law is knowable to all. Here is what he meant. In the first place, Aquinas did not think that we either know something or we don't know. There are, rather, degrees of knowing. For example, you know mathematics and the rules of grammar but could know them more fully. You know your loved ones but could always know them more completely. There are degrees and gradations and kinds of knowing. Even to know that you don't know something requires some degree of knowing. A thing that was utterly unknown to you would be a thing you didn't even know you didn't know.

There are also different ways of knowing things. One way of knowing a thing is by its effects. If you see the sun streaming down on a beautiful café, you don't need to look up at the sky to know that the sun is there. You know it by its effects. Indeed, this is one of the ways we come to know God. We know God by the kind of universe God has made. The universe is not God, however, rather it is something God caused through acts of power and providence. The point, then, is that we all know the eternal law to greater or lesser degrees, and we know it primarily through its effects. But what are its effects? Aquinas explains: "For every knowledge of truth is a kind of reflection and participation of the eternal law, which is the unchangeable truth." Some know more of it and some less, but at the very least, all know "the common principles of the natural law" to which we now turn.[6]

The natural law is the name for our knowledge of the eternal law, which we have by virtue of being rational beings capable of arriving at truth. The natural law refers in the first place to principles or starting points of moral reasoning that are self-evident truths. With respect to speculative reasoning, the principle of noncontradiction, which states that a thing cannot both be and not be at the same time, is a self-evident principle from which more specific truths may be derived through syllogistic reasoning. With respect to practical reasoning, however, the first principle or precept of the natural law is that good is to be pursued and evil avoided. Those things to which we are naturally inclined we apprehend as good, and the

<hr>

[6] *ST* Ia IIae q. 93 a. 2.

contraries of those things we regard as evil. Thus, we regard the preservation of human life and the removal of obstacles to human flourishing as good. Think of all the scientists working to find cures for diseases, or of all the cures or vaccines found for diseases previously thought to be incurable. We naturally regard these as good and pursue them. In a similar respect, we also find it good to come together for the having and raising of children. These natural inclinations we share with the animals, but we rational creatures also want to know the truth about God and to live in society. Thus, we attempt to avoid ignorance, deception, and loneliness. Misanthropic people who hate others, who spread ignorance and deceit wherever they go, and who try to tear apart familial and communal bonds are not only unpleasant, they are living in contradiction to their own nature. There are some groups who think that human beings can become totally depraved – that is, that the law of nature can be annihilated in them. However, Aquinas did not think the law of nature could ever be completely obliterated from the hearts of men. He acknowledged, however, that through "evil persuasions, vicious customs, and corrupt habits" it could be greatly obscured.[7]

Just as, with respect to speculative truths, secondary precepts may be derived from primary precepts, so too with respect to the natural law, which resides in the practical reasoning. Therefore specific moral norms, or secondary precepts, such as "killing is wrong," can be deduced from the primary precepts. Thus we find the "ought" that Hume was looking for; it is the first principle of the natural law. Good ought to be pursued and evil to be shunned. This is the self-evident first principle upon which all practical reasoning depends. Therefore, if the major premise is good ought to be pursued and evil to be avoided, and the minor premise is that pollution is evil, then the specific moral norm "pollution ought to be avoided" is valid according to natural law reasoning. The "ought" claim has not been slipped into the conclusion but follows from the premises. Given that the natural law is a participation in the eternal law, the view that pollution ought to be avoided and the view that pollution is great so long as it makes us a lot of money would not be just two different subjective opinions; rather, one would be objectively right and the other wrong. This we can deduce by our reason. However, our natural capacity to discern right from wrong is perfected by revealed morality, to which we now turn.

---

[7] *ST* Ia IIae q. 94 a. 6. Aquinas treats the natural law in Ia IIae q. 94 aa. 1–6.

REVEALED MORALITY

Perhaps one of the most distinctive claims of the Catholic moral tradition is that revealed morality completes natural morality. In other words, what God has revealed about how we should live does not negate or replace what we can know by the natural law, which we all have by virtue of being rational creatures. Imagine that I had six squares, which I assembled into a three-dimensional cube. It would be inaccurate to say that the two-dimensional squares had been negated, obliterated, or replaced. Rather, they have been taken up into a higher plane of being, the three-dimensional world. It is like that with natural and revealed morality. The latter does not replace the former but elevates and transfigures it in a manner that preserves, rather than destroys, the continuity between what it was and what it becomes. To become a butterfly is not the demise of the caterpillar but rather its perfection.

The source and summit of the Catholic moral tradition, therefore, is the Beatitudes given by Jesus Christ.[8] In them, we find that morality is not just about pursuing good and avoiding evil in our actions but indeed in our entire person. Morality concerns what we do, but also who we are. Additionally, we find that living morally is the key to attaining true happiness. In fact, the Latin word *beatus* means "happy."

We can see the continuity between Christ's moral teachings and the natural law insofar as Christ provides us in the Beatitudes with good things to pursue and bad things to avoid.[9] With respect to the latter, we are to avoid unhealthy attachments to wealth, power, honor, and pleasure. "Blessed are the poor in spirit, for theirs is the kingdom of heaven" teaches us to resist the view that material goods can fulfill our deepest yearnings. Over and against modern views of happiness, which demand that we be in a great mood all the time and say that if we are not then we are not "well-adjusted" or "self-actualized," "Blessed are they who mourn, for they will be comforted" teaches us to avoid a hedonistic way

---

[8] See Matthew 5:3–10 *NAB*. Throughout this book I employ what Servais Pinckaers referred to as the "total" method of scriptural exegesis as opposed to the "fragmented" method. I also follow Pinckaers in reading Scripture in general and the New Testament in particular as chiefly concerned with questions of happiness and salvation. This is an important starting point because, as Pinckaers warns, "when we superimpose our moral distinctions upon the New Testament, we become guilty of an anachronism that vitiates our question and falsifies our research from the start." Servais Pinckaers, O.P., *The Sources of Christian Ethics* (Washington, DC: The Catholic University of America, 1995), 106–7.

[9] See Fr. Robert Barron's reading of the Beatitudes in *Catholicism: A Journey to the Heart of the Faith* (New York: Image Books, 2011), 41–45.

of life. Staying true to the will of God sometimes involves psychological or physical suffering. "Blessed are the meek, for they will inherit the land" teaches us that no amount of worldly power can finally satisfy our deepest desires. How many ruthless dictators have attained power only to die miserable, lonely, and unfulfilled? Finally, "Blessed are they who are persecuted for the sake of righteousness, for theirs is the kingdom of heaven" teaches us that ultimate happiness does not reside in prestige, honor, or celebrity. Leading a righteous life is generally unaccompanied by fame. To be clear, the teaching is not that money, power, honor, and pleasure are evil in and of themselves. It is rather that the human tendency, so easily observed in everyday life, is to set up one of these things or some combination of them as objects to provide us with ultimate happiness and satisfaction. In other words, we make idols of them. In the Beatitudes just reviewed, Jesus is correcting our flawed notion of what will make us happy. He is not removing our natural desire to pursue good and avoid evil, rather he is correcting our perception of what the good truly entails.

Very well then; we are to avoid the evil and destruction that comes from idolatry. What are we to pursue? Jesus tells us: "Blessed are the merciful, for they will be shown mercy," which teaches us the true nature of justice. We are to pursue mercy by showing mercy. To do so is to please God, and to please God should be our ultimate concern, not the acquisition of greater power, wealth, pleasure, or fame. "Blessed are the clean of heart, for they will see God" speaks again to the actuality of morality residing, not only in our acts, but in our hearts, in the reality of who we are on the inside. We may often succeed in giving others misleading impressions of who we really are. We may invent personas and pseudo-versions of ourselves on the Web or on TV, but the divine intellect is never fooled by perceptions. "Blessed are they who hunger and thirst for righteousness, for they will be satisfied" again speaks to the truth that attaining righteousness is the key to true happiness. Our natural instinct to pursue good and avoid evil aligns with our desire for the contentment that comes from living in accord with our nature. Finally, "Blessed are the peacemakers, for they will be called children of God" teaches us to pursue peace rather than violence and conflict.

These teachings may seem very simple and obvious to you, but it is surprising how routinely we all fail to consistently order our lives by them. At any rate, the point for the moment is that these moral teachings revealed by Christ are not some brand new morality that Jesus invented in order to negate our natural sense of morality. Rather, these teachings take that which we naturally know and that to which we are naturally drawn and elevates it to a greater pitch.

Another example that helps illustrate the relation of natural law morality to revealed morality can be seen with respect to marriage. In the *Summa Theologiae*, Thomas Aquinas gives a natural law argument concerning marriage.[10] His argument may surprise you. In Aquinas's view, we observe in nature that there are two groups of species. In the first group, the father participates in the upbringing of the offspring; in the second group, he does not. It is natural for penguin fathers to help in the rearing of penguin babies, for example, but dog fathers do not do the same. These are not moral judgments; it is just the way things happen to be, because animals only follow their instincts. In which group, then, should human beings be categorized?

Aquinas argues that we belong in the first group. In the human family it is natural for the father to participate in the rearing of the children in various ways. Therefore, given that sexuality is ordered to the having and rearing of children, which it is natural for human beings to pursue, we can deduce the specific moral norm that sex should take place within the context of a long-term, committed relationship. Notice that I did not say marriage. From the natural law alone, we do not get to marriage, but only a long-term relationship, a relationship, that is, which lasts at least throughout the upbringing of the child. However, through revealed morality we understand the sacrament of matrimony, which Jesus taught was for a whole lifetime and much deeper and richer than a mere long-term relationship maintained for the sake of the children. This is why the *Catechism of the Catholic Church* holds that "divorce is a grave offense against the natural law."[11] Here the understanding one could gain from natural law alone has been elevated by that which can be known from revelation.

According to the Catholic moral tradition, marriage expresses the deep unity between Christ and his body, the Church, which makes it indissoluble, mystical, and expressive of a love that transcends the natural world. Importantly, then, the Catholic teachings on marriage do not violate the natural law but rather transform and perfect it. Our natural desires to come together for the sake of the having and rearing of children are

---

[10] *ST* IIa IIae q. 154 a. 2. My focus here is on the manner that Aquinas employs natural law and revelation to form his argument. Tracing the history of Christian attitudes regarding marriage is beyond the scope of the current chapter. For more on this topic see Margaret A. Farley, *Just Love: A Framework for Christian Sexual Ethics* (New York: Continuum, 2006).

[11] *CCC* no. 2384.

transformed in the context of the sacramental marital bond. The natural principles of our reason are complemented and perfected, not replaced or contradicted, by faith. If the natural law was all we had, then we could never fulfill the deepest longings of our nature. On the other hand, if morality came from faith alone, then Christian ethics would turn out to be just another form of relativism – morality would be relative to the faith claims of some particular religious sect. By championing both the natural law and revealed morality, the Catholic moral tradition is grounded both in the universality of reason and the particularity of faith.

Having made clear the foundation of Catholic morality, we may now turn to an interrelated but importantly distinct set of issues pertaining to the topic of authority. In brief, the question involves the role that the teaching office of the Church – the Magisterium – plays in assisting individuals in the formation of specific moral norms. It is true that the Catholic moral tradition regards the moral law as inhering within the individual in the form of the natural law, but this does not mean that external authority cannot also play a role in helping shape and guide one's moral judgments.

AUTHORITY IN THE CATHOLIC MORAL TRADITION

In 1968, Blessed Paul VI composed an encyclical entitled, *Humanae vitae.* In it, he treats, among other things, the controversial topics of abortion and contraception. This encyclical caused uproar not only in the larger society, but also among Catholics. We discuss these specific issues at length in a later chapter. At the moment, my focus is only on how responses to this encyclical can help us understand the nature of authority as understood in the context of the Catholic moral tradition. One of the problems that the reception of the encyclical brought to light was the tendency on the part of some ethicists to mistakenly regard Catholic moral teaching as grounded in nothing other than mere appeals to religious authority. However, as explained earlier, the Church understands its moral teaching to be rooted in the natural law, which is the possession not only of Catholics but all people. If we all have the natural law, and the wrongness of abortion and contraception is made clear in the light of that law, then why did the views advanced in *Humanae vitae* appear obtuse to so many people? Is this not evidence that what Catholics call the natural law is, in reality, only a set of subjective, religious opinions?

In response to this problem, John Finnis and Germain Grisez developed a theory, which is commonly referred to as "the theory of basic goods." Finnis and Grisez argued that one did not need to appeal to the authority of revelation as transmitted by the Magisterium in order to form specific moral norms against abortion, contraception, or whatever else. Rather, the theory of basic goods posits the following list of goods: life, knowledge, play, aesthetic experience, sociability, practical reasonableness, and religion.[12] According to the theory, these goods are self-evident. Therefore, activities that further the basic goods are to be pursued whereas those things that endanger them are to be avoided. Finnis and Grisez hold that human beings naturally strive for holistic human fulfillment, which involves respecting each of the basic goods and not deliberately sacrificing any one of the basic goods to another. In other words, the theory of basic goods grows out of a rejection of utilitarianism, which, as we have seen, subordinates all other goods to pleasure. In this way, Finnis and Grisez attempted to advance the view that Catholic moral teaching can be rationally upheld without having to appeal to revelation or religious authority.

Another response to the Pope's encyclical came in the form of the method of Catholic moral theology known as "proportionalism." In most instances, the architects of proportionalism sought to ground their method for evaluating specific moral norms in a revision of the traditional Catholic principle of double effect. The purpose of this principle is to help one determine when it is justifiable to commit an action that one knows will have both good and bad effects (hence the term, "double"). In order to pass the doctrine of double effect, four conditions must be met:

1. The object of the act chosen must be good or indifferent.
2. The intention must be good.
3. The bad effect cannot be the means to the good effect.
4. Proportionality: the good effects must outweigh the evil effects.

In order to better understand what these criteria entail, let us consider two cases: one that passes the principle of double effect, meaning that the action being considered is, according to the Catholic moral tradition, morally justifiable, and another that fails and so cannot be done in good conscience. First, imagine a doctor who wants to prescribe pain medication to an elderly patient who has stage four liver cancer and is daily in extreme pain. Now, he foresees that prescribing her a particular pain medication will (not may) hasten her death. Is it morally licit for him to

[12] John Finnis, *Natural Law and Natural Rights* (Oxford: Clarendon Press, 1980); Germain Grisez, *The Way of the Lord Jesus: Christian Moral Principles* (Chicago: Franciscan Herald Press, 1983). The list of basic goods is sometimes formulated in different ways, but this list is fairly standard.

do so? The first criterion states that the object (this only means what is done) of the act chosen must be good or indifferent. Well, there is nothing intrinsically evil about prescribing pain medication, so it passes that one. The second criterion states that the intention must be good. Surely, relieving someone's pain is a good intention, so it passes that one. The third criterion says that the bad effect cannot be the means to the good effect. In this case the good effect is the pain relief; the bad effect is the hastened death. However, the hastened death is not the cause of the intended pain relief. Hence, it passes the third criterion. Finally, the good effects must outweigh the bad ones. This is hard to determine, but when the doctor adds up the relief of pain, the terminal nature of the condition, the effects on the family, and the medical costs, he may reasonably determine that the good effects outweigh the bad effect of hastened death in this case. Very well then; it passes double effect. The doctor may prescribe the medication in good conscience.

Next, consider a scenario where a different doctor wants to inject the same woman with a chemical that will kill her. It does not pass the first criterion, because murder is intrinsically immoral. It may pass the second, if he is doing so out of a want to relieve her pain and not for a malicious reason. It does not pass the third, as the bad effect (her death) is the means to the good effect (the cessation of pain). And, as is always the case, the fourth criterion is up for interpretation and debate.

We discuss euthanasia at length in the final chapter of this book, but for now the focus is on proportionalism, which tended to regard the fourth criterion of the principle of double effect as suitable for the formation of specific moral norms. For this reason, some came to regard proportionalism as a form of consequentialism, which is basically a pejorative term for utilitarianism. A consequentialist is someone who determines the rightness or wrongness of an act based solely on the consequences that the act produces. Despite the fact that they were often branded as consequentialists, most proportionalists would reject this description of their views. Regarding the subjects of suicide and killing, for example, Richard McCormick, S.J., in his 1973 Hillenbrand Lecture, wrote as follows:

The first thing that must be said is that the issue is not precisely whether suicide and killing are generally wrong. This we grasp spontaneously and prethematically, a point well made by Germain Grisez and John Finnis. In this sense our basic moral commitments are not the result of discursive reflection. The issue is exception making, and the form of moral reasoning that both supports and limits in an intelligible way the exceptions we tolerate.[13]

---

[13] Richard A. McCormick, "The New Medicine and Morality," *Theology Digest* 21 (1973), 315.

Although McCormick is not a consequentialist, as this passage shows, it has been argued that he, nevertheless, embraces what Baruch Brody refers to as "a consequentialist methodology for exceptions."[14] This is because McCormick grounds the legitimacy of "exception making" in only the fourth criterion of the principle of double effect, which, taken in isolation from the other criteria, leaves one with a kind of lesser evil approach.[15] This, of course, raises the question of how the weighing of consequences is supposed to take place.

The proportionalists tended to distinguish between "ontological" or "premoral" evil and "moral" evil. By "ontological" or "premoral evil," the proportionalists meant the deprivation of some basic good. For example, if I walked outside and saw a decomposing human body lying on the ground, I would be in the presence, according to this definition, of ontological evil. Death is the privation of life; evil is the privation of good. Life is a basic good. Therefore, the decaying human body is evil, ontologically speaking. However, this does not mean it is morally evil. According to the proportionalists, a moral evil refers to a deliberately willed act that produces the evil in question. So the decomposing body may be a result of moral evil (somebody murdered him) or maybe he died of natural causes (in which case ontological evil is still involved, but not moral evil). The proportionalists argued that an action, for example, killing, could entail ontological evil without entailing moral evil depending on the consequences the act produced and what was intended. Theoretically, an act may be morally upright, despite the ontological evil resultant from the act. In this way, the proportionalists denied the existence of absolute moral norms (acts that are always wrong regardless of intention and consequence).[16] It is largely for this reason that John Paul II is critical of

---

[14] See his "The Problem of Exceptions in Medical Ethics," in *Doing Evil to Achieve Good*, Paul Ramsey and Richard McCormick, eds. (Lanham, MD: University Press of America, 1985): 54–67. Brody argues, rightly in my view, that the proportionalists in general, and McCormick in particular, are not consequentialists, but nonetheless follow what Brody calls a "consequentialist methodology for exceptions" (56). Brody is not critiquing proportionalism from the standpoint of natural law ethics. Rather, he is an emotivist.

[15] McCormick thinks that certain situations simply leave one no option but "to choose the lesser evil." See McCormick, "The New Medicine and Morality," 311.

[16] The intricacies of the proportionalist claims cannot be fully addressed here. Charles Curran, for example, distinguishes four types of moral norm. First are formal absolute moral norms, such as murder. Second, are general absolute moral norms, such as not causing harm. Third are qualified absolute moral norms, such as harming someone to indulge one's sense of superiority. Fourth, are concrete unqualified absolute moral norms, such as active euthanasia is always wrong. The most fecund ground for debate really concerns the fourth kind, according to Curran. The main point he wants to extol from a proportionalist perspective is that one cannot say with accuracy that there are certain acts that are always and everywhere wrong. Curran appeals to historical consciousness and

proportionalism in his encyclical letter, *Veritatis splendor*, to which we now turn.

Veritatis splendor was promulgated on August 6, 1993.[17] The encyclical has three purposes. The first purpose is "to reflect on the whole of the Church's moral teaching, with the precise goal of recalling certain fundamental truths of Catholic doctrine which, in the present circumstances, risk being distorted or denied" (no. 4). The second purpose is to reiterate the Catholic answer to the foundations question considered at the beginning of this chapter. Third, is to reaffirm the Church's traditional moral teachings. It is primarily this third purpose that requires our attention here. The Pope begins by noting that, despite the desire on the part of some proportionalists to distance themselves from utilitarianism, proportionalism nonetheless entails the view that moral norms can be deduced "solely from a calculation of foreseeable consequences" (nos. 74–75). Now, according to the Pope, the problem with proportionalism is that it entails the view "that it is never possible to formulate an absolute prohibition of particular kinds of behavior which would be in conflict, in every circumstance and in every culture" with the moral values of "revelation and reason" (no. 75). To be sure, there are good things about proportionalism that the Pope affirms; for example, it seeks to "take account of the intention and consequences of human action" (no. 77). Nevertheless, the encyclical declares that proportionalism cannot be "faithful to the Church's teaching, when [proportionalists] believe they can justify, as morally good, deliberate choices or kinds of behavior contrary to the commandments of the divine and natural law." Thus, according to the encyclical, proportionalism "cannot claim to be grounded in the Catholic moral tradition" (no. 76).

Basically, John Paul II is critiquing proportionalism on the grounds that it is not suitable as a method for arriving at specific moral norms.[18] However, this speaks to the larger issue of the relationship of the authority of the hierarchical Magisterium to the formation of individual

---

the turn to the subject as allied in proportionalist thinking to dispel concrete unqualified absolute moral norms. See Charles Curran, "Absolute Moral Norms," in *Christian Ethics: An Introduction*, Bernard Hoose, ed. (Collegeville, MN: The Liturgical Press, 1998): 72–83.

[17] In-text parenthetical citations in this section are to the paragraph numbers of the encyclical.

[18] Assessing rival views of John Paul II's treatment of proportionalism is beyond the scope of the current chapter. See the further reading in the appendix for a sampling of works written from a proportionalist perspective. James Keenan, S.J., argues that, with respect to the reception of the encyclical, one group found it "a worthy challenge to the pervasive culture of contemporary moral relativism," whereas another group "lamented" that the views of the proportionalists "were misrepresented." See Keenan's *A History of Catholic Moral Theology in the Twentieth Century: From Confessing Sins to Liberating Consciences* (New York: Continuum, 2010), 128.

consciences. In the Catholic moral tradition, it is understood that the Magisterium is equipped to help in the formation of individual consciences for two reasons. First, given that "the task of giving an authentic interpretation of the deposit of faith has been entrusted to the living teaching office of the Church alone," the authority of the Magisterium also "extends to those truths necessarily connected with Revelation."[19] Such truths may in a number of cases concern the formation of specific moral norms.[20] This leads us to the second reason why the Magisterium is able to assist in the formation of individual consciences: "An upright and true moral conscience is formed by education and by assimilating the Word of God and the teaching of the Church. It is supported by the gifts of the Holy Spirit and helped by the advice of wise people."[21] Although God has given human beings a participative role in the formation of moral norms through the natural law, this does not mean that we are "on our own" so to speak. As John Paul II made clear, the modern age is marked by a "profound crisis of culture, which generates skepticism in relation to the very foundations of knowledge and ethics."[22] Amidst this crisis, the Magisterium is charged with the task of helping shape the consciences of the faithful and protecting them from errors.[23] And, again, in so doing the Magisterium does not appeal merely to its own authority as grounds for

---

[19] *CCC* nos. 85–100. The quotation is from the USCCB edition of the *Compendium to the Catechism of the Catholic Church* (Washington, DC: Libreria Editrice Vaticana, 2006), no. 16.

[20] However, the Catholic Church does not hold that all its moral teachings are equally authoritative. The topic of authority within the Church is more complex than often supposed. The clearest statement on this topic is probably still the Congregation of the Doctrine of the Faith's 1990 document, *Donum veritatis* (the gift of truth). The document outlines four kinds of magisterial (official) teaching and four corollary levels of assent. First, divinely revealed pronouncements are infallible and thus require theological assent. Definitive magisterial pronouncements are not divinely revealed themselves but intrinsically connected to the content of revelation and, therefore, must be firmly accepted and held. Third, non-definitive pronouncements that elucidate or clarify revelation call for religious submission of intellect and will. Finally, there are magisterial teachings that warn against dangerous opinion and error. These are often conjectural and not guaranteed by the charism of infallibility. Consequently, they require only a response of prudential assent. For further details, see *DV*.

[21] *CCC* nos. 1783–1800; citation from *Compendium* no. 374. See William C. Mattison III, "The Changing Face of Natural Law: The Necessity of Belief for Natural Law Norm Specification," *Journal of the Society of Christian Ethics* 27, no. 1 (2007): 251–77.

[22] *EV* no. 11.

[23] Of course there can arise tensions between individual consciences and the authority of the hierarchal Magisterium. This will be partly addressed in Chapter 4's treatment of prudence. However, a more prolonged treatment of the issue of justified dissent would take us beyond the scope of the current book. For more on this topic see Paulinus Ikechukwu Odozor, C.S.Sp., *Moral Theology in an Age of Renewal: A Study of the Catholic Tradition Since Vatican II* (Notre Dame, IN: University of Notre Dame Press, 2003), especially 44–77.

the moral exhortations it gives. Rather, Catholic moral teaching is rooted in revelation and reason.

Before concluding, I wish to note that I will have given the reader a very wrong impression indeed if he or she takes from this chapter the view that the Catholic moral tradition develops merely through a propositional approach to investigating moral truths without any reference to human experience. This is not the case. However, as Richard R. Gaillardetz has pointed out, experience is not purely subjective; rather, experience refers to "encountering reality in some determinate way." At the same time, "human experience is never complete; we change and grow in our grasp of reality."[24] The same is true with respect to the development of the Catholic moral tradition. It matures over time. Indeed, it matures in a manner similar to the way that human beings mature. Some transitions are greater than others, but a certain continuity always remains between what the thing was and what it becomes. The distance between the two creates the space in which Catholic moral theology happens.

Weaving these strands together, then, here is where the Catholic moral tradition stands with respect to the foundations for moral judgments and responsibility. There is an eternal law of right and wrong. Our participation in this law is called the natural law and it is something we all possess. Revealed morality both fulfills and perfects this law. Although the natural law can be accessed and defended by reason, the hierarchical Magisterium has an authoritative role to play in the shaping of consciences in order to help guide individuals in living out their natural inclinations to flourish and achieve true happiness. The Magisterium is equipped for this role because the tradition it upholds is anchored in the teachings, and, indeed, the very person of Christ. It is for the same reason that the tradition is also capable of maturing over time insofar as it comes to grasp the reality of Christ more clearly.

SUMMARY

In this chapter, we have become acquainted with the natural law tradition. Additionally, we have investigated the capacity of revealed morality to elevate and perfect what we can discern from reason alone. Through our examination of the Beatitudes and the Catholic teachings on marriage, we have seen how the confluence of revealed and natural morality

---

[24] Richard R. Gaillardetz, *By What Authority?: A Primer on Scripture, the Magisterium, and the Sense of the Faithful* (Collegeville, MN: Liturgical Press, 2003), 9.

provides a suitable foundation for moral judgments and responsibility. In addition, this chapter has introduced you to the question of authority in the context of the Catholic moral tradition. We examined basic goods theory, proportionalism, and John Paul II's critique of the latter in the encyclical letter *Veritatis splendor*.

In closing, I wish to make clear that the reason why the foundations for Catholic ethics differ so greatly from the views espoused by the thinkers considered in the previous chapter is not because Catholic ethicists invented their view of ethical foundations to counter the claims being made by Hobbes and Hume or whoever else. Rather, it is the other way around. As Montague Brown has pointed out, "Both Hobbes and Hume (along with Bacon) were caught up in the anti-Roman Catholic and hence anti-Aristotelian mindset of the Reformation. Since Thomas Aquinas and other eminent Catholic theologians made extensive use of the philosophy of Aristotle, a rejection of Catholic theology tended to include the rejection of Aristotelian philosophy."[25] At any rate, the primary purpose of the present chapter has been to provide a clear response to the foundations question according to Catholic ethics. That response is two-fold: revealed morality and natural law. What each entail and the manner in which they are related should now be clear, or at least, clearer than they were before you read this chapter.

---

[25] Montague Brown, *The Quest for Moral Foundations: An Introduction to Ethics* (Washington, DC: Georgetown University Press, 1996), 37.

CHAPTER 3

The River Between: Test Case

The social order requires constant improvement: it must be founded
in truth, built in justice, and enlivened by love.

Gaudium et spes no. 26

It is one thing to consider moral theories in the abstract and quite another
to analyze and assess them in relation to concrete practices. In this
chapter, therefore, we investigate the moral theories heretofore assessed
through an examination of a specific moral issue. Female genital cutting,
or circumcision, is still a common practice in several parts of the world.
Humanitarian critics of the practice describe it as female genital mutilation, or FGM, because the procedure involves removing a portion or all
of the external female genitalia and is normally performed on young girls
as a rite of passage into womanhood. The purpose of this chapter is to test
the theories we have learned up to now in the light of this controversial
practice.[1]

This chapter unfolds in five sections. First, we explore themes found
in Ngũgĩ wa Thiong'o's insightful novel, *The River Between*. Second, we
investigate whether the various versions of moral relativism are helpful with respect to arriving at moral judgments regarding both female
circumcision itself as well as the Western response to it. Next, we consider the natural law argument to be made against female circumcision.
A fourth section shows how norms derived by the natural law elevated

---

[1] Although indirectly, this chapter also draws attention to the topic of race and the global Catholic
Church, which has been a significant source for reflection in Catholic ethics in the post-conciliar
period. Issues arising from these reflections need not be understood as disconnected from the histor-
ical heart of the tradition. Much of this reflection has been taking place at the Catholic Theological
Ethics in the World Church international conferences. See James F. Keenan, S.J., *Catholic
Theological Ethics in the World Church: The Plenary Papers from the First Cross-cultural Conference on
Catholic Theological Ethics* (New York: Continuum, 2007).

and transfigured by the morality of the Gospel provide the most ethically sound solution for the issues raised by the practice of female circumcision. We see how this is actually taking place in modern day Kenya. Finally, a summary section addresses a few misunderstandings that may arise with respect to the fundamental claims of the current chapter and the whole of Part I.

THE RIVER BETWEEN

Ngũgĩ wa Thiong'o is a Kenyan writer whose famous novel, *The River Between*, first published in 1965, offers a vivid depiction of colonialism's impact on East Africa. The setting for the novel is bucolic Kenya, the home of the Kikuyu people. The Honia River, to which the title refers, divides the borders of Kameno and Makuyu. In Kameno lives an important elder, Chege, who is the father of the main character, Waiyaki. The village folk regard Chege as a kind of mystical prophet who speaks with Murungu (God) but never shares what Murungu tells him with the people. To Chege, the Christian teachings of the colonial missionaries are unintelligible. Chege sends Waiyaki to a Christian school to see what all the fuss is about, but not to convert to Christianity.

On the other side of the river lives Joshua, who has converted to Christianity. Since his conversion, he now regards all tribal rituals to be evil. One of these rituals is female circumcision. Joshua refuses to circumcise his daughters Nyambura and Muthoni, because he now regards this custom as contrary to the laws of nature and of God. Violating Joshua's wishes, Muthoni follows the ancient custom and is circumcised, but the tribal leaders cannot stop the bleeding, eventuating in her tragic death.

In the story, so beautifully narrated by Thiong'o, Chege and Joshua are symbols of the moral and ethical divide between two radically distinct cultures. Waiyaki, who is a symbol for the possibility of unity between these differing ways of life, ultimately is unable to bring the two cultures together in a creative synthesis. He must choose between two rival moralities and ways of life despite his efforts to avoid having to make that choice. The novel is a chilling and disturbing reflection on the kinds of unnecessary conflict and cultural misunderstandings that ripped villages in Africa apart during the colonial era as indigenous cultures clashed with traditional European values and Christian ethical norms.

FEMALE CIRCUMCISION AND MORAL RELATIVISM

Let us consider first the case that can be made from the standpoint of the various forms of moral relativism. Indeed, at first glance Joshua's reaction to female circumcision, as depicted in *A River Between*, seems to point to the value of cultural relativism as an ethical theory. Recall Augustine's warning to "pay careful attention to the conduct appropriate to different places, times, and persons" so as to avoid "rash imputations of wickedness." The cultural relativist (which Augustine was not) could argue that the Western European colonists' attitude toward the customs of the Kikuyu people in general, and female circumcision in particular, is a prime example of intolerance, ignorance, and bigotry. If only the colonists could have respected and appreciated the symbolic meaning of female circumcision as understood in Kikuyu culture, then tragedy could have been avoided. Indeed, as Bénézet Bujo has observed, horrific injustice often followed from the fact that the "Europeans regarded themselves from the outset as superior to the unarmed Africans," and this assumed superiority often resulted in dismissive attitudes toward traditional African religions and religious practices.[2]

The problem is that the cultural relativist cannot really decry the evils of colonialism without violating his own principles. If cultural relativism is true, then the fact that the colonists were domineering and intolerant, in instances where that may have been the case, is not morally or ethically wrong. It is just their culture. The fact that they attempted to impose their morality on those they colonized cannot itself have an objective moral value. It is just what Western colonizers in that time period (so we can bring in historical relativism too) happened to do, just like the Kikuyu people happened to practice female circumcision as a rite of passage for womanhood. Thus, neither cultural nor historical relativism is of much help in adjudicating the case of female circumcision as practiced and understood by the Kikuyu people and the colonial response to it. If you want to bring it in to defend the legitimacy of female circumcision for the Kikuyu, then you also have to bring it in to defend the legitimacy of the colonial view that it is morally praiseworthy to impose your morals on others. Furthermore, as a cultural relativist you have to believe that the only way the Kikuyu could learn that FGM was wrong would be by being told so by another culture. In this way, cultural relativism seems to

---

[2] Bénézet Bujo, *African Theology in Its Social Context*, tr. John O'Donohue, M. Afr (New York: Orbis, 1992), 39.

necessitate the kinds of imperialism against which cultural relativists generally find themselves inclined to protest.

Very well then; let's move on to emotivism. The problem here is that one could imagine rival and contradictory emotional responses to female circumcision, both claiming to be grounded in what Hume would call a universal sentiment of benevolence. Perhaps one feels outraged at the practice and the toll it can take on a woman's body and indeed her whole life. There are several instances where female circumcision leads to painful death, infertility, or the impossibility of experiencing sexual pleasure. When you read *A River Between*, you may feel outraged at the people who keep this practice going despite all of its terrible results. On the other hand, you may feel sympathy for the Kikuyu and antipathy for the colonizers who so easily assume their own moral superiority. Or, similar to the main character Waiyaki, you could feel torn between the two points of view. The problem is that emotivism cannot provide us with a foundation to discern which emotions are or are not in line with what is truly morally right. Even if we accept that benevolence is a good thing we ought to encourage, which emotivism on its own principles cannot really tell us, then we still have to ask what benevolence in this particular situation truly entails. If moral emotions-feelings-intuitions-sentiments were uniform, then they may provide a firm basis for moral responsibility; however, they are not.

Social contract theory isn't any help either. Whether female circumcision is legal or illegal, whether it reflects the will of the sovereign, none of that really matters here. The whole question is whether it is moral or immoral. All social contract theory can really tell us is that whoever has power over the Kikuyu, whether that is the Kikuyu themselves or the colonizers, can attempt to impose law. As we saw earlier, however, this itself raises ethical concerns, such as the forceful imposition of an alien moral code on a colonized people. Hobbes's relativizing of morality to power is not helpful in responding to the morality of female circumcision and the colonial response to it. If anything, it only raises more problems.

Utilitarianism does not seem able to provide us much direction with respect to female circumcision either. There is not an objective way to tabulate the pleasures and pains associated with the practice for the individuals who undergo it or for the community as a whole. Beginning with the individual, on the one hand, she risks her life, suffers greatly, and loses the ability to feel sexual pleasure and sometimes to procreate. On the other hand, she feels she has become a woman and kept the ancient traditions of her people. This is why Joshua's daughter, Muthoni, violates his wishes and undergoes the practice without his consent, eventuating in her death. With respect to the larger community, the question is even murkier. What exactly does the greatest good for the greatest number entail here? On the one hand, protesting the practice rips the community apart, and so it would seem that it ought to be maintained. On the other hand, the practice is harmful and dangerous for more than half the individuals of that same community. In what direction does the principle of utility take us? Clearly, we cannot speak to the morality or immorality of female circumcision through a utilitarian calculation. Indeed, these calculations, despite their claims to objectivity, turn out to be every bit as subjective as the other versions of moral relativism.

In sum, the various versions of moral relativism are unhelpful theories with respect to female circumcision as practiced by the Kikuyu and the colonial response to it. These theories are entirely subjective. They either tell us that we have to accept the views of both groups as ethically legitimate, despite the obvious contradiction this entails, or they provide us with equal opportunity to support or reject either view but cannot provide us with a suitable foundation from which to do so. At this point, then, we may proceed to analyze a natural law response to female circumcision.

FEMALE CIRCUMCISION AND NATURAL LAW

From the standpoint of the natural law, female circumcision is an intrinsically immoral practice. We are to pursue good and avoid evil. Our natural inclinations to have and rear children and to preserve the species are good. Threats to this are evil. Thus, the former are to be pursued and the latter avoided. Female circumcision risks the woman's life, seriously jeopardizes her ability to have children, and if practiced universally, would represent a significant risk to the preservation of the human species. In addition, it often leads to early pregnancy, impacting the ability to raise the child, or premature birth, impacting the viability of the child, particularly in a culture that does not enjoy all the benefits of medical science that Westerners take for granted. In any event, the specific moral norm "female circumcision should be avoided" is both valid and legitimate from the standpoint of natural law ethics. The practice is unnatural and immoral.

Additionally, female circumcision does not pass the principle of double effect. First, the object of the act chosen – deliberate and medically unnecessary mutilation of the human body that impairs its functional integrity – is intrinsically immoral.[3] Second, the intention to keep a tribal

---

[3] See *GS* no. 27; also see *EV* no. 4.

custom and respect one's ancestors may be good, but clearly the bad effect is the means to the good effect. It is by performing the female circumcision that the custom is kept. Whether the good effects outweigh the bad effects is up for debate. But whatever the result of that, female circumcision clearly does not meet the first and third criteria and so cannot be morally justified. Nevertheless, the proportionalist might argue that the mutilation is a "premoral" or "ontological" evil, making the action wrong but still morally good considering the intention of maintaining a traditional practice and fostering solidarity within the tribe.

Although Catholic ethics holds that female circumcision is morally evil on the basis of the natural law tradition, recall that Catholic ethics does not rely on the natural law alone. The question, then, is what does revealed morality add to the equation? The answer is love. It is not enough to go about wagging your finger at people and condemning them, even when you are right. You must love and help them. This is precisely the Catholic response to female circumcision in Kenya, as the next section makes clear.

THE CATHOLIC RESPONSE TO FEMALE CIRCUMCISION

As Emmanuel Katongole and Chris Rice have stated, "Christians believe that the world with all its mess is still the province of God's reign and ongoing redemption." As such, Christians are charged with the task of "connecting the brokenness of the world to the story of God and discovering the many gifts that story offers."[4] This is precisely what Catholic aid workers in the town of Meru have been doing by assisting with grassroots movements already begun by native Kenyans. Together, they are working toward the implementation of alternative rites of passage for girls and young women. Instead of female circumcision to introduce the young girls to womanhood, the older women of the tribe teach them how to prepare and serve food and how to use herbal remedies to treat specific medical ailments.

This is not entirely new. Girls in Kenya have always received a traditional training to shape them as future wives, mothers, and women. However, now at the end of this training they enjoy a graduation ceremony and receive a certificate (instead of having part of their genitalia mutilated). This "alternative rite of passage" has been implemented in the

---

[4] Emmanuel Katongole and Chris Rice, *Reconciling All Things: A Christian Vision for Justice, Peace, and Healing* (Downers Grove, IL: IVP Books, 2008), 41.

Catholic diocese of Meru with the help of Catholic Relief Services and other Catholic charities. It is not implemented through force, coercion, and condemnation but through charity, cooperation, and mutual understanding. In this way, an indigenous culture is preserved while a harmful practice is removed.

Additionally, as part of the Catholic outreach, the girls receive an education that corrects some of the cultural myths that circulate about the need for female circumcision, such as, "uncircumcised women cannot become pregnant" and "uncircumcised women are not real women."[5] These, of course, are objectively false claims whatever one's culture. In this way, then, the cultural confluence and understanding that Waiyaki sought but never attained in *A River Between* is actually taking place in modern day Kenya. This attests both to the universality of morality, which transcends culture, and to the Gospel's call for love and understanding. Furthermore, as Agbonkhianmeghe E. Orobator has pointed out, it is this same Gospel understood in the unfolding tradition of the Church that can serve to draw attention to the Blessed Virgin Mary as a powerful symbol of hope and redemption for women in Africa: "From the perspective of our African tradition it would be quite fitting to accord Mary all the honor and the glory as queen mother of God. After all, we say in our African cultures that 'mother is supreme.' "[6]

One further point and I am finished. I will have given the reader the wrong impression if he or she leaves this chapter with the view that some cultures possess understandings of morality that are superior to other cultures. In fact, such a view does not coincide with Catholic moral teaching. Rather, the Catholic view is that, when two cultures collide, learning from each other is a two-way street. Western cultures may be able to offer unique perspectives on the wrongness of something such as FGM, but the native Kenyans who practice this may be able to teach Western cultures something about the importance of ancestral ritual and respect for tradition, even if FGM represents a warped instance of this. The natural law is not the possession of one particular culture or group; it belongs to every member of the human family. None of us keep it perfectly. When differing cultures encounter each other, this is an opportunity for us both to grow from the exchange. A colonial mentality, which glibly assumes

---

[5] There are important parallels here between the way that these women are learning to reclaim their bodies and the way that black women who experienced the horrors of slavery learned to do the same. See M. Shawn Copeland, *Enfleshing Freedom: Body, Race, and Being* (Minneapolis, MN: Fortress Press, 2010).

[6] Agbonkhianmeghe E. Orobator, *Theology Brewed in an African Pot* (New York: Orbis, 2008), 104.

its own superiority, cannot be squared with the Catholic moral tradition. Rather, the Church understands that it can profit from "the riches hidden in various cultures" and that by approaching these riches in a respectful way "new avenues to truth are opened up."[7]

SUMMARY

In this chapter, we have reflected on ethical issues related to female circumcision by examining themes found in Ngũgĩ wa Thiong'o's important novel, *The River Between*. We have seen that the various versions of moral relativism are ultimately unhelpful when it comes to forming a judgment with respect to both the issue of female circumcision itself as well as the Western response to it. Additionally, we have seen how specific moral norms grounded in the natural law elevated and transfigured by the morality of the Gospel have provided an ethically sound solution for the issues raised by the practice of female circumcision. In this way, we see that the Catholic moral tradition's foundations for moral judgments and responsibility – natural law and revealed morality – involve much more than abstract intellectual speculation and theory; these foundations hold up when tested by the storms and challenges of real life.

Before concluding this section, this chapter, and indeed the whole of Part I, I wish to make one further point about the moral law. I realize that several people are not convinced by the kinds of arguments I have been putting forward in this and the previous two chapters. That is, there is a great number of people who think that no matter how sound one's logic or how clever one's arguments, the idea of an objective moral law is simply not tenable. Additionally, some people think that to subscribe to the reality of an objective moral law is not only mean, but also fantastically arrogant. We all know what it is like to speak with someone who seems to care nothing for our point of view. He is so sure that he is right and has all the answers that he does not really take the time to listen to us. Conversations with him, therefore, are unavoidably one-sided. We leave the discussion at least frustrated and sometimes exasperated.

To better understand what I am attempting to describe here, consider the following scenario. Fiona is a college student heading home for Thanksgiving dinner, which she always dreads because her family tends to get into heated religious and political conversations that never seem to go

---

[7] See *GS* no. 44.

anywhere. The two main players are always her dad, a fierce conservative who regards liberals as a threat to the continuation of Western civilization, and her Aunt Sue, who loves all things liberal and thinks conservatives are hateful and intolerant people who will eventually die off, leading to a kind of progressive utopia that she greatly anticipates. Last year, the debate was about gay marriage. The conversation started out innocently enough; Aunt Sue mentioned how pleased she was at her state's recent passage of a bill legalizing civil unions. Fiona's dad immediately took issue with this. The conversation quickly ensued into gasps, flush faces, repeated rolling of the eyes, and Fiona's mother prudently suggesting multiple times (as she does every year) that they change the subject.

This Thanksgiving turns out not to be any different, only this time the subject is abortion rights. Fiona's dad is thrilled that a recent bill to illegalize abortions after twenty-four weeks was upheld, despite the protestations of the pro-choice movement. Aunt Sue objects. She regards the upholding of the bill as a blow to women's rights. Fiona's dad responds that there is nothing sexist about protecting the lives of unborn children, to which Aunt Sue replies that they are not children but merely "fetuses" and that upholding the rights of women is more important than that of a fetus. At this point, a back and forth follows regarding the question of when life begins, but neither party really listens to the other. Each just waits for his or her turn to talk. The argument is like two trains passing in the night. This goes on for a while until Fiona can't take anymore. At a rare pause in the exchange, she chimes in that while she agrees that abortion is morally evil, she does not think that criminalization is the best way to deal with the problem. Her dad and Aunt Sue both take notice of her, nod agreeably, and then go on with their argument as though Fiona wasn't even there. The discussion goes on uselessly, gets more and more heated, and finally Fiona's mom suggests (as she does every year) that they change the subject.

Now, Fiona, very understandably, comes to regard the idea of an objective moral law discernible by human reason as absurd. At least, if there is one, it does not seem very useful in resolving the dispute between her dad and Aunt Sue. Moreover, the whole problem with their futile disputes is that they both are so assured of their own rightness. They are too proud to consider the possibility that the other person may have something constructive to add to the conversation. In other words, the very idea of an objective moral law is to blame. Wouldn't it be much better if Fiona's dad and Aunt Sue agreed to disagree? Wouldn't it be better if they admitted that neither point of view was right or wrong but merely differences of opinion? Wouldn't acceptance of this fact lead to better, or at least friendlier, conversation at Thanksgiving dinner? So Fiona decides that she is not going to be like her dad or Aunt Sue. She is going to reject the idea of "right and wrong" in the objective sense and speak instead of rival opinions and points of view to which all are entitled and which ought to be respected. She finds this far more humble and practical than the alternative.

From the standpoint of the Catholic moral tradition, at least six things can be said with respect to Fiona's objection to the moral law. There are three things about which Fiona is right and three things about which she is wrong. First, she is right in her conclusion that the reality of the moral law, in and of itself, is insufficient to the task of clearing up any given moral disagreement at any given time. There can be gaps in our knowledge, errors, miscalculations, and so forth. Second, what people refer to as "the moral law" or "objective morality" can very often be merely a by-product of their own subjective point of view. We humans have a tendency to think that the very same things that are self-evident to us should be self-evident to all. Sometimes we come to find that things we thought were objective turn out to exist only in our own subjective points of view. Third, being assured of one's rightness does make it difficult for us to regard opposing views as anything more than errors. If we regard the opposing view as utterly devoid of truth, then obviously we are not going to be very receptive to what the other person has to say. About all of this, Fiona is right.

About the following three things, however, Fiona is wrong. First, the reality of widespread moral disagreement does not disprove the existence of the moral law. Indeed, the fact that people find themselves so often divided about moral questions and that such disputes become so passionate and intense itself attests to the importance of this reality in our lives. No one would ever get into a serious dispute over whether Frosted Flakes was a superior cereal to Cheerios, because everyone knows that this is merely a matter of preference. Americans would only jokingly criticize the British for driving on the "wrong" side of the street, because we know that this is simply a societal convention. When we disagree over moral questions, however, we at least act as though there is something important and real in dispute. The fact that we can err in our judgments of the moral law does not mean that no such law exists. For centuries humans believed erroneous things about the nature of the physical universe, such as that the sun revolved around the earth. Even now scientists disagree about whether the fundamental building blocks of the universe are more

like strings or loops, but clearly this does not mean that there are no
such things as facts about the physical universe or natural laws in the
scientific sense.

This brings me to the second point about which Fiona is mistaken.
The fact that people often mix up the objective and the subjective does
not mean that everything is subjective. Indeed, in order for the very
statement that people often make this mistake to be true it would need
to be true in the objective sense. If all was merely opinion, then that very
statement would be only an opinion and hence self-refuting. Finally –
and this is the really important thing – giving up on the reality of the
moral law, however tempting, cannot really lead to better conversations.
In order to understand what I mean to say here, one must distinguish
between quarreling and arguing. Quarreling is merely trying to win an
argument, trying to put the other in the wrong and show off how smart
you think you are. Arguing, on the other hand, means discussing an issue
with someone with whom you disagree in order to attempt to mutually
arrive at more truth than you had before you started the conversation.
The former, quarreling, is adversarial and unpleasant, but arguing is actually a kind of partnering with someone in a quest for greater truth. We
are trying to benefit from the point of view of someone who has a different take on life than we do. Now, the fact that Fiona's dad and her Aunt
Sue quarrel with each other rather than argue is really not the fault of the
moral law. We humans quarrel because we're adversarial and we like the
feeling of being right. On the other hand, if there is no moral law, then
no argument can really take place in the sense just described, because
there is no moral reality to be discovered. If there is no moral law, then
bald disagreement must always and inevitably be the end of every conversation. As Catholic moral theologian Lisa Sowle Cahill has aptly
observed, "radical deconstruction of moral foundations simply leads to a
cultural relativism which enervates real moral communication, intercul-
tural critique, and cooperation in defining and building just conditions
of life for men and women."[8]

To uphold the reality of the moral law does not mean that you think
you have the right answer to every ethical question under the sun or that
you have nothing to learn from those with whom you disagree. Rather,
to uphold the reality of the moral law means that you seek to know that
which you can and are happy to partner with others in this quest when
and where it is possible. Indeed, as *Gaudium et spes* acknowledges, even

---

[8] Lisa Sowle Cahill, *Sex, Gender & Christian Ethics* (Cambridge: Cambridge University Press, 1996), 2.

"pastors will not always be so expert as to have a ready answer to every problem, even every grave problem, that arises." Our responsibility, therefore, is to "try to guide each other by sincere dialogue in a spirit of mutual charity," and we are to do this "under the guidance of Christian wisdom and with careful attention to the teaching authority of the Church."[9]

[9] *GS* no. 43.

PART II

Grace at the Heart of Virtue

CHAPTER 4

The Cardinal Virtues

> Our present discussion does not aim, as our others do, at study; for the purpose of our examination is not to know what virtue is, but to become good, since otherwise the inquiry would be of no benefit to us.
>
> Aristotle, *The Nicomachean Ethics*

The importance of virtue in the history of moral theory is sometimes overlooked in contemporary ethics. Virtue is at the heart of the moral outlook found in classical philosophy, and it plays a comparably significant role in the development of the Catholic moral tradition. The influence of virtue as an ethical theory began to wane in the late Middle Ages, however, and nearly vanished with the advent of modernity. This is partly attributable to the popularity of ethical theories considered in the first chapter of this book: emotivism, social contract theory, utilitarianism, and historicism. However, during the same period, reflection on virtue began to vanish even within the field of Catholic moral theology. At least since the Council of Trent, focus tended to be primarily, if not exclusively, on law and obligation understood from within the framework of the sacrament of penance. In the main, this neglect of virtue as a moral theory marked the decades leading up to the Second Vatican Council. Even in the decades that immediately followed the council, Catholic moral theologians concerned themselves largely with questions of foundation and method – the kinds of questions considered in Part I. Indeed, it was relatively late in the post-conciliar period that virtue returned to a place of prominence in Catholic moral theology.

Before we can appreciate the return, however, we must understand the beginning. Consequently, the current chapter explores the classical account of the cardinal virtues of prudence, justice, temperance, and fortitude. St. Ambrose referred to these virtues as "cardinal," from the Latin "*cardo*," which means "hinge" (such as the hinge on a door), because these are the virtues that open the door to the good life. This chapter develops over seven sections. The first section comments on the relationship of the natural law to the formation of virtue and offers some caveats to ensure that the current chapter is properly understood. The second section examines the soul and its powers – the perfection of which make up the four cardinal virtues examined in subsequent sections. The final section deals with the question of how the virtues are attained.

THE NATURAL LAW AND VIRTUE

Let me begin by commenting briefly on the link between the formation of virtue and the reality of the natural law. Much classical thought is concerned with accurately discerning right from wrong. Indeed, for Socrates, wisdom only meant correct knowledge of good and evil, and he thought that this, wisdom, was the only virtue. All the other virtues he thought of as mere expressions of wisdom in different contexts.

In order to understand why Socrates advocated such a view it is helpful to reflect on the dominant thought of his age, against which he was critically responding. The most influential philosophical school in the period prior to Socrates was the school of the Sophists. Their view, put plainly, was that there is no such thing as objective truth. Sound familiar? All truth, according to the Sophists, is a matter of perception. This is perhaps best expressed in the "man is the measure doctrine" held by one of the leading Sophists, Protagoras. According to Plato, Protagoras taught that, "man is the measure of all things: of the things which are, that they are, and of the things which are not, that they are not." In other words, "as each thing appears to me, so it is for me, and as it appears to you, so it is for you."[1] The same was true, according to Protagoras, with respect to morality, which is to say that Protagoras was a moral relativist. Indeed, most of the leading philosophers in the age before Socrates were relativists. One of the reasons why Socrates and his pupils are remembered by history is because they sought to resist the dominant trend of thought of their time. They sought to communicate, in a convincing way, that deep sense that human beings have that right and wrong, good and evil, are real things.

At the same time, the purpose of the natural law is not merely to help us determine the right rules to follow. The further claim that virtue ethics

---

[1] *Theaetetus* 152 a-b in *Plato: Complete Works*, John Cooper, ed. (Indianapolis, IN: Hackett Publishing Company, 1997).

makes is that morality is about more than discerning our moral obligations correctly and doing our duty. Rather, morality is about living in accord with our nature and purpose as human beings. The virtues are names for the kind of qualities that develop when we do so. Morality, from the standpoint of virtue ethics, is ultimately ordered to human flourishing and happiness. More precisely, morality is ordered to the perfection of the human soul, and such a soul shall attain true happiness. Polus was exasperated when Socrates refused to comment on whether Archelaus, the rich and powerful ruler of Macedonia, was happy or miserable. Socrates refused to do so because he did not know whether Archelaus had or had not lived a moral life.

POLUS: Really? Is happiness determined entirely by that?
SOCRATES: Yes, Polus, so I say anyway. I say that the admirable and good person, man or woman, is happy, but that the one who's unjust and wicked is miserable.
POLUS: So on your reasoning this man Archelaus is miserable?
SOCRATES: Yes, my friend, if he is in fact unjust.[2]

Forming a just soul is the key to attaining true happiness. However, the ancient philosophers were not in a position to understand that ultimate happiness is only possible with the help of God's grace (grace is only a theological word for help).

Suppose that a man was stranded on a desert island and one day a large hunk of plastic floated to shore. The man realizes that he can use it as a sail and so builds a raft, mounts it, attaches the sail, plans his escape, and so forth. And now suppose that he clears the tide and makes it into the ocean paddling and plotting. One day, however, a violent gust of wind rips his sail from his makeshift raft causing it to drift for a while before getting lodged in underwater debris. By this point the man is exhausted, dehydrated, and struggling just to survive. He is stranded in the middle of the ocean helpless and hopeless. He finally gives up, but just before he is about to lose consciousness for the final time a huge ocean liner happens to pass by; it spots him and he is rescued. I know it is a rough analogy, but attaining ultimate happiness by living a virtuous life is a bit like that. From one point of view it seems like it is all up to us. We have to do the planning and plotting, implement our plans correctly, and so forth. On the other hand, without some kind of almost magical help from the outside we will fail. Providence secures the victory. However, this does not

---

[2] *Gorgias* 470 d–471 in *Plato: Complete Works*, John Cooper, ed. (Indianapolis, IN: Hackett Publishing Company, 1997).

make our efforts useless. Our degree of control over the shape of our own lives is simultaneously much more and much less than we sometimes care to admit. Keeping these caveats in place, we may now turn to the ancient account of virtue.

THE SOUL

Most people believe that they possess a soul, but are not quite sure what they mean by the term "soul." What is a soul? Have you ever seen, heard, smelled, touched, or tasted one? If not, then how do you know it is there? Moreover, if you do not know what a soul is, then how do you know you have one? In television and movies, the soul is often depicted as a kind of blurry blob that lives in your chest and floats off somewhere when you die. What is that about? Then, some people are comfortable to leave it undefined or to define it in a vague way as that which makes them who they are or some such thing. Surely your body also plays a role in making you who you are. You don't think that if you switched bodies with some random person you'd go on being you just the same as you were before. So, what is the soul?

When the classical philosophers spoke of the soul, they meant something quite specific, and in order to arrive at a proper understanding of what they meant by virtue, one must first understand their view of the human soul. According to Aristotle, the soul refers to a thing's internal principle of motion.[3] It is that which animates living things. Indeed, the Latin word for soul is *anima*, which is the root of our English word "animate," meaning "to give motion." Hence, Aristotle believed that all things that can move from an internal cause have souls. The tree outside your room, in Aristotle's view, possesses a soul. So does your dog, and so do you. You do not all, however, possess souls in the same way.

Let us begin with the tree. There is some kind of internal principle by which the tree grows, develops, withers, and so forth. This does not mean that external principles do not matter; the tree needs soil, water, wind, and sunlight. Given these things in the proper conditions, it will grow. This kind of soul – the type that enables organic things to grow and develop under the right conditions – Aristotle referred to as the nutritive soul. The tree has it, your dog has it, and you have it; all organic life possesses a

---

[3] This section draws from Aristotle's famous work *De Anima* (On the Soul), tr. Hugh Lawson-Tancred (London: Penguin Books, 1986).

nutritive soul. The coffee cup does not. It can only move by means of an external cause, such as you picking it up to have a drink.

With your dog, however, something else comes into the picture. Your dog has the five senses; it can see, touch, taste, smell, and hear. It also possesses natural instincts, such as the instincts to eat, drink, and reproduce. Interesting research has been done to show that plant life is capable of sensing and interacting with the surrounding environment in a much more complex way then Aristotle could have known, but the basic division between plant life and animal life still holds. The kind of soul that dogs, cows, deer, ducks, and all animal life has, then, Aristotle referred to as the appetitive soul. Your dog does not have an appetitive soul instead of a nutritive soul; he has both kinds, as do you.

There is this great division, then, between plant life and animal life, but one further division remains. In addition to the nutritive and appetitive soul, human beings possess a rational soul. As discussed at great length in Part I, we human beings have the capacity to distinguish true from false and good from evil and to choose between them. If we lacked either of these, then all the things we say about ethics, all our moral judgments, and all laws would just be one huge mistake.

Classical philosophers such as Aristotle understood the soul in terms of its powers. Power here does not mean political power but power in the sense of ability, capacity, or potential. The tree has the potential to grow under the right conditions; the coffee cup does not. The dog has the capacity to interact with its environment through its senses and to desire on the basis of its natural instincts. You have both capacities as well as the capacity to know and choose truth and goodness. Human beings are unique in this sense, but this is not meant to be a disparagement of plants and animals. It is only to say that to discuss the ethics of oak trees or penguins does not make sense, because we believe they lack the capacity to know and to choose – the two cornerstones for ethics. Sometimes a penguin mother may try to take the baby penguin of another penguin mother, but you wouldn't put her in penguin jail. She is only following a natural instinct. Sometimes an oak tree may grow large and crowd out other trees causing them to perish, but you wouldn't have a trial and cut it down. Choice and consent were not involved. So to say that human beings are the only beings capable of knowing and choosing is not meant to deride the animal world or the plant world; it is just a way of describing a fact about the universe. Just think how upside-down the world would be if we acted as though the tree outside your room and your dog had the capacity to know truth and to distinguish good from evil, or that you lacked such a capacity.

We have, then, these powers, some of which we share with plant and animal life, such as the power to grow and the power to desire, but some of which are distinctive to us, such as the powers to know and choose. Virtues refer to the perfections of the powers of the soul, which we can shape through our own actions. When the classical philosophers spoke of virtue, they were not just referring to qualities they happened to find pleasing or useful. They meant something specific. Wisdom is the perfection of the soul's rational capacity, justice is the perfection of the will's capacity to choose, and temperance and fortitude perfect the appetitive desires we share with animals. To perfect one's soul is to live in accord with one's nature, and to live in accord with one's nature is to flourish. This is easy for the tree and the dog. As long as the external conditions are right, they will flourish, but given that we, to some degree, choose how we grow, we decide whether to flourish or to live in a manner that does not coincide with our nature, causing our soul to wither and shrink. Virtues, then, can be thought of as names or descriptions of the flourishing soul. Let us take them now in turn.

PRUDENCE

All the great philosophers and theologians have understood how key wisdom is to living the good life and achieving true happiness, as opposed to the counterfeit happiness that comes from pursuing power, wealth, pleasure, and honor as ends in themselves. Indeed, as I stated before, Socrates believed that wisdom, the perfection of the soul's rational powers, was the only virtue. The other virtues were merely names for the activities of wisdom in different contexts and situations.

Plato furthered this view, as did Aristotle. However, Aristotle made an important clarification. The rational soul is capable both of discerning what the truth is (with the speculative intellect) and also of applying it to particulars (with the practical intellect). The speculative and practical are not two different intellects, but two different functions of the rational power of the soul. Whereas Socrates and Plato rightly understood wisdom, in the moral sense, to pertain to correct knowledge of good and evil, Aristotle clarified that the perfection of the rational soul entailed not merely this knowledge but the proper application of it in a given situation. The ability to rightly apply correct knowledge of good and evil in distinct situations Aristotle called *phronesis*, or prudence, which best translates as moral intelligence.[4] It is one thing to know that $a^2 + b^2 = c^2$,

---

[4] *NE* VI 1. §7 (1139a). See Julia Annas, *The Morality of Happiness* (New York: Oxford University Press, 1994).

but in addition to knowing it, you also need to apply it on the test to the triangle with legs of three and four and to a series of other, different right triangles. It is one thing to know that you ought to pursue good and to avoid evil, but to distinguish the two in the myriad situations of moral significance that confront us in life is an ability that must be cultivated, if we are to live as ethical beings in accord with our nature.

At this point you may be wondering how prudence differs from the more ordinary term with which you are probably more familiar, conscience. Well, in the first place, when people use the term conscience nowadays they usually assume an emotivist point of view. Conscience reduces to a strong feeling to act or not act in a particular way. In the technical sense, though, conscience means something more specific than this. It is the name for the knowledge you arrive at having employed your prudential reasoning in a particular situation. So, again, if the legs of the right triangle are three and four, and you employ $a^2 + b^2 = c^2$ in order to rightly submit that the hypotenuse is five, then, in this analogy, the formula ($a^2 + b^2 = c^2$) is like the natural law; the application of it to this particular triangle with legs of three and four is the prudential reasoning, and arriving at the right answer is conscience (in Latin "conscience" refers to moral knowledge that comes together with proper reasoning from true principles). Very well then; the answer is five. If everyone else in the class thinks it is twenty-five, they are simply wrong. If they think it is yellow, they are very wrong. In the same way, if an entire society comes to think that the wealthy man who tricked the poor widow with the investment scheme did not break the moral law, they are wrong. If they think he should be praised for his cunning, then they are even more wrong.

All of this brings me to the subject of what Catholic ethicists call "erroneous conscience." That is, similar to the fact that it is possible to arrive at the wrong answer in mathematics, so too with respect to moral issues. Nevertheless, one must always follow one's conscience, because this pertains to the capacity God has given us to make right moral choices. According to Catholic teaching (this may surprise you), if anyone, even someone in authority, tells you to act in a way that violates your conscience, you ought to resist. And you can see why. There are numerous instances where we arrive at the right moral judgment on our own but are led off in the wrong direction by misguided friends or corrupt or incompetent authorities. At the same time, following your conscience does not guarantee that you are right, because everyone's conscience can err. This is why it is good to seek out trustworthy sources of external authority to help guide us, as discussed at the end of Chapter 2.

There are two kinds of erroneous conscience. First, there is erroneous conscience with vincible ignorance.[5] This means you did not know any better, but you could have if you would have tried harder. This kind of ignorance means your action is still blameworthy. For example, if I bought my niece a Barbie doll for Christmas when a five-minute phone call with her parents would have informed me that she has no interest in Barbie dolls, then I am still at fault for buying a bad present. The guilt I feel at her disappointment, even if she tries to hide it, is deserved. The other kind of erroneous conscience is with invincible ignorance. This means I am not at fault, because there is no way I could have known better. For example, if I called my niece's parents and learned that she loves Dora the Explorer, and thus bought her a Dora the Explorer DVD, not knowing that her classmate got her the same DVD, then I am not at fault; even though I still may have to go out and buy her a new present later.

Hopefully, the relationship between prudence and conscience is clear. There is one further point to be made about prudence before moving on to justice. Already you understand the main function of prudence, that it is the perfection of the soul's practical reasoning, and you understand its relationship to natural law and conscience, however, another function of prudence is to set things in order. In the moral sense, this means prioritizing the commitments in your life in a proper way by putting them, as it were, into the correct hierarchical scheme. We discuss this much further in the next chapter when we treat the theological virtue of hope, but for the moment it is enough to say that what a person cares most about, his priorities, tells us a great deal about his moral character. Is making money more important than keeping promises? Is feeling respected, or even feared, more important than justice? Is getting what you want more important than someone else's feelings and well-being? Priorities matter. Prudence is also the virtue of rightly ordering one's commitments in the various domains of life. Doing so helps to ensure right relationships with others, which brings me to the next of the cardinal virtues, justice.

JUSTICE

Whereas prudence is the perfection of the practical reasoning, justice is the perfection of the will. It is the virtue that safeguards right relationships with others as well as harmony within the individual soul. Indeed, the Latin word *ius*, from which we get our word justice, only means "proper

---

[5] *ST* IIa IIae qq. 47–56.

harmony" or "right ordering of things." Aristotle spoke of two main kinds of justice: distributive justice, which has to do with giving others what they are due, and rectificatory justice, which deals with setting things right when an injustice has been committed. Given that we treat both of these extensively in later chapters, we may, for the current chapter, focus on justice in the more general sense of harmony or right order with respect to the individual and his or her relations with others.

Let us begin with what it means to be in the right order with others. First and foremost, to be in the right order with anyone, it is necessary to be rightly ordered to God. Indeed, Anselm understood the need for the Incarnation, God becoming man in the person of Jesus Christ, as restoring right relationship with God. The story in Genesis is not about some magic fruit; the whole point is that Adam and Eve, by disobeying God, set the whole human race on the wrong course. God, by virtue of being God, is due our utmost praise, gratitude, worship, adoration, and trust, but in the garden, deceived as they were by the serpent, Adam and Eve withheld these things from God. This created a debt, which is a word for a gap that needs to be filled in order for justice to be restored. This gap, however, was infinite because the one offended was the infinite God who is due infinite praise. According to Anselm, this gap between the human race and God wounded man not only within himself but also in terms of his communal relations. Human society began to fragment along the lines of sex, race, class, tribe, and so forth. Man became divided against himself and against his neighbor. The division between humanity and God led to increasing alienation and dehumanization as society collapsed in on itself.[6]

The debt that needed to be paid was infinite, because the offense was against the infinite God, but a finite human being needed to pay it, because it was finite human beings who first committed the offense. And now do you see why Catholic teaching has always held that Jesus Christ was both fully God and fully man? This was because he needed to be fully man in order to pay the debt on our behalf, but he needed to be fully God in order to pay it infinitely. It is true that God could have fixed the problem in some other way if God wanted, but Christians have always believed that God is a just God, hence God chose to save humanity in accord with God's justice rather than apart from it. The Incarnation, then, is the way God chose to put the human race back into right relationship with God. By being put back into right relationship with God, the proper

---

[6] Anselm, *Why God Became Man* in Anselm of Canterbury the Major Works, tr. Janet Fairweather (Oxford: Oxford University Press, 1998). For Aquinas's treatment see *ST* IIa IIae qq. 57–58. There are other theories of incarnation and redemption, but this is the one I endorse here.

harmony is restored, and right relationship in the normal human relations again becomes possible. Parents have obligations to their children, and children to their parents. Husbands have obligations to their wives, and wives to their husbands. Governments have obligations to their citizens, and citizens to their governments. Friends have obligations to friends, coworkers to coworkers, and so forth. Finally, human beings have obligations to each other and to the created order. The fulfilling of these obligations is prerequisite for right relations and harmony. The most appropriate name for this is justice.

However, right ordering can also refer to the ordering of one's own soul. If you know someone who has an addiction, or if you have suffered from one yourself, then it will be easy for you to understand what I mean. The way the human person is meant to function is as follows: the reason discerns the good to which the will inclines. Choices are thusly made, and the desires conform accordingly. In the addict, however, the reason may do its job of distinguishing the good from the evil, but the will does not incline to the good; indeed it is dragged down and made the slave of the passions. So you find yourself having another drink, lighting up another cigarette, or doing something much worse, even though you know better and a part of you genuinely wants to stop and is pained and scared by your seeming inability to do so. In other words, your soul is disordered. Your reason, which you have by virtue of being a human being, and which is meant to guide you, is being slavishly drug around by your lower passions. The rightful king has been made a slave.

The point here is not so much the blameworthiness of the addict as it is the sadness of it all. The addict is miserable and needs help. He is in a kind of prison of his own making. This is why Augustine said that a disordered soul is its own punishment. The state of his soul is unjust. In order for harmony to be restored, his reason must once again take over the levers of control and subordinate the lower desires to their proper place. As we see in the next section, however, desires, in and of themselves, are not bad things or irrelevant to the moral life. Indeed, desires, too, can share in virtue.

TEMPERANCE

Temperance and fortitude are the perfections of the appetitive soul – the part of the soul that involves desires and fears. Temperance is the perfection of the former and fortitude of the latter. We are generally not accustomed to thinking of emotions as moral or immoral. If we do not have direct control over how something makes us feel, then how could our emotions possibly be blameworthy or praiseworthy? Aristotle acknowledged that we do not have direct control over our emotions. In fact, Aristotle made a distinction between the kind of control we are capable of exercising over our bodies and the kind of influence we are able to exert on our emotions. Aristotle referred to the former as "despotic rule." He did not mean this in a negative way. The point was simply that our bodies obey our commands without resistance. You tell your little finger to wiggle and it wiggles. Emotions, however, come under political rule. They can resist and rebel.[7]

Additionally, we cannot directly command our emotions as we can our bodies. Rather, we shape our emotions indirectly through the choices we make over time. For example, a child may naturally feel an aversion to the smell of cigarette smoke, but if as an adult he or she begins to smoke, then, over time, the smell may instead evoke cravings. If he or she quits, then the smell may again become obnoxious to him or her. The feelings – revolted, attracted, disgusted – were shaped by different kinds of actions over time.

Consider another example. A person who suffers from anorexia may actually come to be disgusted at the sight of food. Obviously, this is an unnatural reaction. Her feelings toward food have been shaped by several psychological factors and choices over time. In order to recover, she will need to retrain her desires through deliberate actions over time. On the other hand, a compulsive overeater suffers from the opposite problem. Certain foods excite in him almost irresistible cravings. Whereas the anorexic's desires for food are too small, the overeater's are excessive. This is why Aristotle said that virtue is always the mean between defect and excess. With respect to the desires, then, temperance means having the right desires to the right degree – not too little or too great.

There are three stages leading up to the possession of the virtue of temperance. The first stage is called "intemperance." This means that one's desires are poorly shaped. The intemperate person, however, is not unhappy. There is a kind of harmony between his choices and his wants. He wants to binge drink every weekend, have one-night stands, and generally live a hedonistic lifestyle without any regard for consequences. He has come to view this kind of life as admirable, and because we humans naturally imitate what we admire, and because we naturally become like that which we imitate (this is Plato's mimetic principle), he becomes more and more the hedonist.

---

[7] *NE* VII 8. §1 (1150b). For Aquinas's treatment see *ST* IIa IIae q. 141. For a helpful treatment of these topics see William C. Mattison III, *Introducing Moral Theology: True Happiness and the Virtues* (Grand Rapids, MI: Brazos Press, 2008), 75–94.

Now, all this may go on for a few weeks, months, or even years. It may even last his entire life. Most people who live this way for a while, however, come to apprehend that the hedonist lifestyle is self-destructive. They realize they cannot go on with it. This is the key insight that moves them from the first stage, intemperance, to the second stage, incontinence, which means lack of control. The incontinent man has realized he needs to stop, but his desires remain disordered from his previous lifestyle. As a result, his choices and his wants no longer line up. He wants to stop binge drinking, but cannot. He wants to have a real relationship with a woman, but has trained himself to regard women as objects for sexual gratification for so long that he genuinely struggles to interact with them as human beings. Incontinence is a miserable stage. It means wanting to live better than you are but lacking the ability to change. It is full of self-loathing, disgust with oneself, fear, and shame.

The transition to continence, the third stage, occurs when one some-how regains control over the levers of power within one's own soul. A just order is returned. One turns away from the harmful behavior. The conti-nent person, however, still is not happy, because the choices and the wants still do not coincide. That secret part of him misses the binge drinking and the womanizing. He remains fearful that he may regress at any moment. He is always watching to make sure he does not put himself in inoppor-tune situations. He is always wondering when he is going to trip up.

Temperance comes when one has lived continently long enough so as to reshape the desires to align with the good. Importantly, temperance does not mean the absence of desire. Desires are natural and there is noth-ing wrong with them. Recall, in the case of the anorexic mentioned ear-lier, the problem was not too much desire but too little. Temperance refers to well-ordered desires. The temperate man does not need to spend the weekend hiding from bars and parties. He does not always feel himself resisting the temptations as so many magnets pulling at him. Rather, he is full of good and healthy desires. He is enjoying a good conversation with his new girlfriend at the coffee shop or playing a game of pool with an old friend. However, in doing this, he is not fighting the overwhelming urge to run back to the old life. The old life is dead. It is not in him anymore. Before, the weeds of misshapen desire would not allow anything inter-esting or beautiful to grow; now the garden is so stuffed full of splendid things that there is no place for the weeds to take root.

Admittedly, several people when first learning of the virtue of temper-ance think it sounds like wishful thinking. People still struggling with powerful addictions or disorders know the feeling that it will never be completely gone. You can never remove it; you can only hope to contain it. Containing it is certainly preferable to letting it destroy you, but better than both is simply getting rid of it. This is difficult but not impossible. Sometimes, the first step to temperance is the courage to believe that it is possible. This brings me to the final cardinal virtue we have left to discuss.

FORTITUDE

As I said earlier, fortitude is the perfection of the part of the appetitive soul that deals with fear. Fortitude is another word for courage or bravery.[8] We are going to discuss this virtue at great length in a later chapter, so I abbreviate my treatment here. Fortitude is the virtue of facing difficulty well. This may involve attack or endurance. There is nothing wrong with aggression for the right reasons and in the right way, aggression, that is to say, ordered by prudence. A soldier, for example, may need to act aggressively to stop an injustice. This does not mean "losing it" in the sense of letting your aggression run wild or take over. Anyone who ever served in the military will tell you that combat training is ordered to controlling your aggression, not letting it run wild, which is dangerous in battle. However, fortitude may also involve enduring suffering for the sake of a just cause. For example, Nelson Mandela spent years in prison for standing up to the heinous injustice of apartheid. When prudence does its job of discerning the good, and justice inclines the will to the proper choice, fortitude ensures that one carries through in the execution of the good despite the dangers this may involve and the harms it may bring. Examining the lives of moral exemplars such as this naturally makes us wonder, "How did they do it?" Indeed, if a theory of virtue does not explain how the virtues are attained, then that theory is merely academic, as the quote at the beginning of this chapter suggests. It is to this topic, then, that we now turn.

HOW IS VIRTUE ATTAINED?

Attaining the virtues is to become good. So how can we attain them? By acting virtuously, of course: "It is right, then, to say that a person comes to be just from doing just actions and temperate from doing temperate actions; for no one has the least prospect of becoming good from failing

---

[8] Aquinas treats fortitude at *ST* IIa IIae q. 123.

to do them."[9] According to Aristotle, the manner that one acquires the right state through repeated right action may be likened to the manner in which an athlete habituates her skills through practice: "This is clear from those who train for any contest or action, since they continually practice the appropriate activities. Only a totally insensible person would not know that a given type of activity is the source of the corresponding state."[10] Thus, our actions are the "sources and means" by which we either "develop each virtue" or fail to do so:

> For what we do in our dealings with other people makes some of us just, some unjust; what we do in terrifying situations, and the habits of fear or confidence that we acquire, make some of us brave and others cowardly. The same is true of situations involving appetites and anger; for one or another sort of conduct in these situations makes some temperate and mild, others intemperate and irascible.[11]

The corresponding situations and actions vary greatly with respect to each discrete virtue, but the one thing all actions that help develop a virtue have in common is that they are in "accord with the correct reason."[12] The virtues grow through repeated action so as to form a *secunda natura*, or more simply put, character of the individual.

In sum, according to Aristotle, actions are key to the attainment of virtue. To become virtuous, one must act virtuously. The acquisition of virtue occurs by degrees over time. As we shall see, Aquinas adopts much of Aristotle's theory into his own account both of the cardinal virtues as well as the manner in which they are attained.

SUMMARY

In this chapter, we have reflected on the cardinal virtues of prudence, justice, temperance, and fortitude. We have seen that these virtues are the names of certain perfections of the soul, and we have investigated what each perfection entails. Additionally, we analyzed Aristotle's theory of how the virtues are attained through acting virtuously. In the next chapter, we examine how this virtue on the natural level is elevated and transfigured by the life of grace.

---

[9] *NE* II 4. §5 (1105b).

[10] *NE* III 5. §10 (1114a).

[11] *NE* II 1. §7 (1103b).

[12] *NE* II 2. §2 (1103b). Indeed, the relation between temperance and prudence is so strong that "temperance (*sōphrosunē*)" is so named because it "preserves prudence (*sōzousan tēn phronēsin*)." VI 5. §4 (1140b).

CHAPTER 5

The Virtues of Grace

> To sum up briefly the general view I have about virtue so far as relates
> to right living: Virtue is the charity by which what ought to be loved
> is loved. This charity exists more in some, less in others, and in some
> not at all; but the greatest charity, which admits no increase, exists in
> no human living on earth.
>
> St. Augustine, *Letter to St. Jerome*

We concluded the previous chapter with a discussion of how the cardinal virtues are attained. There we said that the virtues are acquired
through acting virtuously. In this chapter, we explore another kind of virtue, the virtues infused by grace. These virtues are not earned through
human effort but are given us by God. However, in much the same way
revealed morality does not contravene the natural law but rather perfects
it, grace perfects the cardinal virtues. By grace, the cardinal virtues are
directed to the beatific vision and thus elevated to a higher level. Along
with infused versions of the cardinal virtues, God also infuses the soul
with the theological virtues of faith, hope, and love.[1] The purpose of this
chapter is to explore these virtues of grace.

This chapter develops over six sections. The first section begins where
the previous chapter left off, with an analysis of how the virtues of grace
are attained. Although infused directly into the soul by God, this does
not negate the role of human action in the formation of these virtues.
Second, we analyze the infused versions of the cardinal virtues through
an examination of "the little way" of St. Thérèse of Lisieux. The next three
sections treat the theological virtues of faith, hope, and love respectively.
As this chapter examines the virtue of faith, it presents us with an opportunity to address the issue of modern atheism, which the sixth section

---

[1] See *DCE* (God is Love), *SS* (Saved in Hope), and most recently *LF* (The Light of Faith). The first
draft of *LF* was written by Pope Emeritus Benedict XVI, who had intended to write encyclicals on
all three of the theological virtues. Pope Francis completed *LF* partly in order to complete the project initiated by his predecessor.

does primarily through reference to one of the four Constitutions of the Second Vatican Council, *Gaudium et spes*. This section explores how to respond to the rise of atheism in contemporary culture with faith, hope, and love. We begin, however, with an analysis of the relationship between God's grace and human action.

GRACE AND HUMAN ACTION

Aquinas agrees with Aristotle's account of virtue as attained through the transformational power of acting virtuously consistently over time. Indeed, he helps to clarify how virtuous actions can be accomplished if you have not yet attained the habit of virtue. If I need the habit to do the act, but need to act to acquire the habit, then where do I begin? Aquinas explains:

Virtue is generated by actions which are virtuous in one sense and not in another. The actions that occur before virtue exists are virtuous from the point of view of what is done. The person is doing just or brave things. They are not virtuous from the point of view of how they are done; for before someone has acquired a virtue, he does not do the things that virtue does in the way that a virtuous person does them, that is, readily, without any hesitation, with pleasure, and without difficulty.[2]

According to Aquinas, virtue "is attained out of many good acts, insofar as a subsequent act always occurs by virtue of all the preceding ones – as is evident in drops of water hollowing a stone, where it is not each and every drop that takes away something from the stone, but rather, all the preceding ones are disposing the stone to be hollowed out."[3] Even if a person can act virtuously while lacking virtuous habits, the question remains of the order in which the virtuous habits must be acquired.

As we discuss at greater length in the next chapter, Aquinas does not think the virtues are obtained one by one. Rather, Aquinas equates the growth of virtuous habits to the manner in which a hand grows. As the whole hand grows, the fingers grow "at a proportional rate."[4] Therefore, in order for any given virtuous action to count toward the acquisition of a virtue it must be in accord with right reason, because the other virtues "are possessed along with" prudence.[5] Aquinas explains as follows:

[2] *DVComm* a. 9 ad 13.
[3] *SENT* I. D. 17 q. 2 a. 3.
[4] *DVCard* a. 3 ad. 1. My translation.
[5] *DVCard* a. 2 ad. 10.

Certain virtues, for example, temperance, justice, and gentleness, order us in ordinary areas of human life. In this area, while one is engaged in one type of virtuous activity one must either also be engaged in exercising the other virtues; thus one will acquire all the virtues at the same time; or else do well with respect to one and badly with respect to others. In the latter case, one will acquire a disposition that is contrary to some one of the virtues, and therefore destructive of practical wisdom [prudence]. But without practical wisdom the tendency acquired through acting in accordance with the other virtues will not have the distinctive character of virtue.[6]

According to Aquinas, then, any disposition contrary to a virtue is "destructive of practical wisdom." This is true on the natural level and so remains true with respect to the virtues of grace, which elevate the cardinal virtues discussed in the previous chapter.

The virtues of grace, which include the theological virtues as well as graced versions of the cardinal virtues, are gifts that God infuses into the soul. They are supernatural help from God in living the good life. However, there is still a process of proportional moral growth by which one continues to grow even in these virtues. Actions do not become irrelevant but deepen the virtues, which come from grace. Thus, proportional moral growth remains an apt description even with respect to the attainment of the virtues of grace. This is because God's grace does not obliterate but rather perfects what occurs on the natural level.

Because our actions still impact our character even within the life of grace, Aquinas maintains that serious active sinning and infused virtue are incompatible: "Since charity has for its cause conjunction with God, it is immediately lost by one act [of mortal sin]. And this immediate loss may be found in all accidents that have a cause outside of the subject in which they exist, because nothing can remain in being once it has been separated from its essential cause, as is evident with light."[7] God does not give us virtue to equip us with a sort of invincibility in the moral life. In a sense, the infused virtues are the most fragile, because they can be lost through even one isolated act of mortal sin – that is, sin deliberately done out of hatred for God or even, in some cases, out of weakness.

While on that topic, it is worth briefly summarizing the Catholic view of sin. Understood from the perspective of virtue ethics, sin refers to any action one commits that is destructive rather than perfective of the soul. One is culpable for sin to the degree that one is aware that what one is

---

[6] *DVCard* a. 2 ad. 9.
[7] *SENT* II. d. 31 q. 1 a. 1; see also *ST* Ia IIae q. 63 ad. 2.

doing is sinful and one is acting freely. Ignorance may impede one's knowledge that what he or she is doing is sinful, and extra-volitional factors may impede one's freedom. There are two kinds of extra-volitional factors, external and internal. An example of an extra-volitional external factor is something similar to peer pressure pushing one's will in a particular direction. That is, it is something that is not the will itself (extra-volitional) but is nonetheless exerting pressure on the will from outside (external). An example of an extra-volitional internal factor is addiction. It is not the will itself (extra-volitional) but inheres within the will (internal), predisposing it to certain kinds of acts. In the aforementioned quote, Aquinas is stating that serious sins deliberately committed with full knowledge cut us off from God, who is ultimately the source of all virtue and flourishing.[8] Indeed, as *The Catechism of the Catholic Church* states, this is the very definition of a mortal sin:

Sins are rightly evaluated according to their gravity. The distinction between mortal and venial sin, already evident in Scripture, became part of the tradition of the Church. It is corroborated by human experience. *Mortal sin* destroys charity in the heart of man by a grave violation of God's law; it turns man away from God, who is his ultimate end and his beatitude, by preferring an inferior good to him. *Venial sin* allows charity to subsist, even though it offends and wounds it. Mortal sin, by attacking the vital principle within us – that is, charity – necessitates a new initiative of God's mercy and a conversion of heart which is normally accomplished within the setting of the sacrament of reconciliation.[9]

Again, in order for a sin to be mortal there must be "grave matter, full knowledge, and deliberate consent."[10] Even with all of these caveats in place, it is still the case that human beings, even virtuous ones, sometimes commit mortal sins. This is why the virtues of grace can always be restored through repentance and further virtuous acts. Similar to virtues on the natural level, the virtues of grace advance toward perfection through repeated correct moral action. Furthermore, you can never come to the end of the virtues of grace, because the more we grow in them, the more we are made able to grow still further.[11] In short, the life of grace and human effort are not rivals to each other but rather work in mutual collaboration and harmony toward the goal of beatitude, which is a term used to describe ultimate happiness in unity with God. The virtues grow

---

[8] For more on this topic see Andrew Kim, "Have the Manicheans Returned? An Augustinian Alternative to Situationist Psychology," *Studies in Christian Ethics* 26, no. 4 (November 2013).

[9] *CCC* nos. 1854–1856.

[10] *CCC* no. 1857.

[11] *SENT* III. d. 17 q. 2 a. 4; see also *ST* IIa IIae q. 24 aa. 6–8.

through grace and our response to that grace in the form of virtuous acts. Understanding this, we are now in position to examine the infused virtues more closely.

INFUSED CARDINAL VIRTUES

In a prior chapter, we discussed the relationship of the natural law to revealed morality. There, we said that contrary to the opinions of some, these are not in competition with each other; rather, the latter lifts up and perfects the former. The same relationship holds true with respect to the cardinal virtues and the virtues of grace. The cardinal virtues discussed in the previous chapter are not eliminated by grace but ordered to God, and thus transformed and made perfect. Therefore, in the lives of great saints we should not expect to find the theological virtues of faith, hope, and love instead of the cardinal virtues. To the contrary, we find lives exemplary of both the theological virtues and the cardinal virtues transfigured by Christian love. There are, of course, numerous examples we could speak of, but for the sake of brevity I limit my treatment to Thérèse of Lisieux.[12]

Near the small French town of Lisieux stands an extraordinary basilica dedicated to an astonishing saint. Thérèse was a cloistered Carmelite nun. She was chronically ill for most of her life and died at the young age of twenty-four. At the request of her superior, Thérèse composed her spiritual autobiography, entitled *The Story of a Soul*. In this moving and beautiful account, Thérèse explains that possessing virtue does not always entail being a spiritual exemplar such as her Carmelite predecessors, St. Teresa of Avila and St. John of the Cross. No, "the little way" is not a path for spiritual athletes alone but one for ordinary people also. According to Thérèse, to please God is simply to put all of our trust in God, such as a "little child who sleeps without fear in its Father's arms." To show God's love to others does not always mean doing something heroic. God's love can manifest itself in small, seemingly insignificant acts of kindness, such as taking the time to have a conversation with someone even when you are very busy, or dealing patiently with people who annoy you.

In "the little way" of Thérèse, one can catch a glimpse of the nature of the infused cardinal virtues. Infused prudence reveals the right way to show love to someone in any given situation. Infused justice orders our actions to the good of the other, and infused temperance makes us desire

---

[12] This section draws from Fr. Robert Barron's insightful treatment in *Catholicism: A Journey to the Heart of the Faith* (New York: Image Books, 2011), 204–211.

that good. Finally, by infused fortitude we are able to endure in love even during times of difficulty. Indeed, Thérèse carried on with the little way even after becoming afflicted by the tuberculosis that ultimately seized her life. In this manner, "the little way" of Thérèse is exemplary of the cardinal virtues joined to Christian love and transformed by grace. In addition to the infused versions of the cardinal virtues, the virtues of grace include three virtues relating directly to God, which is why they are called "theological virtues." It is to these virtues – faith, hope, and love – that we now turn.

FAITH

The virtue of faith can be understood in two senses: *fides qua creditur* and *fides quae creditur*.[13] The first sense, *fides qua creditur*, means "the faith by which we believe," that is, the subjective trust we hold in our hearts and place in the Father of our Lord Jesus Christ. *Fides quae creditur* means "the faith which is believed," that is, the objective content of the faith that is what it is and was what it was long before we ever happened to believe it. The objective deposit of faith, *fides quae creditur*, does not change and the Magisterium of the Church is duty bound to preserve and safeguard it, keeping it free from error. One can find it in the Scripture, the Creeds, and the writings of the Church fathers. Subjective faith, *fides qua creditur*, on the other hand, is more like an inner trust. Understood as a virtue, then, faith refers to the good habit of believing true things about God and God's relationship to humanity. Furthermore, it is in the light of these truths that all other truths are illuminated. As Pope Francis observed, "once the flame of faith dies out, all other lights begin to dim."[14]

At this point you may be wondering in what sense believing in something can be understood as a virtue. If belief only means irrational assent to a set of indemonstrable propositions, then it is true that belief in this sense does not pertain to virtue. There is no virtue in making a good guess. On the other hand, faith in the sense of trust can be virtuous when the object in which we place our trust turns out to actually be trustworthy. We can all think of occasions where we failed to trust someone we should have trusted or failed to trust in ourselves and stumbled as a result. It is almost as though the virtue of faith means staying true to a promise once made even when it has become difficult to do so. All bonds are rooted in

---

[13] See *ST* IIa IIae qq. 1–7.
[14] *LF* no. 4.

trust; faith is the name for trust in God. The virtue of faith speaks to the habit of maintaining one's trust when all is well and the sun is shining but also during times of storms and adversity. No one ever said this was easy. None of the virtues are easy. One must work to maintain them the way an athlete works to stay in game shape. Faith is not any different. This is why it is important to nourish one's own faith through prayer, devotions, works of mercy, and the like.[15] Even still, to experience a lapse of faith is not necessarily sinful but can be a part of God's providence. Near the end of her life, Thérèse confessed to serious doubts with respect to the existence of Heaven. However, Thérèse understood this as God providing her with an opportunity to empathize with those who lack faith: "During those joyful days of the Easter season, Jesus made me feel that there were really souls who have no faith…he permitted my soul to be invaded by the thickest darkness." Indeed, similar experiences are attested to by several of the great saints. The strength of their faith is often revealed by weakness and doubt. In an odd way, it sometimes seems as though doubt is necessary for faith to flourish, much like fear is necessary for courage. It is in the overcoming of fear and doubt that courage and faith are made known.

Another comparison may be made with respect to faith and temperance. Recall the previous chapter's discussion of the stages leading from intemperance to temperance. In a similar way, one may think of stages through which one progresses on the way to attaining the theological virtue of faith. The first stage is indifference. Distinctive of this stage is apathy with respect to "big picture" questions. Does God exist? Is Christ God's only Son? Is salvation possible? In this stage, one simply does not care whether a truthful answer to these questions exists or not. People in this stage tend to regard faith as mere subjective sentimentality – comforting opinions that make one feel nice. They have not the slightest interest in whether the opinions are true or not. These may even be people who go to church every Sunday and display several outward signs of faith, even though, in actuality, they possess none.

The next stage is disbelief. In this stage, one has come to regard "big picture" questions as important. Key to the transition from indifference to disbelief is the recognition that how one responds to "big picture"

---

[15] See *CCC* no. 2447: "The works of mercy are charitable actions by which we come to the aid of our neighbor in his spiritual and bodily necessities. Instructing, advising, consoling, comforting are spiritual works of mercy, as are forgiving and bearing wrongs patiently. The corporal works of mercy consist especially in feeding the hungry, sheltering the homeless, clothing the naked, visiting the sick and imprisoned, and burying the dead. Among all these, giving alms to the poor is one of the chief witnesses to fraternal charity: it is also a work of justice pleasing to God."

questions has an enormous impact on one's ability to live a truly fulfill-ing life. A person in the stage of disbelief may be in one of two states. He or she may want to believe, but cannot find a way to do so that doesn't feel like mere guessing. On the other hand, he or she may adamantly dis-agree with Christian doctrine. In either event, the important thing is that in this stage the person has gained the ability to care whether the doc-trines are true or not. The third stage is belief. The transition to this stage occurs when one gains the ability to regard the doctrines of Christianity as true. However, the virtue of faith entails much more than mere intel-lectual assent. The fourth and final stage – the stage in which one gains the theological virtue of faith – occurs when one's intellectual belief in the truth of Christian doctrines spills over into the whole person. Assent becomes ascent. One comes to believe with whole heart, mind, and soul and to live accordingly. As Pope Francis has concisely stated, Catholics believe that "the transmission of faith occurs first and foremost in bap-tism."[16] However, the path leading up to this may vary greatly from person to person. Whatever one's path, the virtue of theological faith is always an infused virtue; it is a gift from God. The same is true of the virtue of hope, to which we now turn.

HOPE

In the previous chapter's section on prudence, I said that one of the func-tions of prudence is to order one's priorities. The theological virtue of hope also involves the right ordering of one's priorities.[17] Our hopes reflect our deepest wants and commitments. Even the lack of hope speaks to the kinds of people we are. A helpful way of understanding this can be gained through an appreciation of the distinction between an "*ad finem*" and an "*in finem*." Both are Latin terms. The former means "for the sake of the end"; the latter means "an end in itself." Determining what things in life we treat as mere means to an end, and which we treat as ends in them-selves, can help us uncover in what we have placed our hopes.

Admittedly, most of the things we do in life are *ad finem*. That is, they are done for the sake of some further end. You read the book the professor assigns in order to do well in the class, to get the grade, in order to graduate, for the sake of the job, and so forth. The *in finem*, the that-for-the-sake-of-which we do most of what we do, is most clearly

---

[16] *LF* no. 41.
[17] See *ST* IIa IIae qq. 17–21.

stated as happiness. We want to be happy. But to what do we look for our happiness? Is it money, power, pleasure, and honor – the four classical temptations referred to in previous chapters? As mentioned prior, there is nothing intrinsically evil about these things, the problem is our tendency to set them up as gods, to think that they can grant us ultimate happiness. Do you think that if you had one billion dollars you would be ultimately happy? If so, then "a billion dollars" has a godlike status in your mind. And there are other things that can come to have this kind of a godlike status even without us realizing or consciously choosing it. For example, marriage or family life could present themselves to one's mind as things that will bring ultimate happiness. Again, of course, there is nothing bad about these things, which are good in and of themselves. The problem is when we make idols of them.

In addition to being morally wrong, idolatry is a recipe for great unhappiness. The whole point is that only God can provide ultimate happiness. Therefore, when you go about seeking to extract it from something else, then that something else is bound to fail. You are doing both you and it, not to mention God, a great disservice. This brings me to what C.S. Lewis referred to as "the fool's way" and "the way of the disillusioned sensible man."[18] These are alternative outcomes, which may follow from the failure to put one's hope in God. The first, "the fool's way," refers to the kind of person who blames the objects for not being able to satisfy his or her deepest longings and so replaces them in frustration. He or she goes from spouse to spouse, or from job to job, and is never satisfied. However, the problem was not with the spouses or the jobs; it was rather with his or her unrealistic expectations. The second way, "the way of the disillusioned sensible man," refers to the kind of person who teaches himself to stop hoping for ultimate happiness. He or she learns to settle for moderate happiness and not to expect too much out of life. This person suppresses his or her longing for ultimate happiness and goes throughout life settling for the mediocre happiness of lesser things.

Now, the point is that both of these are poor responses to two realities: (1) our longing for ultimate happiness, and (2) the fact that only God can satisfy it. The virtue of hope, then, means centering our ultimate hope for happiness and satisfaction in God. When we place God first, when we make God our *in finem*, then all of the other things in our lives become rightly ordered. When God is the center of the wheel, all the other goods of this life – family, play, collegiality, work, and all the rest of it – are like

---

[18] C.S. Lewis, *Mere Christianity* (San Francisco: Harper Collins, 1952), 134–8.

the spokes as life rolls along. The irony here is that the best thing we can do for those we love most is to love God more. I think this is part of the reason why our Lord taught us to love God with our whole heart, mind, and soul, and to love our neighbor as ourselves. Notice the ordering; it is not accidental. This brings us to the greatest of all the virtues, love.

LOVE

Augustine beautifully attests to the primacy of the virtue of love. St. Ambrose, one of Augustine's mentors, rooted all virtue in the person of Jesus Christ, the wisdom that generates virtue in all virtuous people. Ambrose likens the cardinal virtues to the four rivers of Eden, which have God as their source.[19] These virtues orient one toward God. Accordingly, in Ambrose's view, "the virtues are so connected and chained together, that whoever has one seems to have them all; and there accrues to the saints one virtue."[20] This account is confirmed and expanded by Augustine.

In *De moribus ecclesiae catholicae* (On the Morals of the Catholic Church), Augustine puts forward a Christian understanding of virtue and happiness while showing the continuity between the moral teachings of the Old and New Testaments. In *De moribus*, Augustine defines virtue in the following manner:

Temperance, we say, is love preserving itself in integrity and without corruption for God, fortitude is love enduring all things for the sake of God, justice is love serving only God and, therefore, ruling rightly those things subject to man, and prudence is love discerning well between those things that aid it in reaching God and those things which can impede it.[21]

Here Augustine has formulated his view that love is the one true virtue; the other virtues are only names for different activities of love. Again, in the *Enchiridion*, Augustine emphasizes the primacy of love with respect to virtue: "And now regarding love, which the Apostle says is greater than the other two – that is faith and hope – for the more richly it dwells in a man, the better the man in whom it dwells. For when we ask whether someone is a good man, we are not asking what he believes, or hopes, but what he loves."[22] In a letter to his friend St. Jerome, Augustine again clarifies his understanding of love as the very essence of the virtues of grace.

---

[19] *DP* 3.18. Referenced in R.E. Houser, *The Cardinal Virtues: Aquinas, Albert, and Philip the Chancellor* (Toronto: Pontifical Institute of Mediaeval Studies, 2004), 36.

[20] *LUC* tr. Houser, *The Cardinal Virtues*, 2004: 36.

[21] *DM* 2.25. My translation.

[22] *EN* XXXI.

To sum up briefly the general view I have about virtue so far as relates to right living: Virtue is the charity by which what ought to be loved is loved. This charity exists more in some, less in others, and in some not at all; but the greatest charity, which admits no increase, exists in no human living on earth. So long as it admits of increase, what makes it less than it ought is due surely to vice.[23]

In a way, everything that needs to be said regarding Augustine's view of virtue is summarized in this passage. Virtue is love. It is possessed by degrees. It is not absolute in this life. Furthermore, possession of it does not uproot all of the bad effects of our past sins in one triumphant blow, as it were. Rather, it grows in the person by degrees. More is said regarding these aspects of virtue in the following chapter, but for the moment let us continue exploring the nature of Christian love.

C.S. Lewis's book, *The Four Loves*, is also helpful in illuminating the virtue of Christian love or charity.[24] Lewis explains that, in Greek, they have four words for love. The first kind, *storge*, refers to the love we have in familial relations. It is the kind of love you have for your sister or brother, or for Mom and Dad. *Filia* refers to friendship love and *eros* to romantic love. These are the natural loves, and they are so distinct that, in Greek, they have separate words for them, whereas in English, we rely on context to discern. When you say, "I love my girlfriend," I know "love" means something very different than when you say, "I love my aunt."

Now, to be clear, there is nothing wrong or inferior or lesser about these natural loves. God does not view these loves as rivals. Indeed, God has no rivals. However, we humans have two problematic tendencies. First, we are selfish, and selfishness corrodes all our relationships. We need to have our needs met. We need companionship. We need to be loved. We need to love. We want to feel good about ourselves. This element of need in our loves can never be totally removed, although we can sometimes become more selfless. We can learn to love with less attachment and in a more appreciative way as we grow and mature.

The second problematic tendency that afflicts our natural loves is our propensity for idolatry. This can happen with *storge* and *filia* but is nowhere more evident than in *eros*. Just listen to the lyrics of a few love songs, or read Romeo and Juliet, and you will see how we tend to worship at the feet of *eros*. We idolize romantic love and are willing to become lawless and rebellious in pursuit of it. Television shows teach us that the breaking of marital vows, the abandoning of children, or virtually anything else is justified when done for the sake of romantic love.

---

[23] *EP167, The Cardinal Virtues*, tr. Houser, 2004: 214.
[24] C.S. Lewis, *The Four Loves* (New York: Harvest, 1960).

Agape, divine love, is corrective of both the aforementioned tendencies. In the first place, *agape* refers to God's love for us, and Catholic teaching has always held that the love of God is entirely free from need. God did not need to create the universe or the human race or anything at all for that matter. God is not lacking in any perfection. Therefore, it follows that God created the universe out of purely self-diffusive love under no compulsion or necessity. It is by accepting this kind of love that God has for us, this love that God pours out on us whether we deserve it or not, that we learn to love God in return. Again, however, the divine love is not in rivalry with the human loves. Rather, God's love is the only hope the natural loves have of not being consumed by selfishness. By displacing idols as objects of love and by placing God at the center, we shape our relationships according to the divine pattern. In brief, *agape*-charity-love is the virtue of loving God with one's whole heart, mind, and soul, and loving one's neighbor as oneself. Love is both the height and engine of the virtues. It animates all virtue and directs every virtuous act toward God as its end.

RESPONDING TO MODERN ATHEISM WITH FAITH, HOPE, AND LOVE

Before concluding, this is a fitting place to examine the treatment of modern atheism in the Pastoral Constitution of the Second Vatican Council, *Gaudium et spes*.[25] The document begins by outlining the three kinds of modern atheist. First is the apathetic atheist. In many ways this is the most difficult kind of atheism to counter, because it is often subtle and unstated. The apathetic atheist is in the stage of indifference. He or she does not adamantly deny the existence of God. Rather, the apathetic atheist does not care – or at least claims not to care – whether there is a God or not. He or she thinks life can be perfectly happy and lacking in nothing without God. The apathetic atheist just doesn't care and in a sense even wills not to care. He or she refuses to wonder.

The second kind of atheist is the empiricist. At least since Francis Bacon, there have been those who think that objective knowledge can only be arrived at through observation, experimentation, and verification. The empiricist, therefore, cannot subscribe to belief in God, because the existence of God cannot be proven in that kind of a way. He or she

---

[25] See *GS*. The discussion takes place in the very first chapter of the document; it treats modern atheism, kinds, causes (nos. 19–20), and ways in which it can be countered (no. 21).

thinks belief in God is unscientific. Indeed, ever since the Draper-White thesis taught everyone to regard science and religion as perpetually pitted against each other, there has been a kind of scientific triumphalism, which looks down its nose at belief.[26] The Draper-White thesis approaches the past through a conflict myth according to which Western history is marked by an ongoing struggle between religion and science. But this is untrue. There are examples of conflict between religion and science in history, but for every such example there are numerous other examples of mutual collaboration, confluence of ideas, and harmonious working together in the pursuit of truth. Furthermore, the Draper-White conflict myth has no way to account for the myriad examples of important thinkers who were both committed scientists and deeply religious, such as Isaac Newton. Nevertheless, there are those who honestly find it difficult to believe without empirical evidence. They have yet to learn that the absence of evidence is not evidence of absence. The empiricist atheist is stuck in the stage of disbelief.

By far the most impassioned kind of atheist is the moralist/humanist atheist; he or she, too, is in the stage of disbelief. This kind of atheist has an explicit goal of driving religion out of the world. The moralist/humanist atheist blames religion for all the things in the world he or she finds displeasing: exclusivity, strife, war, ignorance, and so forth. At the heart of the critiques is the claim that religion is immoral and demeaning to human dignity, which is why this kind of atheism is referred to as moralist/humanist. In his famous guide for those aspiring to gain power, *The Prince*, the philosopher Niccolò Machiavelli said that the surest way to gain power over people was to offer them a solution to a problem that they did not know they had. Well, the moralist/humanist atheist convinces listeners that what has bothered them all their life is this thing called religion, which is responsible for all their discontent. He or she offers them secular humanism instead, a worldview without God. The method is generally to take all the worst abuses of religion and compare them with the highest ideals of science. The abuses of science and triumphs of religion the moralist/humanist atheist conveniently forgets.

Moralist/humanist atheism has its historical roots in the thought of three influential philosophers of modernity: Ludwig von Feurbach,

---

[26] John William Draper (1811–1882), author of *History of the Conflict between Religion and Science* (1874), and Andrew Dickson White (1832–1918), author of *The Warfare of Science* (1876) and *A History of the Warfare of Science with Theology in Christendom* (1896). Today most historians of religion and science reject the conflict thesis as an overly simplistic nineteenth-century invention, which greatly distorts what is in actuality a multifaceted and complex history.

Karl Marx, and Sigmund Freud. Feurbach gets the ball of modern atheism rolling by merely asserting that God does not exist and then speculating on why the world is replete with belief in God. If one assumes the premise that there is no God, then the varieties of belief about God or gods that populate the world are certainly in need of explanation. Feurbach theorized that people invent gods to meet their deepest longings. God is just a kind of imaginary friend we invent for the sake of comfort.

Marx and Freud ran with this view but also took it a step further. Marx argued that belief in the Christian God was immoral because it taught people to put their cares off until the next world. He thought this would lead to neglect for the demands of justice in the present life and was thus bad for society. Freud focused on the psyche of the individual. Following Feurbach, Freud thought that the Christian God was a mere projection of human wishes. Thus, terms such as "wish thinking," "wishful thinking," or "wish fulfillment" are pejorative; they are meant to demean belief. Freud thought that to believe in God was tantamount to believing in unicorns. Humanity, according to Freud, needed to outgrow religion in order to develop and mature. Obstinately holding true to your beliefs keeps you from growing up and becoming a self-actualized, enlightened member of the human race. Modern atheists are not merely speaking in hyperbole or trying to get attention. The moralist/human atheist really believes that religion is the root of all evil, and he or she really wants to see it plucked from the ground and tossed into the fire. They regard those who possess anything even approaching a robust belief in God as diseased simpletons in need of the Machiavellian cure they have on offer.

The program for responding to modern atheism (particularly the moralist/humanist kind) set forth in *Gaudium et spes* may be summarized with the acronym RENEW, which stands for reveal, engage, nourish, empathize, and witness. First, one must do one's best to reveal rather than conceal God to others. It is true that atheists are responsible for the choices they make, but Catholic teaching acknowledges that atheism is often caused by the bad example of believers. Whether through sheer ignorance of authentic Christian teaching or willful disobedience to this teaching, it is often the behavior of those inside the churches that convert others to atheism in numbers that the atheists themselves could never hope to match. On the other hand, when we live a life true to the Gospel of Jesus Christ it does more to disarm atheism than any intellectualism, rhetoric, apologetics, or set of arguments could ever do.

Second, we are to engage with atheists. It is easy and tempting to just ignore atheists and dismiss them as a group of oddballs, similar to the kids at school that you wouldn't sit next to in the cafeteria. But this will not do. In the first place, atheists often have difficult and challenging arguments that require honest responses and attention. If believers are too busy being pious to respond to them, then it is no wonder that progress isn't made. In the second place, you may find that in some cases the atheist has actually thought more deeply about your own religion than you have. He or she is critical of your religion because he or she has thought through the implications of certain beliefs to a degree that you have not. Also, more importantly, the Gospel requires that we go out of our inner-ring of friends and likeminded people to share our faith with those on the outside. After all, these are the ones who most need to hear it.

Third, we must make sure to nourish our own faith. If your own faith is running on empty, then engaging with an atheist is like jumping into a river to help someone who is drowning when you yourself do not know how to swim. There are numerous instances in the Gospels of Jesus going off by himself to pray, and he exhorts the disciples to do the same. If you yourself do not really take the doctrines of Christianity seriously or firmly hold to them, then it is probably better to focus on what is going on with your own house before you get to work fixing the houses of others.

Fourth, we are instructed to empathize with those who find it difficult to believe. This means trying as best we can to see the world as they see it and understand their obstacles from their own point of view. If you have not put forward the effort to do this, then you shouldn't be surprised when your dialogue with a nonbeliever descends into mere quarrelling. Everyone wants to feel understood, even by people with whom we disagree. C.S. Lewis, one of the leading Christian apologists of the second half of the twentieth century, was himself an atheist before converting to Christianity. Therefore, he was uniquely positioned to argue with atheists because he knew their view "from the inside," as it were. *Gaudium et spes* is not saying that we all need to spend some time as atheists! However, we do need to try and see things from their point of view. As we observed earlier in the chapter, Thérèse of Lisieux understood her own struggles with faith as God providing her with an opportunity to empathize with those who lack faith.

Finally, one of the most effective tools for countering modern atheism is the witness of the Christian communities. Unfortunately, there is much division among contemporary versions of Christianity. When Christians fight, quarrel, bicker, wage war, and generally exhibit behaviors that fall well below the standard set by our Lord, not to mention just the ordinary standard observed by decent people everywhere, then it makes the whole thing appear absurd, hypocritical, and unappealing to the outside world. On the other hand, when Christians show unity, love, forgiveness, extraordinary compassion, and, in short, live Christ-like lives, then it has the opposite effect.

In sum, the way to counter modern atheism is not merely by sitting down and trying to think up clever arguments, although there is some value in this too. The most important thing to do is respond with faith, hope, and love. *Gaudium et spes* instructs us to reveal God to others not merely with words, but in our actions, both as individuals and as a community. Or, as St. Francis of Assisi famously stated, "Preach the Gospel at all times and, when necessary, use words."

SUMMARY

In this chapter, we have explored the virtues of grace. These virtues are not acquired through human effort, but gifted to us by God. By this grace, the cardinal virtues are directed to the beatific vision and thus transformed through the theological virtues of faith, hope, and love. As we have seen, this does not negate the role of human action in the formation of the virtues. Next, we analyzed the infused versions of the cardinal virtues exemplified by "the little way" of Thérèse. We then examined the theological virtues of faith, hope, and love. Finally, we investigated the rise of atheism in contemporary culture as well as the way to counter atheism as set forth in *Gaudium et spes*. Having analyzed the virtues independently, it is essential to make clear what has been alluded to several times to this point. Although we examine the virtues individually for the sake of clarity and for the purposes of analysis, in reality the virtues are never found apart from each other. Whoever has one of them has them all. However, to make clear that this is so and why it matters requires a separate chapter.

CHAPTER 6

The Unity of the Virtues

"A virtue cannot be perfect, as a virtue, if isolated from the others."
St. Gregory the Great, *Commentary on Job*

Having attained a basic understanding of the acquired and infused virtues, we may proceed to a slightly more complicated discussion regarding the interconnection of the virtues. There are two major schools of thought with respect to this topic. Most modern ethicists think that the virtues are not necessarily connected. According to this view, a person may possess courage without temperance, justice, prudence, or even all three; any virtue may exist independently of any other virtue. In this chapter, I refer to this view as the "isolation thesis," because those who support it believe that a person can possess a virtue in isolation from the other virtues. The other view, held by Socrates, Plato, Aristotle, Augustine, and Thomas Aquinas, maintains that in order to possess a single virtue one must possess them all. I refer to this view as the "unity thesis," because those who support it hold that individual virtues are never found apart from each other. The virtues always form a unity. This chapter contends that the unity thesis is true and the isolation thesis false.

This chapter develops in four sections. The first section considers the case for the isolation thesis as well as the two main objections that its supporters make against the unity thesis. The next section replies to these objections and shows that one cannot correctly understand virtue if one denies the validity of the unity thesis. The third section examines the significance of the findings of the first two sections in light of the Catholic moral tradition. Finally, a summary section reviews the major points both of the current chapter and the whole of Part II.

THE ISOLATION THESIS

As stated previously, the majority of contemporary ethicists contend that it is possible to possess individual virtues in isolation from other virtues.[1] Those who support the isolation thesis tend to make their respective arguments through appeals to common sense. Remember that friend you had in high school who seemed brave but often exhibited poor judgment? If the unity thesis is true, then your friend's inability to consistently make sound judgments (imprudence) cancels out his or her courage as well. Isn't this unfair? Consider the following scenario: Forest is sixteen years old and has just obtained his driver's license. He wants to impress Jenny, the pretty girl who lives down the street. He knows that she always goes to watch the illegal drag races, which take place in the adjacent town every Saturday night. Now, Forest does not know how to drag race. Also, his car is not exactly stellar. He bought it for $500.00. It is old. There are no airbags or safety features. Every time he comes to a stop the brakes squeak loudly and emit a bad smell. Lastly, the guy who sold him the car warned him that if he accelerates to more than 75 mph, then there is a good chance that the engine "might" explode.

For all of these reasons, Forest is doubly afraid to enter the drag race. First, he is afraid that he may hurt himself. Second, he is afraid that he may make a fool of himself. These are quite rational fears. Additionally, even if he were to avoid injury, embarrassment, or both, there is no guarantee that Jenny is even going to be impressed or notice that he was there. Maybe she just goes to the drag races to hang out with her friends. Plus, aren't there other, safer, ways to attempt to impress Jenny? Is it really worth breaking the law and risking one's life just to impress a girl that you think is pretty? In short, Forest entering the drag race would be a foolish and rash decision.

"But still courageous!" says the supporter of the isolation thesis. Can't there be such a thing as foolish or imprudent courage? Haven't we known many people who seem to possess just such a quality? Forest's desire to impress Jenny may be causing him to exercise poor judgment. By entering the drag race, Forest may even be further ingraining within himself a tendency to act recklessly in order to gain the approval of others. With all of this the supporter of the isolation thesis can agree, but is not Forest also learning to overcome his fears? The fact is that Forest is committed to what, for him, is the very important goal of impressing Jenny. Those on the outside may think the goal foolish, and they may be right. They may also think that the way Forest plans to impress Jenny is misguided, and they may be

[1] For a representative example see Robert Merrihew Adams, *A Theory of Virtue* (Oxford: Clarendon Press, 2006). See also Jean Porter, "The Unity of the Virtues and the Ambiguity of Goodness: A Reappraisal of Aquinas's Theory of the Virtues," *The Journal of Religious Ethics* 21: 1 (1993): 137–63.

right about that too. But isn't going through with an action despite one's fear the definition of courage? If Forest were to back out at the last second, would we admire his wise discretion or think him a coward? Suppose that Dan also entered the drag race to impress Jenny. Suppose further that his car was even worse than Forest's. Suppose further still that Dan had been in a car accident when he was younger and so was even more afraid than Forest was. But Dan went through with it, and Forest backed out; to whom do you find your admiration tending, Dan or Forest? For all of these reasons, argues the advocate of the isolation thesis, it is clear that courage is isolable from good judgment. Hence, the unity thesis is false.

Now, let us consider a much more serious example. On September 11, 2001, terrorists hijacked American planes and flew them into the World Trade Center in New York. Thousands of innocent people were murdered that day. A couple of days later, a popular political commentator who hosted his own talk show on ABC argued that however much we may disagree with their worldview, we cannot deny that the terrorists displayed courage in giving up their lives for the sake of their beliefs. A national uproar ensued, and the commentator was quickly fired and his show cancelled. Nevertheless, the supporter of the isolation thesis may find him or herself compelled to agree. If one is going to attribute courage to Forest merely for risking possible harm for the sake of impressing a girl, then how could one deny courage to the hijackers who faced certain death out of obedience to what they understood to be the divine will? To be clear, according to the isolation thesis, one can still maintain that the terror-ists possessed a warped understanding of reality – that they lacked pru-dence. One can still hold that the means they employed in pursuit of their ends – the deliberate killing of innocent people – were profoundly unjust. However, the supporter of the isolation thesis asks why we can't simply say that the individuals in question displayed imprudent and unjust courage, but courage nonetheless? If the isolation thesis applies to Forest, then it applies to the 9/11 hijackers too.

From these examples, each of which is revisited in the next section, we may extrapolate the two major objections that supporters of the isolation thesis make against the unity thesis. First, if one has to possess all of the virtues in order to possess even one of them, then no one is actually vir-tuous. Human beings are the sum total of all their qualities, both good and bad. No one's character is wholly good or wholly evil. Just imagine if you had to place all the people you have ever known, and you your-self, into one of those two categories. Would you be able to? Wouldn't you find yourself begging for the option of a middle category? Indeed, an ancient school of philosophers known as the Stoics denied that such a category existed. The Stoics likened unrighteousness to drowning. There is no such thing as "kind of" drowning. One is either drowning or one is not; there is no in-between. The Stoics thought that the same was true of moral character. One either possesses a virtuous character or one does not; there is no such thing as "kind of" virtuous. It was for this reason that the Stoics denied the isolation thesis. If one possessed a single virtue without the others, then that person would be good in a limited sense. However, for the Stoics, one is either fully virtuous or devoid of virtue entirely.[2]

This brings me to the second major objection made by proponents of the isolation thesis. If it were true that everyone was either wholly good or wholly bad, then there could be no such thing as gradual moral progress – the kind of progress, that is, with which most people are familiar. Rather, the only transitions possible would be from wholly evil to wholly good or the reverse. However, that isn't how real life works. Consider it with respect to any other area in life. Does one go from not being able to play the violin at all to becoming a maestro in an instant? Are there not almost uncountable gradations of progress and regress in between? Or think of it with respect to biological development. We sometimes speak, for the sake of convenience, as if the world was populated only by children and adults, but in reality we know that things are much more complex than that. There are multiform gradations of development seamlessly weaved together in the ever-unfolding journey of personhood. If everything else we know consists of spectrums, then why should morality alone consist only in absolutes?

In sum, supporters of the isolation thesis deny the unity thesis, because they think that it negates the possibility of anyone ever being or becoming virtuous. It sets the standard for moral goodness so high that no one could ever hope to reach it. They think that the isolation thesis is the solution to this problem. If it is true, then, at least, I can attribute some level of virtue to almost anyone, even those who are otherwise very imperfect. With respect to all of these arguments, proponents of the isolation thesis are mistaken, as the next section shows.

THE UNITY THESIS

To begin our response to the isolation thesis, let us return to Forest's situation. The first thing to make clear is that to uphold the unity thesis

[2] See J.M. Rist, *Stoic Philosophy* (Cambridge, UK: Cambridge University Press, 1969).

does not commit one to the Stoic view that possessing virtue is an all-or-nothing affair. Thomas Aquinas, for example, believed that one could possess the virtues in unused states. God infuses the habits of the virtues into the souls of infants when they are baptized, but the infants still need to learn how to use them as they mature. Even on the natural level, Aquinas thought that everyone possessed what he referred to as "natural dispositions to virtue." These are good qualities that have the potential to become virtues when joined with prudence, the habit of good judgment. This is where Forest comes in. When I was relaying to you the scenario earlier, you may have found yourself conflicted. On the one hand, you may not have wanted to attribute the virtue of courage to Forest, because his decision seems so foolish. On the other hand, you may have agreed that there is something admirable about carrying through with an action for the sake of something important to you, even when one's judgment is poor. If the Stoics are right, then we can't attribute any courage to Forest. If proponents of the isolation thesis are right, then we have to grant him perfect courage. However, with Aquinas we can draw the more reasonable conclusion that Forest does indeed possess a good quality, the natural disposition to the virtue of courage, but that we can only admire it with reservations because it has yet to be joined to good judgment.

Next, let's reconsider the more significant case of September 11th. As you reflected on the argument for attributing courage to the suicide bombers, there may have been a part of you that began to feel extremely frustrated. There is, after all, a certain logic to the case made by advocates of the isolation thesis. But the part of you that felt frustrated was right to feel that way. The reason why it is wrong to attribute the virtue of courage to the 9/11 hijackers is because virtue is a fine and noble thing, and what they did was neither fine nor noble. This raises a crucial point: virtues are directable only to that which is morally good. They are perfective of the person. Proponents of the isolation thesis have forgotten this and, as a result, do not correctly understand the nature of virtue. They think that virtues are mere instruments, such as hammers, which may be used to build up a house or to destroy one. And there are, indeed, qualities like this. Aquinas uses Augustine's example of a miser to explain. There is a quality similar to prudence by which the miser "devises various roads to gain." The miser has a sense of justice ordered to not taking from others out of fear of consequence. He has a kind of temperance "whereby he curbs his desire for expensive pleasures." He even has the courage to brave the sea, cross the mountains, or go through fire in order to avoid poverty.[3] The point made by both Augustine and Aquinas is that the miser's tendencies are mere counterfeits of virtue, because they are not ordered to a true good but only an apparent good. Coming back to the 9/11 hijackers, the point is the same. Proponents of the isolation thesis may rightly point out that the hijackers possessed some kind of tendency by which they devised and carried out their plan, but these tendencies had not been shaped by a truthful vision of reality and so lack the distinctive character of virtue.

Having responded to each example, we may now reply directly to the two major objections that supporters of the isolation thesis make against the unity thesis. First, it is simply inaccurate to say that if the unity thesis is true, then no one is virtuous. It would be true if everyone who endorsed the unity thesis shared the Stoic assumptions about virtue, but this is not so. As we have seen, Aquinas thought that it was possible to possess virtue in underdeveloped states. The unity thesis only applies to virtues in the later stages of development, which I speak more of later in this section. Furthermore, distinguishing between natural dispositions to virtue and true virtues actually enables one to give a more truthful account of the kind of qualities people possess, as we saw in the case with Forest and Jenny. Were the isolation thesis true, we would have to attribute full courage to Forest despite the fact that this is clearly not the case. Thus, Aquinas's version of the unity thesis still allows us to attribute good qualities to people that are lacking virtue in important areas, but it also gives us the tools to describe these qualities in an accurate way. The same cannot be said for the isolation thesis.

The second objection is also false. Supporting the unity thesis does not commit one to the Stoic view that the only way to become morally good is to instantaneously transition from lacking virtue completely to possessing it entirely. In fact, one of the first thinkers to take issue with this view was Augustine:

It seems to me that the Stoics are wrong in refusing to admit that the man who is increasing in wisdom has any wisdom at all, and insisting that he has it only when he is absolutely perfect in it; not that they refuse to admit the increase, but for them he is not wise in any degree unless he suddenly springs forth into the free air of wisdom after coming up and, as it were, emerging from the depths of the sea.[4]

---

[3] *ST* IIa IIae q. 23 a. 7; Aquinas treats the connection of the virtues at Ia IIae q. 65.

[4] *EP167* cited in R.E. Houser, *The Cardinal Virtues: Aquinas, Albert, and Philip the Chancellor* (Toronto: Pontifical Institute of Mediaeval Studies, 2004), 214. The driving question of Augustine's exchange with Jerome involves the meaning and implications of the Scriptural passage that states that "whosoever shall keep the whole law but offend in one point has become guilty of all."

Augustine did not think that the moral life worked that way. At least, that was not his experience. Rather, becoming good was similar to coming out of a dark cave and slowly adjusting to the light of the sun a little bit at a time. Aquinas agreed, but the metaphor he preferred was the one of biological development I alluded to earlier:

The spiritual increase of charity may be compared with man's bodily growth. We can, doubtless, distinguish many degrees, yet it has certain fixed divisions characterized by actions or pursuits corresponding to that growth. Thus infancy precedes the age of reason; another stage begins with the use of reason and speech; then comes puberty and the possibility of reproduction, and so on until full development. In like manner, the diverse degrees of charity are distinguished according to the different pursuits inspired by development itself. For at first keeping away from sin and resisting concupiscence, which lead in a direction opposed to charity, is the main concern. This concerns beginners, in whom charity has to be nourished or strengthened lest it be destroyed: in the next phase, the main concern is the intention of progress in the good. This is the pursuit of the proficient, whose aim is mainly at strengthening their charity by adding to it. Finally, there is a third pursuit whose chief aim is union with and enjoyment of God. This belongs to the perfect who depart to be with Christ. This is the very law of motion: we see the body distance itself from its point of departure, then progressively approach, and finally, at the end, find repose.[5]

In the same way that we pass through stages of development in our biological life, so too with respect to the moral life. Both Augustine and Aquinas, however, realized that the reality of moral progress is too complicated to be fully explained by any single metaphor. Indeed, as C.S. Lewis observed, this change does not happen to everyone in "a sudden flash – as it did to St. Paul or Bunyan." It is not necessarily similar to the transition from drowning to breathing or from blindness to sight. In fact, "it may be so gradual that no one could ever point to a particular hour or even a particular year." Either way, however, the important thing "is the nature of the change itself."[6]

THE CATHOLIC MORAL TRADITION AND THE UNITY OF THE VIRTUES

As you read through this chapter, you may have wondered what exactly all of this has to do with Catholic theology. One of the reasons Catholic theologians like Augustine and Aquinas saw the importance of the unity

---

Augustine approaches this question by means of what he deems to be the related question of whether the person who has one virtue has them all.

[5] *ST* IIa IIae q. 24 a. 9. For this passage I use the translation found in J.P. Torrell's *Saint Thomas Aquinas Vol. 2 Spiritual Master*, tr. Robert Royal (Washington, DC: CUA Press, 2003), 359–60.

[6] C.S. Lewis, *Mere Christianity* (New York: Harper Collins, 1952), 146.

of the virtues is because they recognized that it speaks to the larger issue of what it means to become morally good. Indeed, one of the reasons why the unity thesis is unpopular today is because our society sets a very low bar in this regard. However, in the Gospels, Christ is depicted as setting a very high standard:

I tell you, unless your righteousness surpasses that of the scribes and Pharisees, you will not enter into the kingdom of heaven. You have heard that it was said to your ancestors, "You shall not kill and whoever kills will be liable to judgment." But I say to you, whoever is angry with his brother will be liable to judgment.... You have heard that it was said, "You shall not commit adultery." But I say to you, everyone who looks at a woman with lust has already committed adultery with her in his heart. If your right eye causes you to sin, tear it out and throw it away. It is better for you to lose one of your members than to have your whole body thrown into Gehenna. And if your right hand causes you to sin, cut it off and throw it away. It is better for you to lose one of your members than to have your whole body go into Gehenna.[7]

Take a moment to reflect on what Christ is saying here. It is, perhaps, not difficult to empathize with someone who, upon first hearing these statements, fails to take them seriously. He may agree that learning not to act on one's anger is both possible and worthwhile, but not getting angry at all? He may agree that not acting on one's sexual desires is sometimes necessary, but not having them at all? And then what of this business of plucking out eyes, lopping off hands, and so forth. He can't be serious; just think how your college campus would look if everyone actually followed this advice.

Despite the disbelief one may initially feel when contemplating Christ's words, I think there are at least three points in need of our attention here. First, becoming morally good is not just about what one does but about who one is. Our society tends to focus more on external behaviors than interiority and character – the stuff a person is made of. Part of this is merely practical. We can observe behaviors; we cannot observe internal beliefs, attitudes, or dispositions. Moreover, it often seems to us as though actions are more important than internal dispositions or states of character. This is because actions have transitive effects. These are effects that impact other people. For example, if a drunk driver crashes into another car, then the transitive effects are whatever pain and suffering the people in that car endure. However, we often fail to consider the intransitive effects of our actions; that is, effects that do not have a direct impact on

---

[7] Matthew 5:20–22a; 27–30 *NAB*.

others. Consider, for instance, the example of looking lustfully. It may be true to say that if a man looks at a woman with lust, then this does not directly cause her harm in the transitive sense. Nonetheless, intransitively, he harms himself, because he further ingrains within himself the destructive tendency of viewing women as things rather than persons. He becomes more like a certain kind of bad man. Furthermore, forming this kind of a character could lead him to treat women exploitatively at some point down the line. Hence, those who think that actions are more important than character are misguided, because the states we acquire inform our actions.

Second, our happiness is ultimately contingent on whether we become morally good or fail to do so. As I said before, most of us are somewhere in between total depravity and total perfection on the spectrum of moral goodness, but with every choice we progress more toward one direction or the other. All of our roads are before us, so to speak. However, at some point we will have to look back at the lives we have lived and feel either contentment or shame. When that time comes, it will not matter how much money we have made or how many honors we have achieved. The only things that will matter are promises either broken or kept, forgiveness offered or withheld, loves honored or betrayed. I think that this is one of the things of which Jesus is reminding us with the bit about plucking out eyes and so forth. He needs to speak in this way to arouse an apathetic world that is still muddling about with pleasure and power, thinking that these things can give them happiness.

Third, and most important, Christ offers us a daunting standard in order to remind us that we can't go it alone. Have you ever wondered if you will make a good wife or husband some day? On the one hand, it would seem that there are some qualities you could start working on now that would help ensure that result: honesty, caring, patience, and so forth. On the other hand, however important these qualities may be, there is simply no way to become a good husband or wife outside of the context of marriage. The relationship itself is the source of this specific kind of goodness. It is the same with God. Because of shame, several people try to put off having a relationship with God until they have become morally good or worthy of just such a relationship, but this is putting the cart before the horse. Being in right relationship with God is the cause, not the result, of moral goodness.

Having understood these three theological points, let us now return to the virtues. Indeed, we can see here how the virtues and Christ's teachings mutually illuminate each other. The virtues are not just about actions but the interior states that produce those actions. Also, the virtues remind us that the good life is not just about keeping a set of rules but achieving true happiness. The acquired virtues are, perhaps, best thought of as the good qualities at which we are capable of arriving from our own efforts. Affirming these qualities reminds us that becoming virtuous is not only for those who know Christ.[8] At the same time, whatever virtue we may attain before being joined to God in sanctifying grace may best be thought of as preparation for the fullness of virtue that God gives to those who accept it.

And now do you see why upholding the unity of the virtues was important to Augustine and Aquinas? The point of the Catholic moral life is to become good through Christ. The unity of the virtues is a description of what that goodness entails. In this way, it helps to illuminate God's will for us. God made us in God's image, with souls capable of knowing truth, doing good, and most importantly, being in the right relationship with God. Furthermore, God intends that we accomplish all three, which is why we are given the habits necessary to do so – the virtues of grace.

Having concluded our formal discussion of the virtues, let us now return to Fiona one final time. When we last left her at the end of Chapter 3, she was dealing with issues concerning the objective moral law. Let us now suppose that she is struggling with issues pertaining to becoming a virtuous college student. As you are well aware, a number of specific issues confront college students in pursuit of virtue. One of the main challenges is that college students tend to regard morality as merely an arbitrary set of rules. Recall the debate between Socrates and Glaucon narrated in Chapter 1 of this book. My chief point in that chapter was that Glaucon, similar to Hobbes, wrongly thought that moral rules are rooted in nothing other than power. We have moral rules because people in authority invent and implement them in society. Socrates, on the other hand, understood that moral rules are not arbitrary inventions of the powerful, but descriptions of what is needed for attaining true happiness. We may now take up this argument again. If Glaucon is right, then keeping moral rules is only a matter of obligation. We may refer to this as the "morality of obligation" perspective. However, if Socrates is right, then following moral rules is something we do in pursuit of our own happiness. We may call this the "morality of happiness" perspective.

---

[8] *ST* IIa IIae q. 23 a. 7. Aquinas says that "we may speak of virtue being where there is no charity, insofar as it is directed to some particular good."

Now, whether one holds a morality of happiness perspective or a morality of obligation perspective is also going to impact one's view of freedom. The view of freedom that follows from the morality of obligation perspective we may call "freedom of indifference." According to this view, to be free means merely to be able to do what one wants with no external or internal constraints. However, from the morality of happiness perspective, one may derive a more truthful understanding of freedom, which Catholic moral theologians refer to as "freedom for excellence."[9]

In order to understand the difference between these rival views of freedom, consider the example of language. When I was a kid I saw the film *Indiana Jones and the Last Crusade*. In this movie, Indiana Jones, the adventurous archaeologist, finds two ancient scrolls written in Latin and quickly translates them to uncover clues in his quest to find the Holy Grail – the legendary cup used by Christ during the Last Supper. I thought this was neat, so I purchased a book to teach myself Latin. I quickly realized that this was no fun at all. Learning Latin begins not with the actual language itself, but with a bunch of boring grammatical rules one must memorize. One learns to distinguish between the nominative and the genitive, active voice and passive voice, the present and the pluperfect, the indicative and the subjunctive, and so forth – no fun at all. Latin seems like just a bunch of constricting grammatical rules. However, once one internalizes these rules, then one is freed to translate sentences – simple ones at first, and later, more complex ones. With more practice and skill, one becomes able to read Augustine and Aquinas in their original languages. This is what is meant by "freedom for excellence." The more one keeps the rules, which admittedly may seem arbitrary and constricting at first, the freer one becomes. It is the same in the moral life. Following moral rules is the key to attaining moral excellence, just like following the rules of Latin grammar is the key to attaining excellence in Latin. As *Gaudium et spes* reminds us, true freedom consists in the ability to do "what is good."[10] This is what is meant by "freedom for excellence."

Returning to Fiona, one of the main struggles college students face is that they tend to assume, without knowing it, both a morality of obligation

---

[9] For an in-depth treatment of the types of freedom considered here, see William C. Mattison III, *Introducing Moral Theology: True Happiness and the Virtues* (Grand Rapids, MI: Brazos Press, 2008), 19–37. See also Servais Pinckaers, O.P., *The Sources of Christian Ethics* (Washington, DC: Catholic University of America Press, 1995), 327–78.

[10] *GS* no. 17.

perspective as well as a freedom of indifference perspective. Often, this is not entirely their fault; our society tends to form us in these perspectives. Consider, for instance, Glaucon's advice to college students written from the morality of obligation/freedom of indifference perspective:

Enjoy these years! Experiment! Eat, drink, and be merry! Some day you will work some 9-5ish job and life will be all about responsibility and obligation. All bills, meetings, money, appointments, mortgages, taxes, anxiety, family picnics and, in short, a whole life of have-to. Say good-bye to fun. The chances are very high indeed that in five or ten years you'll have become a rather boring person with a rather boring life. So at least be able to look back without regret! Say that you denied yourself no pleasure, that you had fun when you could! If you don't wear out your passions when you have the chance, if you deny them, then they will circle back on you later in life. You don't want to find yourself trying to settle into all of the mundane responsibilities of adulthood and then realize that you did not burn out the energies of your youth when you could! Then you'll betray the normal responsibilities of adulthood to try and recapture your lost youth. You'll be the old, out-of-place person amongst the young who are living as you should have lived when you had the chance! But, alas, this time has passed you by. You can never relive it. So party, party, and party before "the real world" comes for you, which it shall. Have fun! No guilt, no shame; you are only living as a person of your age ought to! Take my advice, do not become a person who lives in the cage of regret for the rest of your life!

Do you find that ideas such as this have gotten into your mind from somewhere? Now, consider how different the advice is when written from the morality of happiness/freedom for excellence perspective of Augustine and Aquinas:

Use these years well! Learn how to live life well. I know that these may feel like the days when you have nothing to lose, so you can live as you please without consequence. But this is a lie. Every choice you make now will echo throughout the rest of your life. So live, not as though you have nothing to lose, but as though you have everything to gain. Learn how to build meaningful relationships. Learn how to separate yourself from bad examples and attach yourself to good ones. Learn how to discern between those who deceive and those who instruct. Learn how to treat others as you would like to be treated. Learn how to do the right thing even when no one else is doing it or cares. Learn how to stand up for those who are marginalized and looked down upon. Learn how to love. And, of course, you shall not learn any of these things in classrooms alone but only by doing them. Build virtue now so that you will have it by your side when the real temptations come and when more is at stake. The worst regret is that of the person who finds himself or herself in a station of life in which he or she desperately wants to be, but for which he or she is ill-prepared due to prior poor choices. If you've lived as an adulterer lives, will marriage fix that? If you've lived as a thief, will a job fix that? If you've lived intemperately, will the mere passage of time fix that? Be virtuous today and tomorrow. Start building the virtue appropriate to your age. Don't think you can wear out your passions by refusing to restrain them; you'll only be wearing them in. Then you will find yourself ill-disposed to take part in the finer things of life, and you will regret your very self. Take my advice, do not become a person who lives in the cage of regret for the rest of your life!

The point is that Fiona has to decide whose advice she is going to follow. If she chooses to follow the advice of Augustine and Aquinas, which hopefully she will, then she will need to do the hard work of discovering what precisely the virtues entail during the stage of time in which she currently finds herself. This brings me to my last point. As stated earlier, Aquinas maintained that there were several different ways in which a person could possess virtue. With respect to possessing virtue perfectly, however, Aquinas explained that there were three ways of understanding what this could mean. First, it could mean that one is absolutely perfect in every possible way, but Aquinas argued that only God could be "perfect" in this sense. Second, one could be as perfect as a human being can possibly become – knowing all the truth that humans can know and doing all the good that humans can do. Aquinas did not think it was possible to accomplish this until the next life, although it is still a worthy goal to strive toward in this one. Finally, one can become perfect in virtue relative to the stage of time in which one finds oneself.[11] Faith, hope, love, prudence, justice, temperance, and fortitude are all going to look different in a seventh grader, a college student, a middle-aged professor, and a retired stockbroker. Fiona's quest to become a virtuous college student does not mean that she can't have any fun. Rather, it means she will have to learn how to have fun in the right way, at the right times, to the right degree. If she does so, then she will find herself happier than her peers who have yet to learn the reality of moral rules. She is trying to discern and follow these rules, because, as C.S Lewis said, "it would be idiotic not to try; for every mistake is going to cause you trouble later on … probably to others and certainly to yourself."[12] Developing the virtues is about much more than keeping a set of rules; it is about the attainment of true happiness.

---

[11] *DF* a. 10.
[12] C.S. Lewis, *Mere Christianity*, 70–1.

PART III

Catholic Social Teaching

CHAPTER 7

Justice in the Catholic Moral Tradition

"For I, the Lord, love justice."

Isaiah 61:8

In his first Apostolic Exhortation, *Evangelli gaudium* (the Joy of the Gospel), Pope Francis explains the connection between the unity of the virtues and Catholic social teaching: "Just as the organic unity existing among the virtues means that no one of them can be excluded from the Christian ideal, so no truth may be denied…each truth is better understood when related to the harmonious totality of the Christian message; in this context all of the truths are important and illumine one another."[1] Truths regarding individual morality and social morality are both part of the fabric of the Gospel. We must not focus solely on one set of teachings to the exclusion of the other. Indeed, as we mentioned earlier, the cardinal virtue of justice involves not only the proper ordering of the individual soul, but also the larger community. While the primary emphasis of prior chapters has been on justice as understood in the former sense, the focus in what follows is on justice as it pertains to political, social, and economic issues with respect to communities, nations, and the global family.

As Benedict XVI observed, the principles of Catholic social teaching are rooted in a particular understanding of justice.[2] The purpose of this chapter is to elucidate this understanding. Thus, this chapter examines four prominent themes of justice within the Catholic moral tradition: primary justice, rectificatory justice, justice as right order, and justice as rights. The first section examines the prevalence of these themes in the Old Testament. Next, we see how the New Testament reinforces these themes. Here we find that, contrary to an erroneous view held by some, justice and love imply rather than contradict each other. Indeed, as we

[1] *EG* no. 39.
[2] *DCE* no. 28.

saw in the previous chapter's analysis of the unity of the virtues, there can be neither love without justice nor justice without love. The final section shows how the quartet of themes treated in this chapter is reaffirmed by the Church fathers. These themes form the bedrock for the principles of Catholic social teaching, which we analyze in the next chapter.

JUSTICE IN THE OLD TESTAMENT

Regarding justice, four themes are evident in the Old Testament: primary justice, rectificatory justice, justice as right order, and justice as rights. Primary justice is both the most important of the four themes as well as the most difficult to explain. It is difficult to see the sun, because looking directly at it hurts your eyes, but by it you see everything else. It is like this with primary justice. It is hard to explain exactly what it is. When you try to analyze it directly, it appears abstract and murky. However, if one does not presume a sense of primary justice, then whatever else is said about justice is reduced to nonsense.

In the Old Testament, the Hebrew word for primary justice is "*mishpat.*" This word for "justice" is normally accompanied by the word "*tsedeqa*," which usually gets translated as "righteousness." For example: "let justice [*mishpat*] surge like waters, and righteousness [*tsedeqa*] like an unfailing stream."[3] These terms are ambiguous. Some think that *tsedeqa* operates more like a verb than a noun, it entails "making things right," whereas *mishpat* refers to the state of rightness itself. Others have argued that when the terms appear together they speak to "true" or "actual" justice and righteousness as opposed to counterfeits of the same. For our purposes here, it is enough to say that primary justice is best captured by the Latin term "*ius,*" which refers to the proper order or harmony of human beings in relation to God and to each other. The other three themes speak to specific aspects of these relations. Hence, rectificatory justice refers to the "rectifying" or "correcting" or "making right" of situations where this order has been frustrated. Notice that any idea of rectificatory justice becomes unintelligible absent an accompanying concept of primary or original justice. If there is no such thing as an original set of right relations, then the concept of restoring or correcting those relations becomes meaningless.

Indeed, a key claim of the Catholic moral tradition is that, much like the human soul needs to be healed through the attainment of virtue, so

---

[3] Amos 5:24 *NAB* throughout.

too human relations need to be set right. The story in Genesis about Adam and Eve being tempted by the serpent is ultimately about man's rebellion against God; this is all that is meant by "the Fall of man" in a theological sense. Admittedly, the idea that the human race fell away from God in some idyllic primordial garden solely because of one decision of the progenitors of the human family has been criticized throughout history. There is something that just seems unfair about it. Why should I be punished for the behaviors of my ancient ancestors? The great Christian mystic, Lady Julian of Norwich, responded to this by noting that this objection fails to take account of the divine point of view. To God, says Julian, all of humanity is but one person, and one person is all of humanity.

I think part of what Julian is saying is that the doctrine of the Fall is not merely about an arbitrary list of punishments God conferred on us for breaking a rule. Rather, it is an explanation of the human condition. Much like a just soul can only come about from being in the right relationship with God, so, too, a just society can only come about in the same way. Man's rebellion against God impacts both the individual and the society. It is not only something that happened a long time ago; we reenact the Fall in our daily lives every time we violate the moral law. This is one reason why I find the doctrine compelling; it is the only doctrine I have found that takes the nature of the real world seriously. The real world is replete with unjustifiable suffering, exploitation, and immorality; any attempt to deny this is an exercise in self-deception. The Christian view is simply that God did not make the world this way and does not desire the world to be like this. We should not be surprised, therefore, when we find that Scripture is replete with appeals to rectificatory justice. For instance, consider the following passage from the prophet Isaiah:

> Is not this, rather, the fast that I choose:
>> releasing those bound unjustly,
>> untying the thongs of the yoke,
>> setting free the oppressed,
>> breaking off every yoke?
> Is it not sharing your bread with the hungry,
>> bringing the afflicted and the homeless into your house;
>> clothing the naked when you see them,
>> and not turning your back on your own flesh?[4]

Freeing the oppressed, providing shelter for the homeless, and clothing the naked are not being presented in this passage as mere charitable

---

[4] Isaiah 58:6–7.

exhortations, but imperatives of rectificatory justice. The realities of poverty, oppression, and homelessness, to which we become so easily desensitized, represent an inversion of *ius* and violate the principles of *mishpat*.[5] Thus, the prophet reveals God's will that these injustices be set right or rectified (*tsedeqa*). Indeed, in the Old Testament God is often understood as the one who brings about this justice through the lifting up of the poor, afflicted, and marginalized:

> Who is like the Lord our God,
>   enthroned on high,
>   looking down on heaven and earth?
> He raises the needy from the dust,
>   lifts the poor from the ash heap,
>   to make them sit with princes,
>   seats them with princes,
>   the princes of the people
> Gives the childless wife a home,
>   the joyful mother of children.[6]

Again, the point is not that God is merely nice and likes to help out the less privileged; rather, it is that God brings justice (*mishpat*) and sets things right (*tsedeqa*). Acquiescing to injustice never has been and never will be the prerogative of a follower of God. The Catholic moral tradition has always affirmed that God is just and demands justice for the people of God even though such people are often shunned by the broader society.

Rectificatory justice also entails restoring the right order. Much of what this right order entails can be gleaned from the Ten Commandments.[7] The first three commandments deal with the right ordering of the community to God. Another traditional formulation of justice is the Latin term "*suum cuique*," which means giving others what they are due. That is, God is due the highest adoration by virtue of being God. The right order of the community pertains not only to God, but also to family and neighbor. Hence, children owe honor to their parents, and spouses owe each other fidelity. Extramarital affairs and the dishonoring of parents upset the right

---

[5] As Benedict XVI observed, the Church's social doctrine has always held that "the pursuit of justice must be a fundamental norm of the state." And a "just social order" requires that each person is guaranteed his or share "of the community's goods." See *DCE* no. 26.

[6] Psalm 113:5–9.

[7] (1) You shall have no other gods beside me. You shall not make for yourself an idol. (2) You shall not invoke the name of the Lord, your God, in vain. (3) Remember the Sabbath day – keep it holy. (4) Honor your father and mother. (5) You shall not kill. (6) You shall not commit adultery. (7) You shall not steal. (8) You shall not bear false witness against your neighbor. (9) You shall not covet your neighbor's house. (10) You shall not covet your neighbor's wife. (Exodus 20:3–17)

ordering of familial relations. Finally, neighbors owe each other a commitment to the preservation and procurement of honest relations with respect to life, family, and property. Lying, killing, coveting, and stealing upset the right ordering of the community for obvious reasons. Finally, right order requires respect for the rule of law and for the rulers of a society, as is made clear everywhere throughout the Old Testament. Indeed, much of the Old Testament can be read as relating both the struggle to create and preserve this right order and the facing of the consequences that follow from failing to do so.

At this point, we may move on to the fourth and final theme, justice as rights. You may find it odd that in a book about ethics we are only now for the first time embarking on a discussion of rights. Indeed, for the larger half of the twentieth century, most ethicists believed that the idea of "rights" did not emerge until the seventeenth or eighteenth century, but recent scholarship has demonstrated that this is not true.[8] As it turns out, the idea of human beings possessing "rights" can be found in the Old Testament.

There are several examples of "rights" throughout the Old Testament. In the first place, the very idea of an obligation carries with it an inverse conception of a right. If children have an obligation to honor their parents, then parents have a right to be honored. If we have an obligation to worship God, then God has a right to be worshiped. If one has an obligation not to steal from his neighbor, this implies that the neighbor has a right to security and to his property and so forth. Rights, however, are not only the possession of those higher up in the order of society, they extend down to the lowest stations as well:

You shall not deprive the resident alien or the orphan of justice, nor take the clothing of a widow as a pledge. For, remember, you were slaves in Egypt, and the Lord, your God, redeemed you from there; that is why I command you to do this. When you reap your harvest in your field and overlook a sheaf in the field, you shall not go back to get it; let it be for the resident alien, the orphan, and the widow, so that the Lord, your God may bless you in all your undertakings. When you knock down the fruit of your olive trees, you shall not go over the branches a second time; let what remains be for the resident alien, the orphan and the widow.[9]

The repeated references to immigrants (resident aliens), orphans, and widows have a broader meaning, which extends beyond just these three

[8] See Nicholas Wolterstorff, *Justice: Rights and Wrongs* (Princeton, NJ: Princeton University Press, 2008).
[9] Deuteronomy 24:17–20.

groups. Indeed, these groups are representative of the most marginalized, and therefore vulnerable, within ancient Hebrew society. Therefore, the poor are often not mentioned, because to be an immigrant, orphan, or widow already implies poverty. At any rate, the point is that the most vulnerable in society also possess rights to have their basic needs met. Again, this must be understood in the context of the other three themes mentioned heretofore. The right ordering of a society mutually entails respecting the rights of the vulnerable. This is not optional; it is an obligation. When the obligation is not kept, then rectificatory justice demands the setting right of the proper order.

In sum, the themes of primary justice, rectificatory justice, justice as right order, and justice as rights are everywhere in the Old Testament. These themes cannot be properly understood in isolation from each other, nor are they rivals to each other. They are, rather, the aspects of justice on which the Old Testament is chiefly focused. These themes are also extended into the New Testament, to which we now turn.

JUSTICE IN THE NEW TESTAMENT

Before demonstrating how the themes of primary justice, rectificatory justice, justice as right order, and justice as rights play out in the New Testament, it is necessary first to clear away the wrong idea that the New Testament is not concerned with justice. The second-century thinker Marcion began the view that it is not. In his view, the New Testament was incompatible with the Old Testament. Indeed, he thought that the god of the Old Testament and the god of the New Testament were two separate gods. The New Testament god was the real god – the god of love, mercy, and forgiveness, whereas the Old Testament god was a false god of justice.

The early Church rejected Marcion's teachings as inconsistent with the Gospel, but he enjoyed quite a following just the same. Even today I still hear people, Christians even, refer to the Old Testament god as a "god of Justice" or a "god of wrath" and the New Testament god as a "god of mercy" or the "god of forgiveness." Unfortunately, speaking in this way reinforces a fundamentally flawed understanding of the God revealed by the Faith once given. Christian theology has always held that God's mercy and God's justice do not contradict each other. At any rate, you can see for yourself why Marcion's view must be wrong. Simply try to define the terms "mercy" and "forgiveness" without any reference, direct or indirect, to justice, and you will find that this cannot be done. Mercy entails bestowing a kindness upon someone who has not earned it or is not deserving of it, but "earning" and "deserving" imply an order of justice. Forgiving and reconciling involve the coming together of the injurer and the injured; however, "injury" already entails a sense of primary justice that has been breached, and "forgiveness" and "reconciliation" already entail rectificatory justice, the setting right of the injury. In short, Christian love-mercy-forgiveness is not opposed to justice but perfective of it. To attempt to ground Christian love in a justice-less god is like trying to ride a bike with one wheel. You will have to pedal very hard, you won't get very far, and you'll look rather silly to the people passing you on normal bikes.

If you are still not convinced, consider Jesus's famous parable of the prodigal son.[10] "There was a man who had two sons," the parable begins, "and the younger of them said to his father, 'Father, give me the share of your estate that should come to me.'" This was a great breach of justice. It is as though the son is telling the father that he is dead to him, for inheritance follows after death. In other words, the younger son was violating the order of justice. Now, the son goes off to some ancient equivalent of Las Vegas and squanders the inheritance "on a life of dissipation." He ends up wishing to eat of "the pods on which the swine fed, but no one gave him any." So, longing to be back on his father's estate, he formulates a plan: "I shall get up and go to my father, and I shall say to him, 'Father, I have sinned against heaven and against you; I no longer deserve to be called your son; treat me as you would treat one of your hired workers.'" The idea of worth and deserving is not called into question here. The parable seems to indicate that indeed the son was no longer worthy to be called the father's son. As the parable continues, it says that the father sees the son from a distance, takes compassion on him, runs to him, embraces him, and kisses him. The son says the line he has been rehearsing about not being worthy, but the father replies by ordering his servants to throw him a huge party: "'Let us celebrate with a feast, because this son of mine was dead, and has come to life again; he was lost, and has been found.' Then the celebration began." This angers the elder brother: "Look, all these years I served you and not once did I disobey your orders; yet you never gave me even a young goat to feast on with my friends. But when your son returns who swallowed up your property with prostitutes, for him you slaughter the fattened calf."

Now, those who wrongly think that this story is about the opposition of love and justice say that the elder brother represents justice and the

[10] Luke 15:11–32.

father represents mercy-compassion-forgiveness. According to this view, the main point of the parable is the obvious incompatibility of the two. However, those who think this have not read the story closely enough. There is a right order, which the younger son violates. In having mercy on the son, the father is not turning his back to justice but restoring it. The younger son wrongly thinks that restoration of the relationship is impossible. The elder brother fails to recognize the value of this restoration. It is only the father who understands what true justice entails, the setting right of that which had been severed: "for this my son was dead, and is alive again; he was lost, and is found." Obviously, the father does not literally mean that the son was dead or lost. Rather, the relationship was dead, and the rightful bond of parent and child was lost. In the restoration of this relationship is true justice, which the parent knows and the child has yet to learn. Thus, the parable of the prodigal son is not about the father's compassion turning a blind eye to the demands of justice. Rather, the father's compassion opens his eyes to those very demands, and the right order of parent to child is restored. As Benedict XVI stated, "charity goes beyond justice but never lacks justice."[11]

Before advancing, I wish to make one further comment on the relevance of Jesus and his teachings as regards justice and social morality. The reason I must do so is because a great number of ethicists have wrongly understood the life of Jesus and his teachings as irrelevant to issues beyond individual morality. Those who think so generally endorse some combination of the following three claims. First, Jesus thought that the world was ending, and so did not care about social morality. Second, Jesus was simple and lived in an age unable to address complex political questions. Third, Jesus only cared about the salvation of individuals, and so did not address social morality. These arguments are wrong for the following reasons.[12] First, Jesus formed a community of disciples and told them go into the nations baptizing all in the name of the Father, the Son, and the Holy Spirit; this mandate is not in conflict with the apocalypse of which no man knows the hour. Second, the sociopolitical issues of Jesus's day were different from our own in important ways but also similar. Greed, exploitation, exclusion, tyranny, and poverty are, unfortunately, not unique to any age. Third, it is not true that one has to endorse either individual

---

[11] *CIV* no. 6. The encyclical, similar to the current chapter, is concerned with the foundations of Catholic social teaching.

[12] See John Howard Yoder, *The Politics of Jesus*, 2nd ed. (Grand Rapids, MI: Eerdman's Publishing Company, 1994), 1–59. Yoder lists a six-fold thesis, but I condense the list here to three.

morality or social morality; it is also untrue that social morality is irrelevant to the salvation of individuals. Social morality, individual morality, and salvation are all bound up with each other in important ways.

Very well then; let us leave behind the erroneous ideas that love and justice are opposed and that Jesus's teachings are irrelevant to justice and social morality. Indeed, the themes of primary justice, rectificatory justice, justice as right order, and justice as rights are reaffirmed and reinforced in the New Testament. A simple way to see all four themes beautifully expressed in the same passage is in the *Magnificat* of the Blessed Virgin Mary:

> My soul proclaims the greatness of the Lord;
> my spirit rejoices in God my savior.
> For he has looked upon his handmaid's lowliness;
> behold, from now on will all ages call me blessed.
> The Mighty One has done great things for me
> and holy is his name.
> His mercy is from age to age
> to those who fear him.
> He has shown might with his arm,
> dispersed the arrogant of mind and heart
> He has thrown down the rulers from their thrones
> but lifted up the lowly.
> The hungry he has filled with good things;
> the rich he has sent away empty.
> He has helped Israel his servant,
> remembering his mercy,
> according to his promise to our fathers,
> to Abraham and to his descendants forever.[13]

All four themes are present here. The right order or harmony of human beings in relation to God and to each other (*ius*, primary justice) is being restored (rectificatory justice). The rights of the lowly and the consequences faced by "the arrogant" for not respecting these rights are not ancillary to the text but essential to it. As Luke's Gospel continues, we discover that God, in the person of Jesus Christ, brings justice and sets things right:

He came to Nazareth, where he had grown up, and went according to his custom into the synagogue on the Sabbath day. He stood up and read and was handed a scroll of the prophet Isaiah. He unrolled the scroll and found the passage where it was written:

---

[13] Luke 1:46–55.

> The Spirit of the Lord is upon me,
>   because he has anointed me
>   to bring glad tidings to the poor.
> He has sent me to proclaim liberty to the captives
>   and recovery of sight to the blind,
>   to let the oppressed go free,
> and to proclaim a year acceptable to the Lord.[14]

Here we see the parallel with the theme in the Old Testament of God bringing justice for God's people. In addition we have, again, the idea of a primary justice ruptured as a result of a failure to respect the rights of the lowly.

We see these themes also at work in the example of the Apostles as relayed in the Book of Acts. Without going into details, we get a fairly clear hint here of what an authentically Christian society would be like. In the first place, there are to be no persons along for the ride or leeches. If an able person does not work, then he does not eat. And work here has a technical meaning; it means to produce something good. There are a vast number of people in our society today who either do not work out of laziness or a sense of entitlement (a corruption of justice as rights), or who do work, and perhaps even make a great deal of money, but produce garbage that is either useless or harmful to others. Neither group would feel at a home in a truly Christian society. On the other hand, the Apostles shared everything in common and always made allotments for the marginalized. In this way, those who society shuns and treats as second-class citizens are provided for; the rights of the marginalized are respected. There is a clear mandate here for setting right (rectificatory justice) a perverse social order. At the same time, proper relations are upheld and obedience to the civil order is always insisted upon (justice as right order). Although some theologians have disagreed, Christianity has never been a religion of violent revolution. Rather, it is a religion of transformation, both of the individual and society.[15] This is clear in the Scripture and further evidenced in the writings of the early Church fathers.

JUSTICE ACCORDING TO THE CHURCH FATHERS

The Church fathers were intensely concerned with justice within the communities of early Christians. For example, St. Cyprian, the third-century

---

[14] Luke 4:16–19.
[15] See Congregation for the Doctrine of the Faith, *Instruction on Certain Aspects of the "Theology of Liberation"* (Vatican City: Libreria Editrice Vaticana, 1984), especially VIII, 1–9.

bishop of Carthage, uttered the following proclamation: "[The rich and powerful] add forests to forests and, excluding the poor from their neighborhood, stretch out their fields far and wide into the space without limits....Their possession amounts to this only, that they can keep others from possessing it."[16] This speaks to a violation of the right order required by primary justice; the violation, as it so often does, stems from a failure to recognize and respect the rights of the poor and oppressed.

St. John Chrysostom expresses the same sentiment. Responding to those who have criticized the social and economic outlook of fourth-century Christians in Constantinople, Chrysostom, the Archbishop of Constantinople, responds as follows: "I am often reproached for continually attacking the rich. Yes, because the rich are continually attacking the poor. But those I attack are not the rich as such, only those who misuse their wealth. I point out consistently that those I accuse are not the rich, but the rapacious; wealth is one thing, covetousness another. Learn to distinguish."[17] Recall that the problem is not so much wealth as it is the idolatry of wealth Jesus warned about in the Beatitudes and elsewhere.

The early fathers frequently warned against unhealthy attachments to material goods. To offer one further example, St. Clement of Alexandria reminded his community that Christians are to regard their possessions as gifts from God. These possessions should be used for the benefit of others.[18] It would not be difficult to go on multiplying examples of this kind. Indeed, what I have included in this section are only representative examples of the kinds of things one finds replete throughout the writings of the early fathers down to the present day. From St. Cyprian's appeals to third-century Christians to Pope Francis's Apostolic Exhortation, *Evangelli gaudium*, delivering the harmonious totality of the Christian message to the world has always entailed upholding the hard justice found in the Scripture, even if this makes the modern world uncomfortable.

---

[16] Cyprian of Carthage, *To Donatus*, 12, cited in William Walsh, S.J., and John Langan, S.J., "Patristic Social Consciousness – The Church and the Poor," in *The Faith That Does Justice*, John C. Haughey, ed. (New York: Paulist Press, 1977), 120. This section is indebted to the following work: Jozef D. Zalot and Benedict Guevin, O.S.B., *Catholic Ethics in Today's World* (Winona, MN: Anselm Academic, 2008), see especially 51–4.

[17] John Chrysostom, *Fall of Eutropius*, 2.3, cited in Walsh and Langan, "Patristic Social Consciousness," 128.

[18] Clement of Alexandria, *Quis dives salvetur*, cited in Walsh and Langan, "Patristic Social Consciousness," 120.

SUMMARY

In this chapter we have examined both the Scripture and the thought of a select sample of the early fathers of the Church. Through this analysis, we have arrived at four themes of justice inherent within the Catholic moral tradition. These themes are primary justice (*ius*), rectificatory justice, justice as right order, and justice as rights. We analyzed these themes in the form of *mishpat* and *tsedeqa* in the Old Testament. Next, we saw how these themes are not contradicted but reaffirmed in the New Testament. Finally, we noted the appearance of this quartet of themes in the thought of select Church fathers. With these themes squarely in place, we are now in position to reflect on the principles of Catholic social teaching.

CHAPTER 8

The Principles of Catholic Social Teaching

> We should recognize how in a culture where each person wants to be bearer of his or her own subjective truth, it becomes difficult for citizens to devise a common plan which transcends individual gain and personal ambitions.
>
> Pope Francis, *Evangelli gaudium* no. 61

Although Catholic social teaching (CST) is anchored in the understanding of justice found in Scripture and the reflections of the early Church fathers, the beginning of CST in its modern form is usually traced back to Leo XIII's 1891 encyclical, *Rerum novarum* (On Capital and Labor). Pius XI's encyclical, *Quadragesimo anno* (In the Fortieth Year) followed in 1931. Next came John XXIII's *Mater et magistra* (Mother and Teacher) in 1961 and Paul VI's *Populorum progressio* (On the Development of Peoples) in 1967. John Paul II authored a trilogy of encyclicals pertaining to CST: *Laborem exercens* (On Human Work) in 1981, *Sollicitudo rei socialis* (The Social Concern) in 1987, and *Centesimus annus* (One Hundredth Year) in 1991, which marked the one-hundred-year anniversary of *Rerum novarum*.[1] Subsequent to that was Benedict XVI's 2009 encyclical, *Caritas in veritate* (Charity in Truth). The most recent statements on CST are Pope Francis's 2013 Apostolic Exhortation, *Evangelli gaudium* (the Joy of the Gospel), and encyclical *Lumen fidei* (the Light of Faith). In some respects, all of these documents either anticipate or confirm and expand the presentation of CST put forward in the Second Vatican Council's Pastoral Constitution on the Church in the Modern World, *Gaudium et spes*, promulgated on December 7, 1965.[2]

---

[1] See *DCE* no. 27. This list is representative, not exhaustive.

[2] Thus, the primary focus of this chapter is on this document. This chapter is indebted to Jozef D. Zalot and Benedict Guevin O.S.B., *Catholic Ethics in Today's World* (Winona, MN: Anselm Academic, 2008).

Having gained a greater appreciation of the roots of CST in the previous chapter, we may now move on to examine the trunk and branches as understood from the standpoint of the aforementioned documents. The three principles of CST that make up the trunk are human dignity, community, and the common good. The five principles that make up the branches are participation, subsidiarity, preferential option for the poor, stewardship, and solidarity. The quartet of themes of justice analyzed in the previous chapter forms the roots that inform the three core principles, the trunk of CST – human dignity, community, and the common good. The other five are the branches that both stem from and contribute to the core. The purpose of this chapter is to ruminate in greater depth on these interconnections. Thus, we analyze the principles of CST in turn noting the links to each other and to the quartet of themes analyzed in the previous chapter as we go. By so doing, we come away with a greater appreciation of CST. The final section of the chapter presents a test case. We investigate the practicality of CST through an analysis of the common practice of large multinational corporations employing sweatshop labor.

HUMAN DIGNITY

In the previous chapter, we analyzed the themes of primary justice, rectificatory justice, justice as right order, and justice as rights. Now, let us examine how these themes impact the first core principle of CST, human dignity. Beginning with primary justice, the point to be made here is that the Catholic moral tradition has always affirmed that God made the human race *imago Dei*, in the image of God. This means that we are capable of knowing truth and doing good. Thus, our dignity is inextricably rooted in our status as creatures made in the image of God, and this dignity extends to all persons. As we see in later chapters, there have been several attempts both throughout history and in contemporary times to deny dignity to certain groups of human beings, but any such attempt meets stiff opposition in the Catholic moral tradition.

Now, because we are made in the image of God, and because we therefore possess dignity as human persons, we also have rights to certain basic goods: life, knowledge, sociability, reason, religion, and such like. Thus, we see how this first core principle of CST draws from the four themes of justice treated in the previous chapter. Primary justice entails the dignity we possess by virtue of being created in God's image. We are not only created by God, however, we are created in the right order to God, by which we are also rightly ordered to each other. This entails the respect of the rights intrinsically connected to the dignity we possess as human persons made in the image of God. Rectificatory justice, then, demands the correcting of abuses to human dignity. This is already attested to in the Scripture and the writings of the early fathers of the Church, as we saw in the previous chapter. As we see in subsequent chapters, however, examples of the trampling of these rights, stemming from a willful refusal to recognize the inherent human dignity of some particular group or groups, remain ubiquitous in the modern world:

The varieties of crime are numerous: all offenses against life itself, such as murder, genocide, abortion, euthanasia and willful suicide; all violations of the integrity of the human person, such as mutilation, physical and mental torture, undue psychological pressures; all offenses against human dignity, such as subhuman living conditions, arbitrary imprisonment, deportation, slavery, prostitution, the selling of women and children, degrading working conditions where people are treated as mere tools for profit rather than free and responsible persons: all these and the like are criminal: they poison civilization.[3]

The Catholic Church stands firmly against all such abuses. In order to be a just society, the human dignity of all its members must be respected. This brings us to the interrelated principles of community and the common good.

COMMUNITY AND COMMON GOOD

In order to illuminate the principles of community and common good, both of which are firmly grounded in the right order theme of justice, an analogy from the writings of C.S. Lewis is helpful. In *Mere Christianity*, Lewis says to imagine "a fleet of ships sailing in formation." He then sets forth three criteria that must be met in order for the voyage to be a successful one. First, it is necessary that "the ships do not collide and get in one another's way." Second, each ship must be seaworthy and "in good order." Third, the fleet must make it to wherever they intended to get to: "However well the fleet sailed, its voyage would be a failure if it were meant to reach New York and actually arrived at Calcutta."[4] Drawing on this analogy from Lewis, the second criteria, that the ships do not collide with each other, pertains to what is meant here by "community." Human beings are communal creatures by nature, not meant to live on islands of

---

[3] See *GS* no. 27; also see *EV* no. 4.
[4] C.S. Lewis, *Mere Christianity* (San Francisco: Harper Collins, 1952), p. 71–2.

self-absorption but in harmony with family, friends, and the larger society (right order).

This communal aspect of our nature is not altogether isolable from our virtue as individuals. As Lewis says, "If the ships keep on having collisions they will not remain seaworthy very long. On the other hand, if their steering gears are out of order they will not be able to avoid collisions."[5] Thus, in one sense, all those virtues discussed in Part II may be seen as ordered to the good of the broader community. They keep us in formation (the nautical term for right order) with the other ships. In addition, the community is ordered to the formation of the individual virtues. A just community or society is simply one that amplifies the opportunities and occasions for these virtues to be formed. An unjust society is one that does the opposite. As may be observed in the quote that begins this chapter, the moral relativism we discussed in Part I is related in some way to the economic mentality that pervades much of the modern world.

Community is ordered to the common good – the third criteria in Lewis's ship analogy just mentioned. In the context of CST, the common good refers to "the sum of those conditions of social life which allow social groups and their individual members relatively thorough and ready access to their fulfillment."[6] In other words, the common good is the goal to live in a society marked by a respect for the basic goods, which make up what it means to be a human person made in the image of God. It is the goods we seek not only for ourselves as individuals but for the broader communities of which we are a part. The five principles remaining to be discussed – participation, subsidiarity, preferential option for the poor, stewardship, and solidarity – are descriptive of particular aspects of how such a community would function.

PARTICIPATION

In the first place, as many members of the community as possible would have a role to play in the decision-making process relative to issues that face the community as a whole. This is the root of the democratic principle and it is upheld by CST: "the choice of the political regime and the appointment of rulers are left to the free decisions of the citizens."[7] At the same time, we are not to forget that "by its nature and mission the

---

[5] Ibid., 71.
[6] *GS* no. 26.
[7] *GS* no. 75.

Church is universal in that it is not committed to any one culture or to any political, economic, or social system."[8]

The CST principle of participation is squarely grounded in the theme of justice as rights. Unlike societies where all the decisions are made by a relative handful of individuals in comparison to the throngs that they rule, a society that truly fostered the principle of participation would give voice to every level of society including the lowliest. Corrupt forms of government are certainly a threat to this, but they are not the only threat. There are several mechanisms the powerful use to shut out, exclude, shun, and marginalize others. Politicians, the media, and the wealthy elite can all shift the balance of power toward a minority ruling class set apart and isolated from the broader community. It is for this reason that *Gaudium et spes* calls on all regimes to respect "the basic rights of the person and the family, and the requirements of the common good."[9] Political and economic power should be widely dispersed and not concentrated in the hands of only a few; this is one of the most basic and fundamental principles of CST.

To be clear, the principle of participation is not suggesting that every member of a given society should occupy some kind of post in the government. It is actually the reverse. The idea here is to reduce the scope of governmental reach so that individual citizens are freer to make their own decisions and thus "participate" in the general direction of the society as a whole. In other words, the principle of participation endorses limited government. Delimiting the scope of government reach and influence helps to ensure that ordinary citizens can have a role to play in the larger society. As stated in *Gaudium et spes*, "Citizens, either individually or in association, should take care not to vest too much power in public authority nor to make untimely and exaggerated demands for favors and subsidies, lessening in this way the responsible role of individuals, families, and social groups."[10] The principle of subsidiarity, which we analyze next, also speaks to the need for limited government.

SUBSIDIARITY

Whereas the principle of participation is grounded in the theme of justice as rights, the principle of subsidiarity is grounded in the theme

---

[8] *GS* no. 42.
[9] Ibid.
[10] *GS* no. 75.

of justice as right order. Consider the following hierarchical ordering: child-parent-local government-state government-federal government. There are spheres of authority and power that should not, whenever possible, be impeded upon by the higher spheres. Imagine a seventh grader who wore a shirt to school with an antireligious symbol that other students found offensive. The school calls the parents who do nothing, so local government officials (the school board) intervene and demand the child not wear the shirt to school. So the child appeals the decision to a state court who upholds the determination of the local officials. Finally, the case goes all the way to the U.S. Supreme Court who determines that not allowing the child to wear the shirt to school violates his or her first amendment rights and so overturns the decisions of both lower courts. By this time, the seventh grader is now a sophomore in college and no longer even owns the shirt. At any rate, whether you agree or disagree with the decision of the U.S. Supreme Court is irrelevant; the point here is that justice is generally better served when the sovereignty of smaller entities of power – family, local, state governments, and so forth – are respected and not interfered with by larger entities of power – federal, international, and so forth. This is not always the case; there could be a compelling reason for interference in special circumstances. Generally, however, the right order entails noninterference and respect for the principle of subsidiarity.

It should be stated that one often encounters people who hold a kind of backward view of subsidiarity. That is, they think that the individual exists for the sake of the family, which exists for the sake of the local community, which exists for the sake of the state, which exists for the sake of whatever the highest echelon of centralized secular authority (the federal government, some international organization, etc.), and so forth. However, the principle of subsidiarity reminds us that the reverse is actually the case. The "bigger," more powerful entities are only there for the sake of securing and protecting the freedoms of the smaller ones. The point is beautifully made by C.S. Lewis in the following passage:

The State exists simply to promote and to protect the ordinary happiness of human beings in this life. A husband and wife chatting over a fire, a couple of friends having a game of darts in a pub, a man reading a book in his own room or digging in his own garden – that is what the State is there for. And unless they are helping to increase and prolong and protect such moments, all the laws, parliaments, armies, courts, police, economics, etc., are simply a waste of time.[11]

---

[11] C.S. Lewis, *Mere Christianity*, 1952: 198–9.

Lewis rightly notes how easy it is to get "muddled" about this point. That is, we can come to regard the collective as more important than the individual. This mistake is called "totalitarianism," and it has always been rejected by the Catholic faith. While we are on this point, it is important to make clear that the Church applies the principle of subsidiarity to itself also. As Lewis states, "the Church exists for nothing else but to draw men into Christ, to make them little Christs. If they are not doing that, all the cathedrals, clergy, missions, sermons, even the Bible itself, are simply a waste of time. God became Man for no other purpose. It is even doubtful, you know, whether the whole universe was created for any other purpose."[12] The Church knows that it is ultimately individual souls that must stand before God at the last judgment: "it is the human person that is to be saved, human society which must be renewed."[13] At the same time, the Church does not endorse the opposite extreme of totalitarianism, which is called "individualism." This view says that each person is so unique that everyone is an island unto him or herself. Rather, we are all like organs in a body – dissimilar from one another and each providing what no other could. The Church's view, properly understood, is neither totalitarian nor individualist. Nevertheless, ideologues on both sides of the aisle will always try to identify the Faith with politics, despite the fact that the Church denies all such associations: "The Church, by reason of her role and competence, is not identified with any political community nor is it tied to any political system. It is at once the sign and the safeguard of the transcendental dimension of the human person."[14] Perhaps no principle of Catholic social teaching is misused by ideologues more frequently than the one to which we now turn.

THE PREFERENTIAL OPTION FOR THE POOR

The preferential option for the poor is grounded in the principle of justice as rights. It calls for one to pay special attention to the plight of the most marginalized elements of a given society, who are normally the poor and impoverished. Importantly, this does not entail favoritism or a French Revolution style inversion of oppression. The Scripture writers go out of their way to guard against such a misunderstanding. For example, Moses warns the people, "You shall not follow the crowd in doing wrong. When testifying in a lawsuit, you shall not follow the crowd in perverting justice.

---

[12] Ibid.
[13] *GS* no. 3.
[14] *GS* no. 76.

You shall not favor the poor in a lawsuit."[15] Again, in Leviticus 19:15, Moses declares, "You shall not act dishonestly in rendering judgment. Show neither partiality to the weak nor deference to the mighty, but judge your neighbor justly." And in Deuteronomy 1:16–17, Moses again orders the Judges to act impartially: "Listen to complaints among your relatives, and administer true justice to both parties, even if one of them is a resident alien. In rendering judgment, do not consider who a person is; give ear to the lowly and to the great alike, fearing no one, for the judgment is God's." Hence, the preferential option for the poor calls for deliberate and sustained attention to the rights of the poor because these are the rights most regularly trampled on by the powerful. This, however, does not entail a skewed redistribution of injustice but a striving to eliminate injustice without partiality, as the Scripture makes clear. The preferential option for the poor is a counterbalance to the preferential option for the rich that marks the status quo.

STEWARDSHIP

The principle of stewardship takes us back to the right order theme of justice. The first chapter of Genesis states that God has given the human race stewardship over the creation. Given the abilities that we have to gain ever-expanding control over the natural order, we have a unique responsibility to maintain that order in a manner that is not exploitative and violent. It is as though nature is a precious gift that has been placed in our care. In one sense, it is true that we may do whatever we wish with it; after all, it has been given to us. In another sense, however, the very nature of stewardship entails not merely watching over something but watching over it as if it were your own. If your friend asked you to house-sit for the weekend, you would make sure that the house was not trashed when he returned. Part of the right order of the universe entails that we humans have a providential role to play in the care for creation. To neglect this duty is to participate in great injustice.

SOLIDARITY

Last but not least is the principle of solidarity, which is again grounded in the themes of justice as right order and justice as rights. In one respect, solidarity may be understood as the culminating principle of CST; it entails having compassion for others and taking deliberate steps to act

---

[15] Exodus 23:2–3 *NAB* throughout.

on that compassion in a manner that fosters community. For example, it is one thing to feel bad for the plight of the homeless and quite another to volunteer at a homeless shelter. Whereas the former, in and of itself, does not further solidarity, the latter does. Again, for the Christian, this is not merely optional charity but a demand of justice understood as rights for those members of society who have been marginalized by poverty and other factors. John Paul II clarified that solidarity is "not a feeling of vague compassion or shallow distress at the misfortunes of so many people both near and far." To the contrary, solidarity "is *a firm and preserving determination to commit oneself to the common good*; that is to say to the good of all and of each individual, because we are all really responsible for all."[16] Solidarity is but another name for the right order entailed by primary justice, which entails the recognition of inherent rights; rectificatory justice involves taking deliberate steps to reinforce these rights where and when they have been trampled on.

At this point, I'd like to take a guess at the reaction you may be having to the principles of CST as I have just explained them. One group of readers may think that these principles all seem like wishful thinking. That is, you may think that they all sound great in theory, but economic and political realities are messy things and not amenable to the kind of principles heretofore discussed. Political and economic realities are always going to orbit around greed, selfishness, exploitation, and, in a word, the realities of human nature. Underestimating these realities is dangerous and naïve. Another group of readers may have been moved by these principles and felt a great sense of desire to work toward the implementation of them. The only dangerous thing, for this group, is to ignore the regular injustices of a status quo that routinely ignores these very principles. I think both groups are on to something important. Put succinctly, the question is whether the principles of CST are practical, and, if so, what would need to take place in order to see them instantiated in the modern world. The purpose of the following test case is to pursue this question.

TEST CASE: SWEATSHOPS

Jim Keady, a Fair Labor activist, made a documentary titled "Behind the Swoosh," which, last I checked, can still be viewed on YouTube. Keady gained media attention after he refused to wear Nike products, which

[16] John Paul II, Sollicitudo rei socialis, in *Catholic Social Thought: The Documentary Heritage*, David O'Brien and Thomas Shannon, eds. (Maryknoll, NY: Orbis, 1995), no. 38 [emphasis in the original].

he was required to do as a soccer coach at St. John's University. Keady claimed that Nike labor practices violate every principle of CST, and hence that their products should not be endorsed by St. John's, given that it is a Catholic university. After being compelled to resign for his adherence to CST over university policy, Keady traveled to Indonesia to examine Nike factories firsthand. It is this visit that makes up the content of "Behind the Swoosh." During the eight weeks that Keady spent living in the conditions of the Nike factory workers and earning their wages of $1.25 a day, Keady also documented their accounts of violence, compulsory overtime, and exploitation. Keady subsequently committed his life to further exposing the injustices of multinational corporations such as Nike. The exploitation taking place in Indonesia is not confined to a few locations; it is a pervasive result of globalization.

In response to Keady's efforts, some Catholic universities have turned to brands that respect principles of social justice such as Alta Gracia. Brands such as these are committed to upholding the basic rights of its employees. By not engaging in expensive endorsement deals and by regulating corporate pay, Alta Gracia has been able to turn a profit and keep prices down in a manner that does not violate the demands of justice and the principles of CST. Despite this success, most people and most brands simply ignore Keady as a kind of zealot or idealist who for some strange reason is concerned about the plight of foreign people in third world nations.

Keady's war with Nike raises the fundamental question of whether CST is practical. As mentioned earlier, there is a certain kind of reader who is likely to regard the principles of CST as hopelessly unrealistic. As I stated before, this is not entirely false. The world is replete with routine violations of justice that we have become so desensitized to that we no longer think about them or even recognize them as injustices. We have been deceived and consumed by the widely circulated lie that human dignity is not universal but limited to some select group. I call this "the assumption of selective human dignity" and we meet with it again in later chapters.

In order to understand the assumption of selective human dignity, just ask yourself this question: "Why would I not agree to work in a sweatshop fourteen hours a day, seven days a week, doing menial labor for $1.25 a day (not an hour)?" Several reasons come to mind. I couldn't pay my bills or even meet my basic needs. My quality of life would be severely diminished. At the bottom of it, however, even beyond these concerns, wouldn't you be offended at the mere thought of working such a job? Do you not have a sense that it is beneath your dignity to be turned into a kind of human production machine in a factory? Is it not beneath your dignity to have your unique intellectual, artistic, or creative talents ignored? Is it not beneath your dignity to be treated as a mere means to an end as opposed to an end in and of yourself with inherent rights and worth? There is nothing wrong with answering "yes" to all of these questions and working toward a career that will not violate your dignity in these respects. But here is the issue: if your inherent self-worth and dignity as a human being ought to be respected, then why is it permissible to routinely violate the same dignity of people in impoverished countries?

Catholics believe that all human beings are made in the image of God and possess dignity, and it is this principle that informs Catholic business ethics. The implication of this principle is that businesses should prioritize the well-being of individuals over the maximization of profit. Pope Leo XIII made this point forcefully when he stated that "to exercise pressure for the sake of gain upon the indigent and destitute, and to make one's profit out of the need of another, is condemned by all laws, human and divine."[17] Thus, it is not difficult to see that sweatshops by their very nature violate human dignity and therefore the foundation of Catholic business ethics.

To be clear, my point is not that community, the common good, participation, subsidiarity, preferential option for the poor, stewardship, and solidarity are not also violated by sweatshops. Clearly they are, particularly the preferential option for the poor; these principles of CST also all apply to Catholic business ethics. My point is that of all of these, it is the refusal to recognize the human dignity of particular groups of people that blinds us to the injustice of it all. It is this assumption of selective human dignity, based on arbitrary criteria, which allows us to look the other way and feel no shame. Thus, the issue is really not whether CST is practical. I know that there are certain fundamental social problems that are not going to go away just by refusing to wear the products of a particular company, boycotting, protesting, and so forth. Rather, the point is that, because we strive for justice in our own lives, we ought to be concerned about justice for others. Because we seek to preserve our own dignity, we ought to respect the dignity of others. This is the very nature of solidarity. Rectifying the routine violations of justice that mark the modern world, respecting the rights of the marginalized, and working to restore right order are not special interests or stimulating political ideas; they are mandates of justice according to the Catholic moral tradition.

[17] Leo XIII, On the Condition of Labor, in *Catholic Social Thought: The Documentary Heritage*, David O'Brien and Thomas Shannon, eds. (Maryknoll, NY: Orbis Books, 1995), nos. 15–17.

At the same time, all of this being stated, it is unclear how best to bring about the kind of societal transformation for which the Catholic moral tradition calls. Clearly, government programs alone, whether national or international, are not the solution. If people lack virtue, then they will carry out the same old schemes regardless of whatever set of policies or governmental program is implemented. I suppose the surest thing we can say is that there will not be sweeping societal transformation independently of many individual transformations, but at present certain societal trends and generally accepted practices in the status quo make it harder for such transformations to occur or even for us to recognize the need for them. Perhaps this is what John Paul II meant when he stated that a just society is simply one that makes it easier for an individual to become good. An unjust society is one that makes it harder. At the moment, the state of the world seems, sadly, to be the latter. In such a world, it seems that social change is only likely to begin with individual conversions of the heart.

SUMMARY

In this chapter, we have investigated the trunk and branches of CST. Human dignity, community, and the common good are the core principles. The principles of participation, subsidiarity, preferential option for the poor, stewardship, and solidarity branch out of these. All would wither if not deeply rooted in the biblical themes of justice analyzed in the previous chapter. This chapter has sought to trace the complexity and interconnections among them. This chapter has also examined sweatshops in order to respond to the claim that CST is impractical. We observed that CST is more concerned with justice than it is practicality.

CHAPTER 9

The Just War Tradition

> War must be, while we defend our lives against a destroyer who
> would devour all; but I do not love the bright sword for its sharp-
> ness, nor the arrow for its swiftness, nor the warrior for his glory.
> I love only that which they defend.
>
> J.R.R. Tolkien, *The Two Towers*

The Catholic teachings on war are complex and multifaceted enough to
require a separate chapter. Although a part of CST, the just war tradition is often treated separately from the quartet of themes examined in
Chapter 7. This is odd because "just war tradition" even has the word
"just" in it, which seems to necessitate a grounding in a particular understanding of justice. Therefore, this chapter draws attention to how the
just war tradition is rooted in the themes of justice set out in Chapter 7.
Before doing so, however, it is necessary both to explore what the just
war tradition entails and how it differs from rival moralities with respect
to the topic of war. First, we investigate the total war mentality. Next, we
analyze pacifism. The just war tradition is somewhere beyond these two
poles. A third section presents a test case; we analyze whether the use of
predator drones in the context of the War on Terror can be squared with
the Catholic just war tradition. The final section makes summary clarifica-
tions with respect to the current chapter and the whole of Part III.

TOTAL WAR

The "mentality of total war" refers to ethical claims that two specific rules
of conduct do not apply in warfare: proportionality and discrimination.
Proportionality means not visiting destruction upon the enemy to a
degree that exceeds the amount needed to restore justice. Discrimination
refers to not deliberately attacking noncombatants (i.e., discriminating
between combatants and noncombatants). The total war mentality says

that these caveats are not applicable in warfare. You do what you need to do to win and then salt the earth so that the enemy never again even thinks of messing with you.

There are several examples of the total warfare mentality at work throughout history. When I served as an officer in the United States Navy, I met several people who still held this view, and I could see why. The idea is that if you try to follow rules in war, particularly rules that the enemy either has never heard of or deliberately breaks, then you put yourself at a disadvantage. Imagine a football game where one side had to follow all the rules while the other was free to pull facemasks, dish out illegal hits, and so forth. The team trying to follow the rules would probably lose. Additionally, there is always a kind of ends justify the means utilitarianism, which says that whatever results in victory is therefore justified, even if it involves nuking an entire population or handing out germ-infested blankets to Native Americans, both of which obviously involve breaking the rules of proportionality and discrimination.

We have already dealt with utilitarianism, so I respond here to the "you put yourself at a disadvantage" argument. This argument is true when one considers the short term, but it is false with respect to the long term. It is true that if you ignore proportionality and discrimination you may more quickly win the present battle or even bring a quicker end to the war, but in so doing you are simultaneously sowing the seeds for future wars. The current War on Terror is a chilling example in this regard. This war is actually rooted in the Sabra and Shatila massacre, which took place in Palestinian refugee camps in Beruit, Lebanon, over a two-day period in September of 1982. The death toll was 3,500 civilians. The massacre was viewed as revenge for the assassination of newly-elected Lebanese president, Bachir Gemayel, the leader of the Lebanese Kataeb Party. However, Palestinian militants had not carried out the assassination. We know now that it was native, pro-Syrian militants. Now, the United States was erroneously perceived as having been behind the massacre, so ever since that time it has drawn the ire of terrorist groups in the Middle East. This was, in many ways, the beginnings of the War on Terror, at least in its modern form.

Even if the United States had been behind the Sabra and Shatila massacre, it would still not justify the total war mentality of terrorists who intentionally target noncombatants. However, the point here is that it is in the strategic interest of American foreign policy to quell the perception that several have of the United States as an unjust enemy aggressor. On the border of North Korea and China, there exists a museum with phony exhibits of a supposed "bacteriological" attack that the U.S. Air

Force visited upon Chinese civilians during the Korean conflict. There is no evidence of this atrocity ever having taken place, but the communist government likes to keep it around to stir up anti-American sentiment and distrust of outsiders. It is a mechanism they use to preserve the power and control they exercise over the wider population. Now, there is nothing the United States can do to eliminate the spread of fictional propaganda. However, sound foreign policy ought to avoid supplying potential adversaries with atrocities that can be used as recruitment tools for generations to come. In brief, the argument that a total war approach, because it gives the United States a strategic advantage in warfare, is necessary takes insufficient notice of the long-term impact that failure to respect the principles of proportionality and discrimination has on foreign relations.

However, there is another reason why the total war mentality ought to be avoided, which we find clearly stated in the Scripture. In Genesis 18, God declares judgment against Sodom and Gomor'rah. The city is to be destroyed. Abraham asks God, "Will you really sweep away the righteous with the wicked? Suppose there were fifty righteous people in the city; would you really sweep away and not spare the place for the sake of the fifty righteous people within it? Far be it from you to do such a thing, to kill the righteous with the wicked."[1] God affirms Abraham's understanding of justice by declaring that, indeed, God would spare the city for the sake of the fifty righteous people. However, Abraham is not finished: "See how I am presuming to speak to my Lord, though I am only dust and ashes! What if there are five less than fifty righteous people?"[2] The dialogue proceeds this way until God acknowledges that even for the sake of ten righteous God will not destroy the city. Now, it is true that "righteous and unrighteous" is not necessarily the same as "noncombatant and combatant," but it seems reasonable to infer a prohibition against indiscriminate killing from this passage. At this point, then, we may leave behind the total war mentality as inconsistent with the Catholic moral tradition and move on to another rival perspective with regard to the subject of morality and war. This is the view generally referred to as pacifism.

PACIFISM

It should be acknowledged from the threshold that a large group of Christians understands the Gospel as containing a moral injunction

---

[1] Genesis 18:23–25 *NAB* throughout.
[2] Genesis 18:27–28.

against war and in favor of pacifism. Let us begin our analysis of pacifism, therefore, by considering an argument to this effect made by the prominent Christian ethicist, Stanley Hauerwas. In his "Should War Be Eliminated? A Thought Experiment," Hauerwas constructs a dichotomy between competing histories: God's history and the history of war.[3] In light of this division, he challenges the Catholic just war tradition while upholding the view of Christian pacifism advocated by John Howard Yoder.[4] The stated purpose of his essay is "to help us understand morally how we arrived at a situation where our so-called safety can be ensured only if we are willing to will countless deaths and destruction" (395).

Hauerwas begins with an analysis of John XXIII's *Pacem in Terris* (1963) and the Pastoral Letter of the American Roman Catholic Bishops, *The Challenge of Peace: God's Promise and Our Response* (1983). In his analysis, he seeks to make explicit what he regards as implicit in the documents, namely, an understanding of war as morally positive. After criticizing *Pacem in Terris* for its partial reliance on the natural law tradition, Hauerwas goes on to juxtapose this to *The Challenge of Peace*, in which he finds an appeal to "the Gospel rather than natural law" (400). Although Jesus stands against war, eschatological peace has yet to arrive. Sin and war, which are linked together, mark the present age. Thus, even though pacifism may be a legitimate response to war in some instances, the bishops advocate the just war tradition as a moral alternative. According to the bishops, Christians "must recognize the paradox we face…living in the context of the world as it presently exists; we must continue to articulate our belief that love is possible and the only real hope for all human relations, and yet accept that force, even deadly force is sometimes justified and that nations must provide for their defense" (402). On this basis, Hauerwas critiques the pastoral letter as turning the Gospel's commitment to peace into "an unrealizable ideal" (403).

In Part I, we analyzed the Catholic understanding of the relationship between revealed morality and natural law. However, according to Hauerwas, these operate in *The Challenge of Peace* as conflicting ethical perspectives, although the conflict is either not recognized or not

---

[3] "Should War Be Eliminated: A Thought Experiment," in *The Hauerwas Reader*, John Berkman and Michael Cartwright, eds. (Durham, NC: Duke University Press, 2001): 392–425. Parenthetical citations in this section are to this work.

[4] John Howard Yoder, *The Original Revolution* (Scottdale, PA: Herald Press, 1971).

acknowledged: "From the perspective of the former [revealed-Gospel morality], war is the unambiguous sign of sin and can never be called a good. From the perspective of the latter [natural law], war can sometimes be a good, indeed a moral duty, necessary to preserve human community" (403). Hauerwas does not see how one can affirm both positions at once. Hence, a dichotomy is formed between Catholic just war tradition, on the one hand, and Christian pacifism on the other. The just war tradition is more or less discarded in favor of a pacifist ideology linked to "the Gospel ethic" (404).

However, Hauerwas wants to make the case for the possibility of morality in war as strong as he can in order to counter it more effectively. What is it about war that captures the moral imagination? What is it about war that makes us want to regard war as good? Hauerwas wonders:

There is no question that war makes marvelous history to read. We like to read about war, I think, not simply because there are sometimes good and bad guys, winners and losers, but because war, unlike most of our lives, seems to be more coherent. To be sure, in the middle of a battle the participants seldom know what is going on or what they are doing, but looking back on the confusion, an order emerges that reassures us that, whether we won or lost, we still have a damn fine story to tell. Not only to tell but to be. It is a particular story to be sure, and perhaps we tell it with a good deal of bias, but it is nonetheless ours....War is our ultimate comfort in a world without a history, for it provides us with a story. To be sure, it may be a hard and even gruesome story, but such a story is better than no story at all. (409)

Hence, the pastoral letter, according to Hauerwas, is at best inconsistent in its support of pacifism as a legitimate individual option and at worst disingenuous. And this is because either consciously or unconsciously the bishops operate on the assumption that "states are the bearers of our history, and nations rely upon war or the possibility of war to sustain our history" (416).

Over and against the inconsistent natural law/Gospel hybrid presented in *Pacem* and the pastoral letter, Hauerwas champions "the peace brought by Jesus' life, death, and resurrection." He clarifies that such a peace "is not simply the absence of war, but rather it is a peace that is itself an alternative to a world at war" (418). Christ has declared "the reality of a new age," which entails a Christian commitment to nonviolence (420). Accordingly, Hauerwas regards the just war tradition and pacifism as mutually exclusive moral stances because "they draw on different assumptions about history and its relation to God's kingdom" (421). At this point

Hauerwas states the dichotomy between God's history and the history of the world in binary terms:

Christians believe that the true history of the world, that history that determines our destiny, is not carried by the nation-state. In spite of its powerful moral appeal, this history is a history of godlessness. Only the church has the stance, therefore, to describe war for what it is, for the world is too broken to know the reality of war. For what is war but the desire to be rid of God, to claim for ourselves the power to determine our meaning and destiny? Our desire to protect ourselves from our enemies, to eliminate our enemies in the name of protecting the common history we share with our friends, is but the manifestation of our hatred of God. (421)

Pacifist Christians are equipped with their own true history over and against the world's false history of godlessness. The false history of the world can only be exposed as false in the light of the true history of the Gospel. Despite the arguments of Yoder, Hauerwas, and other Christian pacifists, the Catholic moral tradition has never issued a blanket condemnation of war as intrinsically evil. A war can be just given the presence of certain conditions to which we now turn.

JUST WAR

The Catholic moral tradition does not hold that there is something inherently illicit about military service. In fact, *Gaudium et spes* states just the opposite: "All those who enter the military service in loyalty to their country should look upon themselves as the custodians of the security and freedom of their people; and when they carry out their duty properly, they are contributing to the maintenance of peace."[5] At the same time, one must learn to distinguish carefully between when war is just and when it is not. The Latin term *ius ad bellum* means "justice in going to war." In order for it to be just to go to war, seven conditions need to be met. These conditions are grounded in rectificatory justice. In the Catholic just war tradition, going to war involves rectificatory justice by means of military force. The conditions of *ius ad bellum* are as follows:

1. Just Cause: rectificatory justice sometimes requires force. If the only way to restore primary justice in the sense of right order or the restoration of rights that have been abused is through force, then the cause (the restoration of *ius*) is just.

---

[5] *GS* no. 79.

2. Comparative Justice: if both parties have been injured, the harm to one side must be significantly greater to justify that side's use of force.

3. Legitimate Authority: your next door neighbor cannot declare war unless your next door neighbor is also the commander in chief or the duly constituted public authority of some other nation state.

4. Right Intention: those with a total war mentality can sometimes fall into the wicked state of actually enjoying visiting needless and excessive cruelty on others. The intention in just war can never be a mere want to do violence for violence's sake. It must be for the restoration of *ius*.

5. Probability of Success: this does not mean success in the sense of simply winning the war, but actually restoring justice. You have likely heard the term "pyrrhic victory," which refers to a military victory where so much had to be lost in order to attain the victory that the victory ends up actually being a defeat. If the use of military force is futile to the restoration of justice, then military force ought not to be employed. Particularly in a nuclear age, sometimes the only way to win the game is not to play.

6. Proportionality: the good to be achieved must outweigh the evils that always come from war.

7. Last Resort: all efforts of diplomacy and sanctions must have been exhausted in order to justify the use of military force.

These, then, are the conditions that need to be met in order to go to war. The conditions that need to be met in order to maintain just conduct once in war, or the *ius in bello* conditions, we have already considered. They are noncombatant immunity, proportionality, and right intention. Noncombatants may not be deliberately targeted. One cannot visit undue harm on the enemy, and the intention must always remain the restoration of *ius*; one must not let it drift into spite, cruelty, vengeance, or hatred as easily happens in war. With respect to pacifism, then, I suppose the Catholic just war response runs something like this: It is true that unjust war – total war – is intrinsically evil. This is why *Gaudium et spes* unequivocally condemns it as does *Pacem in Terris* and *The Challenge of Peace*. However, it is possible to be on the just side of a war ordered to the restoration of *ius* even when this requires the use of military force. Some cases, on the other hand, may be better served by a nonviolent response. Nevertheless, even when one accepts the Catholic principles regarding just war, this does not mean they are easy to apply, as the following test case makes clear.

TEST CASE: PREDATOR DRONES

Predator drones are remotely controlled unmanned aircrafts employed by the military for surveillance and missile attacks on terrorists. The U.S. drone program was initiated by the Bush administration and has been continued and frequently utilized by the Obama administration. Because of the relative novelty of this practice, a consensus has yet to emerge among Catholic moral theologians. Some argue along pacifist lines that the use of predator drones is intrinsically immoral and so can never be done in good conscience. Others say that it is not intrinsically immoral, but that when conducted in noncombatant areas, where terrorists often reside, it could be immoral depending on the likelihood of bringing injury or death to noncombatants. In order to determine who is right, let us now consider the ethics of using predator drones through an examination of *ius in bello* and the principle of double effect.

To begin with, it ought to be acknowledged that it is not self-evident that the use of predator drones is intrinsically immoral. As we have seen, the use of lethal force is sometimes justified according to the just war tradition. Predator drones, aside from the scary name, do not really add anything to the nature of traditional bombing campaigns. The only real difference is that they can target enemies with more precision, which would seem helpful with respect to the end of not violating the principle of discrimination; that they are unmanned aircraft does not change the moral dimensions of bombing. The aircraft is still under the control of human agency, just via remote.

The real issue with predator drones is that they generally target enemies who attempt to blend in with civilian populations, thus raising the risk of collateral damage. This is not an entirely new issue. In 1944, John Ford, S.J., published the famous and influential article, "The Morality of Obliteration Bombing," which addressed this very subject.[6] The point of the article was to respond to the "militarized culture" argument, which was being used by the Allied forces to justify the bombing of civilian cities in Europe. This justification, along with several others, ended up carrying over to Hiroshima and Nagasaki. The argument basically ran like this: we will discriminate between combatants and noncombatants, but even belonging to the enemy culture makes you a combatant. Hence,

---

[6] John Ford, S.J., "The Morality of Obliteration Bombing," *Theological Studies* 5 (1944): 259–309.

lip service is given to the principle of discrimination, but the distinction between combatant and noncombatant is, for all intents and purposes, eliminated, thus rendering it useless. As stated in no uncertain terms by prominent contemporary Catholic moral theologian, William C. Mattison III, "Efforts to redefine all a nation's inhabitants as combatants should be seen for what they are: a self-protective and deluded way to justify the desire to kill the innocent among the enemy, despite an unstated recognition that the innocent should not be intentionally killed. Americans do well to remember our justified outrage when our enemies make just such self-deluding claims."[7] In brief, obliteration bombing violates the Catholic principle of discrimination and so does not square with *ius in bello*.

On the basis of what has been said, it could be argued that the use of predator drones is unjust because of their tendency to be used in areas populated by noncombatants, presuming that the militarized culture argument is illegitimate. However, this issue really has to do more with the nature of the War on Terror than it does with anything specific to predator drones. At issue is whether or not the bombing of military targets is justifiable even when one can foresee that this will result in unavoidable collateral damage (the demise of noncombatants). In order to assess this question one must turn to the doctrine of double effect. Recall that in order for an action to pass the doctrine of double effect, four conditions must be met:

1. The object of the act chosen must be good or indifferent.
2. The intention must be good.
3. The bad effect cannot be the means to the good effect.
4. Proportionality: the good effects must outweigh the evil effects.

As we have already discussed, Catholic just war tradition holds that the use of military force is not intrinsically evil. Hence, the use of predator drones passes the first condition. Second, if the intention is to restore justice, not merely to seek vengeance or display power, then the intention is good. In addition, the intention here could be to protect citizens from a future terrorist attack, which is also a good intention. Third, collateral damage is not the means to the good effect of stopping future terrorist attacks or restoring justice to the global order. In fact, predator drones

---

[7] William C. Mattison III, *Introducing Moral Theology: True Happiness and the Virtues* (Grand Rapids, MI: Brazos Press, 2008), 170.

are able to target enemies with more precision, which already implies the intention of avoiding collateral damage for the sake of the strategic advantage referred to earlier. Moreover, if a drone strike successfully took out a target without any collateral damage, you wouldn't need to go back and target the civilians in order to achieve the desired effect. So clearly the bad effect (collateral damage) is not the means to the good effect (restoration of *ius*, protection from future attacks).

Finally, there is the question of whether or not the good effects outweigh the evil effects. This is tough. In order to say that the good effects outweigh the evil effects, it seems to me that one would need to presume that the lives of the civilians, which will be destroyed by collateral damage, are somehow less valuable or less important than the lives of those one aims to protect by taking out terrorist suspects. This is another instance of the assumption of selective human dignity and therefore wrong. Either everyone has dignity or no one does. Therefore, we must conclude that predator drone strikes violate the Catholic just war tradition in instances when collateral damage is foreseeable and unavoidable. Collateral damage, in and of itself, despite however one seeks to justify it, further disrupts *ius*. In addition to being immoral, failing to discriminate between innocent civilians and enemy perpetrators is also bad foreign policy for the reasons referred to at the beginning of this chapter.

In sum, then, the argument that the use of predator drones is intrinsically immoral fails. However, it can be shown that the use of predator drones violates *ius in bello* when collateral damage is unavoidable and foreseeable, even if it is an unintended side effect. Killing innocent civilians, whether intentionally or unintentionally, disrupts *ius* and thus cannot be squared with the Catholic just war tradition.

SUMMARY

Christians disagree amongst themselves as to whether Christ laid out a foreign policy program and if so what this policy entailed. I suppose all Christians, whether pacifist or not, are agreed in rejecting total warfare as a legitimate moral option. In this chapter, we have analyzed the Catholic just war teaching with respect to this subject. We have seen how this teaching is grounded in the themes of justice analyzed in Chapter 7. We concluded by evaluating the use of predator drones in the context of the War on Terror and determined that drone strikes in civilian populations cannot be squared with just war tradition if collateral damage is foreseeable and unavoidable. According to the Catholic moral tradition, the only time when the use of force is justified is when there is no other way to restore or defend justice. Without justice, there can be no peace.

The purpose of the chapters of Part III has been to clarify key aspects of Catholic social morality. And now, before I conclude, I am going to venture on a conjecture as to how these chapters have impacted any who have read them. My guess is that there are some liberal people among them who are rather upset that we have not moved further down that path, and some people of a contrary kind who are irritated because they think it has gone considerably further down that path than they would like. If this section has impacted the reader in one of these two ways, then I think it has done what I intended it to do. This is because I do not believe that Catholic social teaching squares neatly with either of the prevailing political ideologies of the current age. I imagine that if a group of extreme liberals and extreme conservatives could be magically transported to a fully Christian society, then they would both find certain aspects of it extremely disagreeable. This is because both parties, for quite some time, have been distorting Christianity to fit into the mold of their respective ideologies.

Until this pattern ceases, both parties will go on trying to convince us that their program squares with Christianity more than the other party's. The truth is, however, that neither party seems very interested in conforming to the norms of faith; they are rather more concerned with conforming Christianity to the norms of their respective political platforms. So long as this goes on, we will not get much closer to a political or economic system that aligns with the principles of Catholic social teaching. Those who conflate the Faith once given with a particular political ideology need to be reminded yet again that "the Church, by reason of her role and competence, is not identified with any political community nor is it tied to any political system. It is at once the sign and the safeguard of the transcendental dimension of the human person."[8]

One further point and I am finished. If anyone thinks that Catholic social teaching can be pursued in lieu of individual morality, then that person is mistaken. As *Gaudium et spes* makes clear, "the betterment of the person and the improvement of society depend on each other."[9] A Christian society is not going to arrive without the individuals of that society truly desiring it. And they are not going to want it unless they

[8] *GS* no. 76.
[9] *GS* no. 25.

themselves are fully Christian. Social morality, as C.S. Lewis states, drives us "on to something more inward – driven on from social matters to religious matters. For the longest way round is the shortest way home."[10] Both as individuals and as members of society, CST reminds us of the important role we have to play when corrupt social institutions overstep "the limits of the natural law and the law of the Gospel."[11]

[10] C.S. Lewis, *Mere Christianity* (San Francisco: Harper Collins, 1952), 87.
[11] *GS* no. 74.

PART IV

Bioethics

CHAPTER 10

The Dignity of the Human Person

God created mankind in his image; in the image of God he created
them; male and female he created them.

Genesis 1:27

Bioethical debates stem from competing notions of human dignity.[1] The
fundamental principle of Catholic bioethics states that "the dignity of a
person must be recognized in every human being from conception to natural death."[2] I refer to this as the principle of universal human dignity. The
purpose of the current chapter is to elucidate this principle by contrasting
it with what I referred to in previous chapters as the "assumption of selective human dignity."

This chapter unfolds in four sections. First, we examine the "capacities approach," which attempts to provide philosophical justification for
the assumption of selective human dignity, and we analyze the manner in
which the Catholic moral philosopher, John Finnis, critiqued this view.
Based on this analysis, we are able to discern a way for defending the principle of universal human dignity apart from appeal to revelation or divine
authority. Next, we turn to the treatment of human dignity in *Gaudium et
spes* in order to examine the manner in which revelation once again lifts up
and perfects what can be found from reason alone. Third, we investigate
examples, historical and contemporary, of injustices perpetrated under the
banner of the assumption of selective human dignity. Through reference
to Thomas Merton, we see how the assumption of selective human dignity is rooted in the sinful tendencies we possess as human beings. Finally,
through an analysis of the parable of the Good Samaritan, we observe
how a commitment to the principle of universal human dignity is needed

---

[1] S.F. Gilbert, "Ecological Developmental Biology: Developmental Biology Meets the Real World,"
Developmental Biology 233 (2001): 1–12.
[2] *DPer* no. 1.

to combat these injustices. With this understanding of dignity in place, we will then be equipped, in the remaining chapters, to treat select issues in bioethics from within the framework of the Catholic moral tradition.

The title of this chapter is "The Dignity of the Human Person," and the use of the term "human person" is intentional. This may seem odd to you, but there is an entire school of philosophers and legal scholars who make a distinction between what it means to be "human" and what it means to be a "person." Basically, their argument runs like this: the term "human" is a biological description. To say that you are a human being is only to describe the particular kind of biological life you possess, as when I call an ant an ant or a penguin a penguin. To call you a human being, then, is not to make any assumption about your inherent worth, dignity, rights, status under the law, and so forth. However, the term "person" is really more of a legal, rather than biological, description. To refer to you as a "person" entails all the things that the mere biological descriptor does not (worth, dignity, rights, status under the law). Therefore, it is possible to be a human person, which refers to your biological and legal status, or to be a human nonperson, which means that, although you are biologically human, you do not possess the same worth, dignity, rights, and status under the law as a human person does.

The obvious issue that arises is the manner in which one is to distinguish between a human nonperson and a human person. This is where we come to the capacities approach, that is, the formal philosophical/legal version of the assumption of selective human dignity, sometimes associated with the constitutional scholar and philosopher Ronald Dworkin. According to this view, what makes a person a person is the capacity to appreciate and value one's own existence. If you lack this capacity, then you may indeed be human, but you are not a person. You are a human nonperson. The capacities approach, then, becomes an ethical and legal justification for abortion, infanticide, and euthanasia. Because a fetus and even an infant, according to those who endorse the capacities approach, cannot value their own existence, they are human nonpersons lacking worth, dignity, rights, and status under the law. With respect to euthanasia, whether voluntary or involuntary, if the patient lacks the capacity to appreciate his or her own existence for whatever reason – he or she is in a coma, a persistent vegetative state, suffering from a terminal disease, has dementia – then he or she, again, is a human nonperson without worth, dignity, rights, or status under the law. In this way, the capacities approach provides a philosophical and legal framework for the practices of abortion, infanticide, and euthanasia.

In his essay, "A Philosophical Case Against Euthanasia," John Finnis takes issue with the capacities approach.[3] Given that he is arguing with thinkers who do not accept the authority of revelation or the Catholic moral tradition, it would be of little use to appeal to that authority in his argument. Hence, despite the fact that he is a Catholic moral philosopher, Finnis argues from reason alone because this is the only standard his opponents recognize. Therefore, Finnis even accepts, for the sake of argument, the assertion that the capacity to appreciate and value one's own existence is the sole criterion for personhood. According to Finnis, however, this distinction does nothing to overturn the fact that, "Every living human being has this radical capacity for participating in the manner of a person – intelligently and freely – in human goods" (31). Therefore, "every human being is equal precisely in having that human life which is also humanity and personhood, and thus that dignity and intrinsic value" (32). Here Finnis is defending the principle of universal human dignity.

So, is Finnis arguing that a fetus or a person with dementia or in a coma values and appreciates his or her own existence in just the same way as a healthy adult? No, but what does this have to do with the *capacity* to do so? Think about it. When you fall asleep every night you lose the capacity to appreciate and value your own existence in quite the same way as you could when you were awake. This does not mean you lack the capacity; it only means the capacity is impaired by sleep. In the same way, the fetus and the infant do not lack the *capacity* to value and appreciate existence; rather, they possess this capacity in an undeveloped state of potential. Someone with dementia does not lack the capacity to appreciate and value existence; rather, they possess the capacity in an impaired state. In other words, the assumption of some that the capacity to appreciate and value existence is an absolute state not subject to gradation is in error. There are a variety of ways in which this capacity can be possessed. And there are, indeed, degrees of possession, as is the case with virtue. It is possible, therefore, to affirm the principle of universal human dignity by appealing to reason alone, yet when we turn to revelation we find the principle elevated and perfected. It is to this that we now turn.

---

[3] In *Euthanasia Examined: Ethical, Clinical, and Legal Perspectives*, John Keown, ed. (Cambridge: Cambridge University Press, 1995). Finnis is replying to John Harris, an advocate of the capacities approach whose essays are featured in the same edition. All in-text parenthetical citations in this section are to Finnis.

THE HUMAN PERSON MADE IN THE IMAGE OF GOD

The principle of universal human dignity is by no means new. It is what theologians have always inferred from the teaching in Genesis that the human race was made in the image of God. Thus, when humanist/moralist atheists try to argue that God is a threat to human dignity, they are cutting off the branch on which they are sitting. This is why *Gaudium et spes* makes clear that God is not a threat to human dignity but the source of it: "Human dignity rests above all on the fact that humanity is called to communion with God."[4]

As indicated in previous chapters, human beings generally do not have a problem affirming the dignity of their own group. Indeed, you've probably noticed already, and we see further examples later, that those who distinguish between human persons and human nonpersons always make sure to do so in a manner that places themselves in the protected category. If there is only one God, however, then the same God is Lord of all. And if the same God is Lord of all, then all are equal in dignity, as all are equally called to the very communion that is the source of that dignity: "Hear, O Israel: The Lord is our God, the Lord alone. Therefore, you shall love the Lord, your God, with your whole heart, and with your whole being, and with your whole strength."[5] This I take as scriptural affirmation of the principle of universal human dignity.

In brief, when we turn to revelation, we find that the principle of universal human dignity, which can be discerned from reason alone, is elevated to a higher level. As it turns out, our dignity is grounded in much more than our own capacities to think, feel, value, and so forth. As important as these capacities are, it is what they attest to that is even more important. We are made in the image of God. There is nothing any philosopher, court of law, or multinational power can do to change that, and even if every human living on earth decided to forget this truth it would remain true just the same. We were not made merely to value and appreciate our own existence; rather, we were made for communion with the very fount of existence itself. A blind and mindless universe that is not even aware that you happened to pop into being cannot confer you with any dignity. God can and did. This is what the Catholic moral tradition upholds.

---

[4] *GS* no. 19.
[5] Deuteronomy 6:4–5 *NAB* throughout.

VICTIMS OF THE ASSUMPTION OF SELECTIVE
HUMAN DIGNITY

Having clarified the principle of universal human dignity, the purpose of this section is to make clear that this entire argument is about much more than a kind of intellectual tennis match. There are grave consequences that follow from the assumption of selective human dignity. We have already seen two possible examples of this in previous chapters – sweatshop workers and collateral damage from predator drone strikes or other military campaigns. This is the assumption of selective human dignity being applied to certain kinds of people. In this section, we examine two further historical applications of this assumption: slavery and anti-Semitism.

Historically, slavery was always justified by an appeal to the assumption of selective human dignity and even a kind of proto-capacities approach.[6] Slavery in the Unites States was not any different. Those Americans who upheld the practice (let us not forget that there were also those who opposed it) argued that the African slave lacked the rational capacity to govern him or herself or to live as a free person in civil society. There was a great deal of pseudoscience used to attest to lies of this kind. You can even see this understanding codified in law in the form of the three-fifths compromise. Slaves were seen as only three-fifths of a person. In other words, they were regarded, for all intents and purposes, as human nonpersons. This is what was used to justify the demeaning, degrading, disgusting, immoral, wicked mentality of slavery.

The same is true with respect to anti-Semitism, only here the depersonalizing process was attributed more to religion than race. For too many centuries and in too many cases, Christian governments and societies perpetuated the idea of the Jews as an inferior people who were guilty, as a race, for the death of Christ. Those who wanted to perpetuate the assumption of selective human dignity in order to demean Jews drew from Scripture to justify their warped view. In Matthew 27:25, a crowd of Jews gathered at the trial of Jesus. In response to Pontius Pilate's hesitance to have Jesus crucified, they shouted, "His blood be upon us and upon our children!" This was used to justify persecution and discrimination

---

[6] See Bryan N. Massingale, "A Parallel that Limps: The Rhetoric of Slavery in Pro-Life Discourse of the U.S. Bishops," in *Voting and Holiness: Catholic Perspectives on Political Participation*, Nicholas P. Cafardi, ed. (New York: Paulist Press, 2012): 158–77. Massingale critiques rhetoric that makes parallels between "the evil of African slavery in the United States and the practice of terminating fetal life" (158). My emphasis here and in the next chapter is not on the practices as such but the assumptions that underlie them.

against Jews for centuries. In the Second Vatican Council's Declaration of the Church on the Non-Christian Religions (*Nostra aetate*), the council fathers acknowledged and repented for these errors: "The Jews should not be spoken of as rejected or accursed as if this followed from Scripture. Consequently, all must take care, lest in catechizing or in preaching the word of God, they teach anything which is not in accord with the truth of the Gospel message or the spirit of Christ." The document continues, "Indeed, the Church reproves every form of persecution against whomsoever it may be directed. Remembering, then, its common heritage with the Jews and moved not by any political consideration, but solely by the religious motivation of Christian charity, it deplores all hatreds, persecutions, displays of anti-Semitism leveled at any time or from any source against the Jews."[7]

We could go on multiplying examples, and we see further examples in the final two chapters of this book, but for now the point is simply that no one is safe from the assumption of selective human dignity. Whether it is on the basis of age, aptitude, class, ethnicity, gender, intelligence, race, religion, sex, sexual orientation, or whatever else, those who, consciously or unconsciously, hold the assumption of selective human dignity – those who for whatever reason seem incapable of affirming their own dignity in a manner that does not deny the dignity of those outside the preferred group, may decide that you are not a person after all.

Indeed, depersonalization can occur even on seemingly trivial grounds. There was a fascinating study conducted by researchers at Yale University regarding the morality of infants.[8] In the study, babies were sat down in front of a puppet show. In what followed, a nice puppet displayed helping behavior, and a mean puppet displayed obstructive behavior. The babies tended to look longer at the nice puppet. Given that prior studies have proven that babies look longer at things they like, this seems to indicate the babies prefer kindness to meanness, justice to injustice, and so forth (an interesting test case for natural law). However, further studies showed that when the mean behavior was directed at a puppet, which they regarded as different from themselves, then they preferred the mean behavior. For example, if a given baby preferred graham crackers to cookies, and then was shown that a particular puppet shared his or her preference, then the baby wanted to see that puppet rewarded. If the puppet

---

[7] *NA* no. 4.
[8] J. Kiley Hamlin, Karen Wynn, & Paul Bloom, "Social Evaluation by Preverbal Infants," *Nature* 450 (2007): 557–9.

did not share the baby's preference, however, if it preferred cookies, then the baby wanted to see it punished. Age, ethnicity, gender, religion, and political affiliation are some of the more common categories we use to create "us" and "them," but not always. We can all think back to times in our lives when we found ourselves curiously to be on the inside or outside of some group. We were cool or uncool. We were in the in-group or the out-group. We were worthy or unworthy of social accolades. When we have made it inside, we tend not to ask why; we're just happy to be out of the cold of exclusion. When we are on the outside, however, we wonder why. We wonder if there is something wrong with us. However, I think (this is only a guess) that in the majority of cases the reasons why we find ourselves in or out are as random and arbitrary as whether we prefer graham crackers or cookies. Some person with social cache chooses to invite us in or target us for exclusion. There seems to be a kind of randomness to it all. In many cases, we can't really control what we become in the perceptions of others.

What we can do, however, is resist this human tendency we all possess, resulting from the Fall, to demean through exclusion. Let us not pretend that it is only some one particular group of humans that suffer from this tendency to which all others are immune. It is rather the common tendency of sin. We sinners first tickle our pride by imagining our group atop the mountain, then we work to climb higher still so that we can look down even on those within our own group. Even if the love of God is atop the mountain, we throw that down as well. Thomas Merton, who I quote here in full, depicts this pattern of sin in a beautiful and disturbing passage:

When I think now of that part of my childhood, the picture I get of my [younger] brother John Paul is this: standing in a field, about a hundred yards away from the clump of sumachs where we have built our hut, is this little perplexed five-year-old kid in short pants and a kind of a leather jacket, standing quite still, with his arms hanging down at his sides, and gazing in our direction, afraid to come any nearer on account of the stones, as insulted as he is saddened, and his eyes full of indignation and sorrow. And yet he does not go away. We shout at him to get out of there, to beat it, and go home, and wing a couple of more rocks in that direction, and he does not go away. We tell him to play in some other place. He does not move.

And there he stands, not sobbing, not crying, but angry and unhappy and offended and tremendously sad. And yet he is fascinated by what we are doing, nailing shingles all over our new hut. And his tremendous desire to be with us and to do what we are doing will not permit him to go away. The law written in his nature says that he must be with his elder brother, and do what he is doing: and he cannot understand why this law of love is being so wildly and unjustly violated in his case.

Many times it was like that. And in a sense, this terrible situation is the pattern and prototype of all sin: the deliberate and formal will to reject disinterested love for us for the purely arbitrary reason that we simply do not want it. We will to separate ourselves from that love. We reject it entirely and absolutely, and will not acknowledge it, simply because it does not please us to be loved. Perhaps the inner motive is that the fact of being loved disinterestedly reminds us that we all need love from others, and depend upon the charity of others to carry on our own lives. And we refuse love, and reject society, in so far as it seems, in our own perverse imagination, to imply some obscure kind of humiliation.[9]

In the end, there is not one simple explanation for why we sinners like to exclude and demean, but these lines from Merton are the best elucidation I have found. The assumption of selective human dignity is not always some formal intellectual philosophy to which we ascribe, as with the capacities approach. More often it is unconscious. Or we do not even know we have it until it spills over into actions in some situation, or memory seizes upon it as with Merton. The effects are in how we regard and treat others, similar to the first signs of a cancer.

COMBATTING THE ASSUMPTION OF SELECTIVE HUMAN DIGNITY

Sin is a kind of sickness, yet this sickness, as John Paul I remarked, provides us with "yet another claim to be loved by the Lord."[10] Indeed, the principle of universal human dignity may be thought of as a kind of medicine to cure a spiritual disease. One can see Christ, the good doctor, giving the medicine in, among other places, the parable of the Good Samaritan.[11] After a lawyer attempts to test Jesus by asking him, "What must I do to inherit eternal life?" Jesus replies, "You shall love the Lord your God with all your heart, with all your being, with all your strength, and with all your mind, and your neighbor as yourself." But trying to find a lawyerly way to violate the commandment, he asks Jesus, "And who is my neighbor?" In asking this, the lawyer is trying to find some way to make a distinction so as to designate some group or groups to whom the commandment does not apply. But Jesus replies with the parable of the Good Samaritan:

---

[9] Thomas Merton, *The Seven Storey Mountain: An Autobiography of Faith* (New York: Harvest Books, 1948), 26.

[10] *AN.*

[11] See *DCE* no. 25b.

A man fell victim to robbers as he went down from Jerusalem to Jericho. They stripped and beat him and went off leaving him half-dead. A priest happened to be going down that road, but when he saw him, he passed by on the opposite side. Likewise a Levite came to the place, and when he saw him, he passed by on the opposite side. But a Samaritan traveler who came upon him was moved with compassion at the sight. He approached the victim, poured oil and wine over his wounds and bandaged them. Then he lifted him up on his own animal, took him to an inn and cared for him.[12]

The choice to make the Samaritan the hero of the story was not arbitrary. To Jesus's audience, the Samaritans were a group regarded as subhuman and lacking dignity. It is as though Jesus was telling the parable at a Ku Klux Klan gathering and deliberately made an African American the hero of the story. At any rate, the message of universal human dignity is always the same: they – yes, even they – possess dignity and are made in the image of God.

I recall here a friend of mine who served in the second Iraq War under the Bush administration. His job was to stand in an alley about twenty-five feet wide and stop every car that came down the alley in order to make sure that it did not have explosives in it. Many of the people with whom he had to interact in this way hated the American presence there. They saw him, understandably, as a symbol of that presence as well as an instrument of restrictions on their freedoms, which they resented. Consequently, when they drove by, many of them would spit at him and shout insulting things. Several would make threatening gestures, such as running their index fingers across their throats. My friend experienced this all day long for weeks and weeks at a time. I asked him once if he hated these people. His response was that, as a Christian, he was called to love them just the same as he loved his friends and family back home. I asked him how he could possibly do this given the abuse and stress he put up with all day. He replied that it was only possible through prayer. He felt hatred sure enough, but when he prayed, he said to God, "I know you love these people, but I sure don't. Please help me to see them as you do." This is the principle of universal human dignity at work.

SUMMARY

The purpose of this chapter has been to elucidate the principle of universal human dignity affirmed in the Catholic moral tradition. We have seen how this principle is accessible through reason and brought to completion

---

[12] Luke 10:25–37.

in divine revelation. Furthermore, we have seen how this principle is violated by the assumption of selective human dignity rooted as it is in what Merton referred to as "the pattern and prototype" of human sinfulness. In the subsequent two chapters, we see that it is this unwavering and even stubborn commitment to the principle of universal human dignity that distinguishes the Catholic response to particular bioethical issues from alternative responses, such as those informed by the capacities approach.

CHAPTER 11

Beginning of Life Decisions

The Church's commitment to human dignity inspires an abiding concern for the sanctity of human life from its very beginning, and with the dignity of marriage and of the marriage act by which human life is transmitted.

United States Conference of Catholic Bishops,
*Ethical and Religious Directives for
Catholic Health Care Services
Introduction to Part IV*

In this chapter, we analyze bioethical topics having to do with the beginning of life. The main focus is on contraception, abortion, and commercial surrogacy. Our goal is to gain clarity as to the Catholic teaching and to see how these teachings are grounded in the principle of universal human dignity examined in the previous chapter. I wish to say that I am aware that these issues, particularly the first two, can evoke strong reactions whether on the part of those who affirm the Catholic teachings or from those who vehemently dissent. Therefore, allow me to make a caveat. Nothing in this chapter is intended as a moral judgment on any particular individual: "Stop judging, that you may not be judged. For as you judge, so will you be judged, and the measure with which you measure will be measured out to you."[1] Obviously, however, this passage does not mean to refrain from making moral distinctions. The very passage itself makes such a distinction between judging and not judging. Let us advance, then, to the subject of contraception.

CONTRACEPTION

In order to make clear the Catholic teaching on contraception, let us begin with a hypothetical thought experiment. We know that in acts of

---

[1] Matthew 7:1–2 *NAB.*

sexual intercourse there is a chemical released called oxytocin. Sometimes referred to as the "love hormone," it is a chemical that furthers the emotional bonding of the couple. Now, imagine that a pharmaceutical company in Sweden successfully produced a pill that could block the release of oxytocin that naturally occurs during the sex act. Why would someone want to use such a pill? Well, just think of all the television shows and movies you have seen that suggest how great it would be if you could remove romantic attachment from sex via mutual agreement in order to just be "friends with benefits." In all the television shows and movies this never works though because those bothersome emotions get in the way. However, our Swedish pharmaceutical company has solved that problem with its invention of the oxytocin suppression pill, the street name for which is the "emotion control pill."

Continuing with our thought experiment, imagine that, when the emotion control pill first hits the market, the reactions to it are mixed. Some people think it is great and cannot see any problem with it. However, the majority thinks there is something rather unnatural about removing emotions from human sexuality. The Pope issues an encyclical stating that it violates human nature and will have harmful consequences for society. Some feminists argue that the pill will be bad for women because it will assist men in dehumanizing them and using them as sexual objects. Other feminists argue that it will be good for women, because with the emotion control pill they will now be able to "have sex like a man" (which means, to their minds, like a bad man) without forming emotional bonds and without concern for ethics and morals.

So the arguing goes on. The politicians take their sides on the basis of how the broader societal debate is taking shape. Over time, however, certain companies begin making more and more money and the emotion control pill is mass-marketed, making the use of it increasingly common. It is only those stubborn Catholics and a few other oddballs who, for whatever outdated reason, still have a problem with it.

I have spent some time with this thought experiment because, today, most people take for granted that there is nothing wrong or unnatural about using contraception. If you went back in time, however, you would find a very different view on these matters. Now, we could be historical relativists and just say that what was good for one generation is not good for another, and that those who still hold the older view just need to get on board with the new morality. Disturbingly, I have heard some people callously talk as though, once the older generation dies off, these issues will simply go away.

There are a number of problems with this view. In the first place, it is untrue. There are a great many people from the older generation quite on board with the new morality and quite a few young people who refuse to get on board with it. Second, the mere fact that something is newer does not automatically make it better. Several older cars are superior in many respects to several new ones. Third, the view that the new is always superior to the old is elitist. It suggests that one group is entirely right and another group entirely wrong. This kind of generational elitism is uniquely intolerant in this respect.

Let us, then, consider the Catholic teachings on contraception afresh. Actually, a number of the objections that the Catholic moral tradition brings against contraception are similar to some objections that may have crossed your mind when I asked you to imagine the fictional emotion control pill. First, there is something unnatural about it. Emotional attachment seems like it is intrinsic to the meaning of sexuality rather than an optional, arbitrary component of human sexuality. Well, all the Catholic teaching is really saying is that it is the same with procreation. It is an inherent, rather than arbitrary, aspect of human sexuality.

John Paul II attempted to express this reality with the terms "procreative" and "unitive."[2] The unitive aspect of sexuality only means that there is something natural about emotional bonds of love and sexuality coinciding. There is something inherently unnatural about the idea of emotionless sex, which is why an emotion control pill would be an odd thing. To deliberately will the unitive aspect out of sexuality is unnatural and therefore immoral according to the Catholic moral tradition. Now, the same is true for the procreative aspect; it, too, is an inherent part of sexuality. Furthermore, the procreative is intrinsically linked to the unitive. Deliberately withholding the procreative element of sexuality from one's partner is similar to signing a prenuptial agreement before marrying them. It is just another way of feigning full commitment.

To be clear, the Church teaches that non-procreative sex is only immoral when it is willfully non-procreative, that is, when some deliberate choice on the part of the couple has rendered it so.[3] If someone is infertile through no fault of their own for whatever reason, then they could still be open to procreation, even though, sadly, they are unable to have children.

---

[2] See John Paul II, *Man and Woman He Created Them: A Theology of the Body* (Boston: Pauline Books and Media, 2006); Karol Wojtyla, *Love and Responsibility*, tr. H.T. Willets (New York: Farar, Straus and Giroux, Inc., 1981); see also *HV* no. 12.

[3] See *HV* no. 11.

It all comes down to what is taking place in the will of the individual couple. In some cases, the use of certain kinds of contraception could also be valid for health reasons depending on the circumstances. The Church also holds that it is possible to responsibly plan pregnancies using the method known as Natural Family Planning (NFP) or Fertility Awareness.

Having summarized the Catholic teaching on contraception, let us now examine how this teaching is grounded in the principle of universal human dignity. The United States Conference of Catholic Bishops preface their treatment of beginning of life issues with the following statement: "The Church's commitment to human dignity inspires an abiding concern for the sanctity of human life from its very beginning, and with the dignity of marriage and of the marriage act by which human life is transmitted."[4] Contraception, then, violates the dignity of "marriage and of the marriage act." This, by the by, is the same reason why the Church disapproves of sex outside of marriage. True respect for the dignity of the act requires the context of full commitment. To capriciously remove the procreative and the unitive aspects of sexuality is to degrade our dignity as persons. Human beings do not have trouble accepting the pleasure that is inherent to sexuality. We realize, too, that sex rightfully involves emotional attachment. The procreative is not any different. It is an inherent, not arbitrary, aspect of human sexuality, which is debased by contraceptive practices. This is the Church's teaching on contraception.

ABORTION

In a way, abortion is the most self-evident violation of human dignity, but it is also the least. This is because people disagree over whether the fetus is a human person or a human nonperson. For those who regard the fetus at all stages of life as a human person, abortion self-evidently refuses the basic good of life to someone, which is the greatest violation of human dignity possible. For those who do not regard the fetus as a person, no such violation takes place. So how do we determine who is right? You could rely on authority, but when there are competing authorities, how is one to choose? The Catholic Church teaches that direct abortion is intrinsically evil.[5] The government says it is legal and a matter of

---

[4] *ERD* IV, Introduction.

[5] See *HV* no. 14. In rare cases, an indirect abortion may be licit based on the principle of double effect. For example, if a woman has an ectopic pregnancy (the fertilized ovum has attached to the wall of the fallopian tube), then surgically removing the part of the fallopian tube that has the baby in it is licit, even when the doctor can foresee that the baby will not survive. The object of

private judgment. In America, the states all have different laws as to when abortion is permissible. One state says it becomes impermissible after twenty-four weeks; another says twenty-six. Still another says thirty-two. Is it up to the state to decide when a human becomes a person? Is it just up for vote? Is it merely a matter of consensus? Then, there is the odd fact that many people who support abortion rights still talk as though it is a harmful and unseemly thing that should be avoided whenever possible. Make it "safe and rare" they say. This is the only example of a "negative right" throughout all of history. Rights have historically been regarded as "goods" to which one is entitled, not dangers to be avoided.

One of the problems with the current abortion debate, at least in the United States, is that both sides tend to begin with their conclusions rather than their premises. The statement, "Abortion is immoral," is not a self-evident premise (hence the debate), but rather a conclusion. In the same way, "Abortion is not immoral," is a conclusion, not a self-evident premise. Therefore, what really needs to be discussed are the premises. I take the first syllogism to run something like this:

A. Murder is immoral (major premise).
B. Abortion is murder (minor premise).
C. Therefore, abortion is immoral (conclusion).

I do not think those in favor of abortion rights oppose the major premise as self-evident. Rather, it is their minor premise, and therefore, conclusion, which differ. Their syllogism runs like this:

A. Murder is immoral.
B. Abortion is not murder.
C. Therefore, abortion is not immoral (at least not in the sense that murder is immoral).

Now, it needs to be admitted that both syllogisms are valid. The conclusions follow from the premises. If the premises are true, then the conclusions are

---

the act, removing a part of the body with a pathology, in this case a section of the fallopian tube, is not intrinsically immoral. The intention, the welfare of the mother, is a good one. The bad effect, the death of the baby, is not the means to the good effect, the saving of the mother. If somehow the baby survived the operation, this would not detract from the end of saving the mother. The good effects outweigh the evil effects. Importantly, the teaching here is not that direct abortion is permissible in this case. Rather, only an indirect abortion has taken place. For more on this topic, see Nicanor Pier Giorgio Austriaco, O.P., *Biomedicine and Beatitude: An Introduction to Catholic Bioethics* (Washington, DC: CUA Press, 2011), 43–72. There is also interesting work being done on the question of whether indirect abortion may be permissible in instances of rape. See Charles Camosy, *Abortion: Beyond Polarization* (Grand Rapids, MI: Eerdman's, Forthcoming 2015).

true. However, both conclusions cannot be true because of the principle of noncontradiction. So we need to find where the respective minor premises come from, and it seems to me that these, too, turn out to be conclusions from prior premises. The first would go like this:

A. All humans are persons.
B. A fetus is human.
C. Therefore, a fetus is a human person.

And the other one runs like this:

A. All human persons appreciate their own existence.
B. A fetus does not appreciate its existence.
C. Therefore, a fetus is a human nonperson.

All this reasoning has really done, then, is take us back to the assumption of selective human dignity versus the principle of universal human dignity. The Church holds the latter and so also that direct abortion is immoral. Abortion rights advocates, it seems to me, must hold the former and so draw lines differently as to when personhood is achieved (26 weeks, 28 weeks, etc.). In other words, Catholic teaching on abortion is grounded in the view that abortion violates the inherent dignity of "human life from its very beginning." For my own part, I do not believe it is possible to advocate for abortion rights without endorsing, explicitly or implicitly, the assumption of selective human dignity. Thus, I find myself compelled to stand against abortion for the same reason I stand against sweatshops. Either everyone is made in the image of God and has dignity or no one does.

Before advancing to our next topic, I wish to make clear an additional point. Although there is a great chasm between Catholic teachings on abortion and the views of the pro-choice movement, I do not believe that this precludes the possibility of fruitful convergence between both sides. Indeed, it would be remiss for me not to draw attention here to a contemporary phenomenon that demands such a convergence – abortion and gendercide.[6]

---

[6] See Andrew Kim, "A Catholic Appeal to the Pro-Choice Movement in the U.S.," The Catholic Moral Theology Blog, entry posted February 13, 2014, http://catholicmoraltheology .com/a-catholic-appeal-to-the-pro-choice-movement-in-the-u-s/ [accessed April 7, 2014]. My argument here is not intended to suggest that abortion is only harmful to women in the context of gendercide. Rather, as Pope Francis states, "Abortion compounds the grief of many women who now carry with them deep physical and spiritual wounds after succumbing to the pressures of a secular culture which devalues God's gift of sexuality and the right to life of the unborn." Vatican, "Pope's Discourse to South African Bishops," *Zenit.com*, April 25, 2014, http://www.zenit.org/en/articles /pope-s-discourse-to-south-african-bishops [accessed April 27, 2014].

In modern day India, an estimated fifty thousand female fetuses are aborted monthly because of gender partiality for boys. Since 1980, an estimated forty million girls have gone "missing" as a result of sex-selective abortion, abandonment, or slaughter. Whether killed in the womb or thrown in the trash after birth, gendercide takes many forms and has been referred to alternatively as "India's dirty little secret" and "India's national shame." Consequently, the Indian government has criminalized both the use of ultrasounds for identifying the sex of the child as well as sex-selective abortion. However, these laws are seldom enforced. This is at least partly because of the fact that the practice is generally the privilege of the wealthy and educated who can afford to pay for the ultrasounds and subsequent abortions.

There are women in India who are fighting against gendercide. Networks of orphanages called "cradle-houses" are springing up throughout the country. They take in baby girls abandoned in dustbins, wells, drains, garbage cans, and "drop-boxes." Some of the baby girls are very sick because their mothers attempted, unsuccessfully, to have late-term abortions by using drugs designed for that purpose. The nurses who work in the orphanages refer to these as "medicines for the killing." Still other women are attempting to change the culture in India. It is a culture in which women are often pressured by their husbands and mother-in-laws to engage in sex-selective abortion – to abort their own daughters.

Indian women against gendercide are fighting for choice. They want to be able to choose not to use the ultrasound as an instrument ordered to the abolition of women. They want to be able to choose not to be pressured into procuring dangerous late-term abortions. They want to be able to choose both to have their daughters and to have them grow up in a culture that does not devalue women.

The pro-choice movement in the United States often presents itself as fighting a war ordered to protecting women's rights and freedoms. If they wish to be consistent in this regard, then they should protest the non-enforcement of anti-abortion laws in India with the same vehemence that they protest laws designed to restrict abortion in the United States. Were this to occur, then the Catholic Church, which is generally regarded as the chief adversary of the pro-choice movement, may turn out to be an important ally of the very same movement in the context of Indian gendercide. Another threat to women is the growing market of international surrogacy, to which we now turn.

COMMERCIAL SURROGACY

I begin this section with a quote from John Paul II's mediations on the Blessed Virgin Mary: "At the moment of the Annunciation, by responding with her *fiat*, Mary conceived a man who was the Son of God, of one substance with the Father. Therefore, she is truly the Mother of God, because motherhood concerns the whole person, not just the body, nor even just human nature."[7] Commercial surrogacy is a growing industry that seeks to radically redefine the essence of motherhood as expressed in the previous passage.[8]

At this point, some background information is helpful. In 1978, the first "test tube baby" was born. The egg and sperm of a married couple were mixed outside the body and a successful fertilization took place. The fertilized egg was implanted in the wife, who carried it through gestation and delivery. This process of *in vitro* fertilization was a watershed moment for new reproductive methods or "assisted reproduction technologies" (ARTs).[9] These ARTs allowed married, unmarried, and same-sex couples to have children regardless of their physical capacity or willingness to conceive and carry a child to term. An estimated 30.2 to 120.6 million women between the ages of 20 and 46 are unable to conceive. Of these, 12 million to 90.4 million are likely to seek medical assistance in order to have a child. Consequently, commercial surrogacy, which sometimes goes by the names of "reproductive tourism," "fertility tourism," or "reproductive outsourcing," has grown into a highly profitable international industrial market.

Commercial surrogacy entails a contractual agreement between a commissioning client and a woman who carries the client's child as a surrogate. The surrogate receives monetary compensation for the renting of her womb, and the client receives parental rights. Clients in wealthy

---

[7] *MD* no. 4. Thank you to Walsh University graduate student Paulette Popovich for helping me compile the research for this section.

[8] See Andrew Kim, "The Mother of God and Commercial Surrogacy," The Catholic Moral Theology Blog, entry posted September 27, 2013, http://catholicmoraltheology.com/the-mother-of-god-and-commercial-surrogacy/ [accessed April 7, 2014].

[9] In order to achieve a high rate of success, physicians generally inject the woman with artificial hormones in order to create an abnormally high number of oocytes. When the oocytes are fertilized, they are screened for abnormalities. If abnormalities are found, then they are discarded. Additionally, multiple embryos are transferred into the woman's uterus to increase the probability of implantation. However, if multiple embryos do implant, then the couples are pressured to selectively abort all but one or two of them so as to decrease risks associated with multiple births. For these and other reasons the Catholic Church opposes IVF. See *DP* no. 15.

countries are renting the wombs of women from poor countries at an alarming rate. The prime example of this is, again, in India.

India's surrogate industry, which was legalized in 2002, generates an estimated $445 million annually.[10] Surrogates are typically poor, uneducated women with families of their own.[11] Indeed, there are two reasons why clients from developed countries seek out surrogates from developing countries. First, it is cheaper. Second, whereas in developed countries surrogates enjoy legal rights to appeal, even in cases where they have given up those rights via contract, poor women in developing countries lack legal recourse, and contracts are not subject to regulatory oversight. Some developed countries prohibit their female citizens from acting as surrogates for ethical reasons. The French government, for example, decries the practice on the grounds that "the human body is not lent out, is not rented out, and is not sold." However, globalization has meant that such prohibitions, which are relatively rare, are not slowing down the practice of commercial surrogacy on the international scale.[12]

Despite its widespread practice, commercial surrogacy has not escaped ethical analysis. As may be expected, the advocates of the practice tend to argue from a kind of utilitarian point of view. Commercial surrogacy is good because the surrogate gains access for upward economic and social mobility by participating in the surrogacy arrangement. On these grounds, several feminists take the stance that illegalizing or regulating surrogacy would violate a woman's right to use her reproductive capabilities as she wishes. According to this view, "fair monetary compensation, combined with freedom of choice, obviates any ethical concern."[13]

On the other hand, there are several feminists who argue that the practice of commercial surrogacy is degrading and dangerous to women. They

---

[10] N. Shah, "Race, Class, Gender and Economics: A Discussion about the Indian Commercial Surrogacy Boom," *Fem* 2 (2012).

[11] See G. Palattiyl, et al., "Globalization and Cross-border Reproductive services: Ethical Implications of Surrogacy in India for Social Work," *International Social Work* 53.5 (2010), 686–700.

[12] M. Chang, "Wombs for Rent: India's Commercial Surrogacy," *Harvard International Review* 31.1 (2009), 11–13.

[13] Raywat Deonandan, "The Ethics of Surrogacy," *India Currents* (February 3, 2012). Deonandan's essay challenges the libertarian view by bringing to light the "classic tension between autonomy and exploitation, in that a desperately poor person can be co-opted to express her autonomy in such a way that it leads to her exploitation." For more on this topic, see Donna Dickenson, *Property, Women, and Politics: Subjects as Objects* (London: Polity Press, 1997); see also C. Shalev, *Birth Power: The Case for Surrogacy* (New Haven, CT: Yale University Press, 1989). There is, of course, disagreement about whether freedom of choice can exist under a coercive economic model that contrasts the socially elite in developed countries to "breeders" in undeveloped countries.

argue that it furthers gender inequality and so ought to be prohibited.[14]
The Catholic view is made quite clear in *Ethical and Religious Directives for Catholic Health Care Services*:

Because of the dignity of the child and of marriage, and because of the uniqueness of the mother-child relationship, participation in contracts or arrangements for surrogate motherhood is not permitted. Moreover, the commercialization of such surrogacy denigrates the dignity of women, especially the poor.[15]

I wish to take this occasion to relate this teaching to the Blessed Virgin Mary. In the Catholic tradition, doctrines about Mary are intrinsically bound to the centrality of Christ; they are not a rival to that centrality. Also, the doctrines about Mary are rooted in the actual person to whom the doctrines are related. Mary is the immaculately conceived Mother of God who was assumed body and soul into Heaven, but these truths about Mary do not exhaust the person of Mary.

So who is the person behind the doctrines? Blessed Paul VI describes her as "a strong and intelligent woman, one who had the wits to question back when the angel addressed her, one who experienced poverty and suffering, flight and exile." In addition, "she consistently gave active and responsible consent to the call of God, made courageous choices, and worked to strengthen the faith of others." She was not a submissive handmaiden in the manner that prior ages conceived, but one who proclaimed a God "that vindicates the humble and the oppressed, and removes the powerful people of this world from their privileged positions."[16] Indeed, with respect to the *Magnificat*, the Catholic theologian Elizabeth Johnson has noted as follows:

Mary's song is the prayer of a poor woman. She proclaims God's greatness with her whole being because the Holy One of Israel, regarding her low estate, has done great things for her. The term for lowliness, *tapeinosis* in Greek, describes misery, pain, persecution and oppression. In Genesis it describes the situation in the wilderness of the escaping slave woman Hagar, whom God heeds (Gen. 16:11); in the exodus story it describes the severe affliction from which God delivers the people (Exod. 3:7). Mary's self-characterization as lowly is not a metaphor for spiritual humility but is based on her actual social positions. Young, female, a member of a people subjected to economic exploitation by powerful ruling

[14] See Debra Satz, *Why Some Things Should Not Be for Sale: The Moral Limits of Markets* (Oxford: Oxford University Press, 2010).
[15] *ERD* no. 42.
[16] *MC* no. 37. I draw here from the analysis of Elizabeth Johnson. See her *Truly Our Sister: A Theology of Mary in the Communion of the Saints* (New York: Continuum International Publishing, 2003), 132–3.

groups, afflicted by outbreaks of violence, she belongs to the semantic domain of the poor in Luke's gospel, a group given a negative valuation by worldly powers. Yet it is to precisely such a woman that the call has come to partner God in the great work of redemption.[17]

The reference to Hagar, the first surrogate in recorded history, is noteworthy. It is but one instance of a pivotal theme throughout all of Scripture – the unity of the omnipotent God with the marginalized and oppressed over and against structures of injustice. The story of Mary exemplifies this theme. Mary partners with God in opposition to structures of oppression and exploitation. Her *fiat* is not so much the timid act of a helpless girl as it is a declaration of war on structures of sin embraced and perpetuated by worldly powers. Mary takes her place in the liberating tradition of her people. As we observed earlier, "In the psalms and the prophets, the Holy One of Israel protects, defends, saves, and rescues these 'nobodies,' adorning them with victory and life in the face of despair."[18]

When Mary's motherhood is divorced from her personhood, however, she becomes a mere surrogate. God is the client. Gabriel is the broker. Her *fiat* is as free a choice as the consent of a choiceless nobody without dignity and rights. She becomes an incubator who happens to breathe. Mary is not the Mother of God or even the handmaid of the Lord; she is a means to an end, an object of use, a faceless name. Indeed, I have often heard it uttered that once science and technology make it possible to create and sustain fetal life in an incubator, then the whole issue of commercial surrogacy will become moot, as surrogates will no longer be needed. However, this reveals that surrogates are currently viewed and treated as little more than human incubators. The fact that they are human only means they have to be paid: "Fair monetary compensation, combined with freedom of choice, obviates any ethical concern."[19]

Commercial surrogacy is grounded in a flawed anthropology of women. It is one that holds that the reproductive capacity of women can be divorced from the context of motherhood and indeed the very person of the mother. It understands women as reproductive machines.[20] Consequently, from Hagar to the present, surrogates tend to come from disempowered classes. In this sense commercial surrogacy is, similar to all

[17] Johnson, *Truly Our Sister*, 265.
[18] Ibid., 266.
[19] Deonandan, "The Ethics of Surrogacy," 2012.
[20] This is also one of the reasons why the Catholic Church opposes human cloning. As Catholic bioethicist Nicanor Pier Giorgio Austriaco, O.P., has stated, "cloning leads to the radical exploitation of women, who are reduced either to egg-making factories or to wombs to gestate a clone." Austriaco, *Biomedicine and Beatitude*, 103.

forms of social injustice, a tool for exploitation. This is why it is significant that God's calling of Mary does not align with the worldly valuations of the powerful. It is, rather, a repudiation of these same structures. Her *fiat* is demonstrative of the kind of power God has. This is a power so great that it does not need to violate or make an instrument of free will in order to accomplish its purposes, unlike the coercive power of the world. Mary is united to God in grace, and in the *Magnificat* she speaks for the nobodies on whom the world regularly tramples and exploits. It is this coming together of the infinite power of God with the socially exploited that the brokers of power most fear.

To sum up, John Paul II remarked that contemplation of Mary should invite consideration of all "women who have been wronged and exploited."[21] The women who have been wronged by the industry of commercial surrogacy belong to this class, or so this section has argued. Their dignity is routinely violated by those who have the financial coercive power to do so. When contemplating Mary, we should contemplate them.

SUMMARY

This chapter has attempted to elucidate the Catholic teaching on beginning of life issues such as contraception, abortion, and commercial surrogacy. We have seen that these teachings are rooted in the principle of universal human dignity examined in the previous chapter. The goal has been to help you understand why the Catholic moral tradition declares what it does with regard to these matters. If you still do not find these teachings persuasive, at least you may now find them intelligible. In the very least, hopefully you can see that these cannot be easily dismissed as mere "religious opinions." Rather, they are grounded in the principle of universal human dignity. As I warned earlier, holding consistently to it is to draw the ire of both sides of the political aisle. For this reason, it is very rarely done. One last point and I am finished. One of the major problems with current attitudes toward the beginning of life issues discussed in this chapter is that people of today tend to regard having a child as a right. In reality, no one is entitled to a child, because a child is a person, not a piece of property. Augustine's son was named Adeodatus. You probably have never met anyone with this name, but you may have met someone with the Greek equivalent, Theodore. Both names mean "gift from God." This seems to me a much saner way to think about bringing new life into the world.

---

[21] *MD* no. 19.

CHAPTER 12

End of Life Decisions

By Christ's Passion man knows thereby how much God loves him,
and is thereby stirred to love God in return, and herein lies the completion of human salvation.
St. Thomas Aquinas, *Summa Theologiae* IIIa q. 46 a. 3

The word "euthanasia" means "mercy killing." In the latter part of the
twentieth century advocates of the practice sought vigorously to get it
accepted as a legal medical procedure, which normally involved injecting
a patient with lethal chemicals meant to induce painless death. There are
two kinds of euthanasia: voluntary and involuntary. The former means that
the patient has given formal consent either through an advanced directive or, if they are conscious and lucid, directly to the doctor. Involuntary
euthanasia generally involves patients in comas or severely impaired states
who are not physically capable of giving consent. The movement to legal-
ize euthanasia in the United States had mixed results. Its most vocal advocate and practitioner, Jack Kevorkian, was imprisoned but also is seen as a
martyr by euthanasia advocates. The two-fold purpose of this final chapter
is both to make clear why Catholic teaching condemns this practice and
to respond to the significant problems euthanasia raises in a unique way
regarding human suffering.

THE CATHOLIC RESPONSE TO EUTHANASIA

To begin with, let us clarify the Catholic teaching. This is more complicated than some suppose. It is true that euthanasia clearly violates the
Catholic moral tradition: "Euthanasia is an action or omission that of
itself or by intention causes death in order to alleviate suffering. Catholic
health care institutions may never condone or participate in euthanasia
or assisted suicide in any way" (no. 60).[1] Seems clear enough, right? But

[1] All in-text references to *ERD*.

what is this "omission" business about? Well, suppose that a patient needs some kind of artificial life support like a ventilator, hydration, or a feeding tube. To intentionally omit these things in order to cause death is still a form of euthanasia. This is what the directive is saying. With respect to assisted nutrition and hydration (ANH), however, things do become a bit more complicated. If the patient "can reasonably be expected to live indefinitely if given such care," then this care is morally obligatory (no. 58). However, ANH becomes "morally optional" when it "cannot reasonably be expected to prolong life or when [it] would be 'excessively burdensome for the patient or [would] cause significant physical discomfort, for example resulting from complications in the use of the means employed'" (no. 58). And it is normally up to the patient, in consultation with the doctors, of course, to exercise his or her own prudential judgment as to when ANH becomes "excessively burdensome" or futile: "The free and informed judgment made by a competent adult patient concerning the use or withdrawal of life-sustaining procedures should always be respected and normally complied with, unless it is contrary to Catholic moral teaching" (no. 59). Additionally, "A person may forgo extraordinary or disproportionate means of preserving life. Disproportionate means are those that in the patient's judgment do not offer a reasonable hope of benefit or entail an excessive burden, or impose excessive expense on the family or the community" (no. 57).

In brief, Catholic moral teaching holds that voluntary and involuntary euthanasia are always morally wrong whether done by commission through lethal injection or omission through the removal of AHN or other life support mechanisms. However, such removals can be morally acceptable when certain conditions are met, such as: the means for preserving life are extraordinary or disproportionate, the means do not offer reasonable benefit, the means entail excessive burden, or the means impose excessive expense on the family or the community. When these conditions are met is to be determined on a case-by-case basis, normally by the patient him- or herself. The decision is left up to his or her prudential judgment. In other words, the distinction between ordinary and extraordinary means is not a medical but a moral one. In situation X, dialysis may be an extraordinary means of preserving life, because the patient has very little hope for recovery, is in extreme pain, and is bankrupting the family. In situation Y, however, dialysis may be an ordinary means of preserving life, because the patient is relatively healthy, has hope of recovery, and can afford it. This judgment is to be decided on a case-by-case basis by patients and their caregivers.

All of this raises the following question: if you are going to let a person gradually wither away by removing ANH, then why not just inject him or her with a lethal drug to kill him or her quickly and painlessly? Would not this be more humane and dignified than allowing them to slowly starve to death? Indeed, one of the reasons why dealing with euthanasia is tricky is because its advocates ground their claims in appeals to mercy, humane treatment, and the dignity of the patient. In recent years, Dr. Philip Nitschke has been pioneering a modern day euthanasia movement that involves the distribution of a pill (the so-called peaceful exit pill) called Nembutal. The idea is that a doctor could prescribe it, but then the patient administers it to him or herself. This way it is no longer, according to the advocates of this practice, assisted suicide, but just plain suicide. Which is more dignified, ask the modern day advocates of euthanasia, to gradually starve to death in a generic hospital room or to take a pill at home or wherever you want, whenever you want, with whomever you want beside you, and peacefully drift into eternal sleep?

There are two Catholic responses to this. The first is practical. No one ever said death has to take place in a hospital bed. The Catholic teaching holds that: "Patients should be kept as free of pain as possible so that they may die comfortably and with dignity, and in the place where they wish to die" (no. 61). Also, pain medication can and should be used, even if this accelerates death: "Medicines capable of alleviating or suppressing pain may be given to a dying person, even if this therapy may indirectly shorten the person's life so long as the intent is not to hasten death" (no. 61). This is a real-life application of the principle of double effect. The object of the act (giving pain medicine) is not intrinsically immoral. The intention of relieving pain is good (not the intention of shortening life as stated earlier). The bad effect (hastened death) is not the means to the good effect (the diminishing of pain), and, in myriad cases, there is proportionate reason.

At this point you may be asking yourself, "If you are going to hasten death with pain medication, why not just give lethal injection?" Because it is morally wrong to kill an innocent person. According to Catholic teaching, lethal injection is killing; prescribing pain medication with the foreseen but unintended side effect of hastening death is not. But how does this apply to a doctor who prescribes "the peaceful exit pill" in places where this is legal? Or how does it apply to someone who sells the pill?

I argue that the manufacturer, the doctor who prescribes the pill, and the person who sells it are all complicit in the death of the individual who takes it, and hence, this is still a form of assisted suicide. This is because death is the only intended usage of the pill. A gun shop owner or a gun manufacturer is not necessarily complicit for the deaths of people killed by guns they sold or produced, although they may be in some instances, because a gun has other uses. A car salesman or manufacturer is certainly not guilty for car accidents unless the manufacturer was negligent or the salesman knew there was something dangerously defective about the car and sold it nonetheless. However, the "peaceful exit" pill is intended only to bring death; it has no other purpose. A less euphemistic name for it is "the death control pill."

I said earlier that there are two Catholic responses to the "euthanasia offers death with dignity argument." The first we just reviewed. The second is more involved and deals with a properly theological question having to do with the problem of human suffering. This requires a separate treatment to which we now turn.

THE PROBLEM OF SUFFERING

Catholic teaching holds that "patients experiencing suffering that cannot be alleviated should be helped to appreciate the Christian understanding of redemptive suffering" (61). Well, what is "the Christian understanding of redemptive suffering?" In order to approach this question, it is helpful to take a step back and analyze an old theological problem. It is a problem that philosophers and theologians have been wrestling with for centuries. C.S. Lewis phrased it well in his book, *The Problem of Pain*: "If God were good, He would wish to make His creatures perfectly happy, and if God were almighty He would be able to do what He wished. But the creatures are not happy. Therefore God lacks either goodness, or power, or both. This is the problem of pain, in its simplest form."[2] Is it a problem with a solution? How would you solve it?

The first thing to take notice of is that there is a sense in which this is a distinctively Christian problem. If you did not believe in God or believed in a god that lacked goodness, power, or both, then you still may object to the ubiquitous presence of human suffering throughout the world, but this would just be a fact about the universe – such as gravity. It wouldn't stand in contradiction to anything. There is no self-evident reason why a mindless time and chance universe should produce creatures such as us, who both suffer and resent the fact of our own suffering. Nor would the fact of our suffering be contradicted by a god who was good and

---

[2] C.S. Lewis, *The Problem of Pain* (San Francisco: Harper Collins, 1940), 16.

empathized but simply lacked the power to do anything about it, or by a god who was malevolent. In his very sad book, *A Grief Observed*, Lewis states, "The conclusion I dread is not 'So there's no God after all,' but 'So this is what God's really like. Deceive yourself no longer.'"[3] Lewis is writing in the wake of the tragic death of his wife, Joy, and he is explaining what the grief is doing to him, how it is making him feel. Again, in *The Problem of Pain*, he describes, in words more powerful and jarring than anything produced by the modern atheists, how the presence of suffering in the world once made it difficult for him to believe in the existence of the Christian God. I quote his remarks here in full:

Not many years ago when I was an atheist, if anyone had asked me, "Why do you not believe in God?" my reply would have run something like this: "Look at the universe we live in. By far the greatest part of it consists of empty space, completely dark and unimaginably cold. The bodies which move in this space are so few and so small in comparison with the space itself that even if every one of them were known to be crowded as full as it could hold with perfectly happy creatures, it would still be difficult to believe that life and happiness were more than a byproduct to the power that made the universe. As it is, however, the scientists think it likely that very few of the suns of space – perhaps none of them except our own – have any planets; and in our own system it is improbable that any planet except the Earth sustains life. And Earth herself existed without life for millions of years and may exist for millions more when life has left her. And what is it like while it lasts? It is so arranged that all the forms of it can live only by preying upon one another. In the lower forms this process entails only death, but in the higher there appears a new quality called consciousness which enables it to be attended with pain. The creatures cause pain by being born, and live by inflicting pain, and in pain they mostly die. In the most complex of all the creatures, Man, yet another quality appears, which we call reason, whereby he is enabled to foresee his own death while keenly desiring permanence. It also enables men by a hundred ingenious contrivances to inflict a great deal more pain than they otherwise could have on one another and on the irrational creatures. This power they have exploited to the full. Their history is largely a record of crime, war, disease, and terror, with just sufficient happiness interposed to give them, while it lasts, an agonized apprehension of losing it, and, when it is lost, the poignant misery of remembering."[4]

Lewis goes on for a while this way before explaining how he changed his mind, but the point here is that a universe so understood is only properly a problem when contradicted by the infinite goodness of an almighty God. It is reasonable for a square god to produce a universe of squares. It

[3] C.S. Lewis, *A Grief Observed* (San Francisco: Harper Collins, 1961), 7.
[4] C.S. Lewis, *The Problem of Pain* (San Francisco: Harper Collins, 1940), 1–2.

is reasonable for a circle god to make a universe of circles. For a square god to make a universe of circles stands in need of explanation, and, according to Lewis, it is Christianity more than any other worldview that insists on holding to the proposition that an infinitely good and powerful God is behind this universe replete with the kind of things just described.

The Christian response to the problem of suffering is articulated in the following way by Thomas Aquinas: "This is part of the infinite goodness of God, that He should allow evil to exist, and out of it produce good."[5] The theological term for this is "providence." Now, it is only in the light of a theology of providence that the Christian understanding of redemptive suffering can be seen. God does not cause our suffering out of meanness or spite, nor does God allow it because of incompetence, indifference, or impotence. Rather, God allows the evil of suffering that good may follow. This is redemptive suffering. To be clear, this does not mean that we should seek out or romanticize suffering for suffering's sake. This would be sadistic, unnatural, and unscriptural. Rather, it means that when the dark times come we are to trust in God to get us through them, reaching out in faith and hope, as it were, asking for deliverance and the strength to move forward a day, sometimes an hour, sometimes a minute at a time. In the midst of tragic suffering, prayer is often for the will to take the next breath.

Whether you are Christian or not, you can probably think of examples of redemptive suffering in your life. That is, you can think of instances when you experienced something difficult that seemed like purposeless misery, but which, with the benefit of time, you are now able to see turned out to be good for you. But what of suffering that seems purposeless? You may have memory of this too. What of seemingly purposeless suffering you witness in others and rightly empathize with? If an elderly person with severe dementia and stage-four pancreatic cancer is slowly withering away, spending every moment in crippling pain, what possible good could come from preserving his or her life? Is it not just pointless suffering that it would be kinder to snuff out as you unhesitatingly would even for an animal? The Christian answer to this is not easy. It is that life is God's to give and God's to take. Even when our darkest moments come, when we can find no worth or meaning in our own lives, we must remember that our lives are gifts to us from God. We must try, difficult as it may be, to look beyond our present despairs to the Giver of good gifts who

---

[5] *ST* Ia q. 2 a. 3 ad. 1.

created, sustains, and awaits us. If the fullness of our dignity is anywhere it is here at its source. There have been thinkers who believe that some suffering is "dysteleological," by which they mean that it serves only to break "the victim's spirit," and therefore, has no redemptive value.[6] However, the Catholic moral tradition holds that, in the present life, all suffering can be joined to the sufferings of Christ and thus become redemptive.

Before concluding, I wish to make clear that I myself am not very good at doing what I have just been espousing. But I have known others that are. I suppose if you want to grow in this regard, then this will involve learning from the example set by Christ. Grace and prayer will be essential as will patience. As for the actual doing, however, my best advice is to seek out those who are able to make clear the nature of redemptive suffering in the way they live their lives and ask them how they do it. Try to emulate them. Most of us spend our lives trying to avoid suffering by any and all means. We raise our fists angrily to the sky at the slightest hint that suffering may be on the way let alone already within the gates. Nevertheless, as Lewis notes, "When pain is to be borne, a little courage helps more than much knowledge, a little human sympathy more than much courage, and the least tincture of the love of God more than all."[7]

All of this brings us to a very important point: God remains God both in good times and bad. Have you ever read the Book of Job in the Scripture? In the beginning of the story, the enemy comes before God and issues a challenge (people often mistake this as a wager). Job is a righteous man who praises God but, surmises the enemy, if you took away all of the good things in his life, then he would curse God. Do you see the claim the enemy is making? Can you see the challenge? The claim is that God is only worthy of love insofar as God can provide us with good things. God is not intrinsically lovable simply as God. Rather, according to the enemy, God needs to buy our love with presents and treats.

So God allows the enemy to take from Job his family and his livelihood but not, at first, his health. Job refuses to curse God. He suffers, he mourns, but he keeps his trust in God. Next, God allows the enemy to take his health, but not to kill him. Job breaks out with rashes all over his body. Then, his friends (who are all amateur theologians like so many people in our society today) show up. They prattle on with their theories about why God is doing this. Surely it is punishment for some sin

---

[6] Robert C. Mesle, "The Problem of Genuine Evil: A Critique of John Hick's Theodicy," *Journal of Religion* 66 (October 1986): 423.
[7] Lewis, *The Problem of Pain*, xii.

of which Job needs to repent, or perhaps God is testing Job's faith. Job rightly rejects these explanations. It seems a good God would not visit suffering on an innocent person in these ways.

Now, at the end of the story, God himself appears to Job and his friends. God begins by chastising the friends for talking nonsense about God, as many well-intentioned people have a propensity to do. And then God gives a long speech to Job, the point of which is simply to remind him of who God is.

> Where were you when I founded the earth?
>> Tell me if you have understanding.
> Who determined its size?
>> Surely you know?
> Who stretched out the measuring line for it?
>> Into what were its pedestals sunk,
>> and who laid its cornerstone,
>>> while all the sons of God shouted for joy?
> Who shut within doors the sea,
>> when it burst forth from the womb,
> When I made the clouds its garment
>> and the darkness its swaddling bands?
> When I set limits for it and fastened the bar of its door
>> and said: Thus far shall you come but no farther,
>> here shall your proud waves stop?[8]

By the end, Job remembers the majesty of God: "By hearsay I had heard of you, but now my eye has seen you. Therefore I disown what I have said, and repent in dust and ashes."[9] The term "disown" in this context means "forget." Sometimes in our hardest moments we understandably get caught up in speculative questions about why God is allowing these awful things to happen. Even when things are going relatively well in our own lives, a quick glance at the morning newspaper may raise the same question. Our own pain, or even the pain of others, can create a great fog blinding us from the reality of God. Sometimes the idea of God not existing is of more comfort than the thought of God being there and able to stop it but not doing so. At least, it's easier to understand.

The Christian teaching on providence does not say that we will understand every bit of suffering that comes our way and easily be able to reconcile it with God's plan for our lives and so take it in stride. Indeed, thinking that we can rely on a set of stock responses to human suffering – God is

[8] Job 38:4–11 *NAB* throughout.
[9] Job 42:5–6.

punishing us, God is testing our faith – is precisely the mistake made by Job's amateur theologian friends. Sometimes we are left in the dark, and our options are either to turn our backs on God or praise God for who God is, regardless of our present circumstances. Trusting in God's providence simply means believing that, impossible as it may seem, somehow in some way, whether in this world or another, God will set right the evils of the present age and, indeed, of all ages. God will repair that which has been destroyed. God will restore that which appears forever lost. I admit that I myself often find it hard to believe in such things, but if God can make stars, then perhaps these things are possible too.

SUMMARY

The two-fold purpose of this chapter has been to make clear why Catholic teaching forbids euthanasia and to respond to the problems euthanasia raises in a distinctive way regarding human suffering. In addition to the practical ethical directives we have examined, we have seen how it is only through a theology of providence that these issues can truly be addressed from a Christian point of view. The claim here is not that these teachings are easy or even pleasant. Rather, the goal has been to help you understand what they are and why they are what they are.

Before I end, I wish to make sure that one key point regarding Catholic bioethical teachings is not lost on the reader. This point has to do with the relationship of Catholic bioethics to the content of Parts I–III. Put succinctly, the Catholic moral tradition holds that human acts in accordance with the natural law and revelation (Part I) are good, and they lead to the perfection of the soul and to the attainment of true and lasting happiness (Part II). However, because we are also social beings who live in community (Part III), our flourishing is invariably linked to the wider nexus of social conditions, which enable people as individuals and as groups to reach their own fulfillment. Bioethical reflection is important because it focuses on the host of questions that the advance of medicine and technology force us to confront, not just for the sake of intellectual speculation, but for the sake of guiding both individuals and society in the right direction, providing science and technology with an ethical compass sometimes lost in the hustle and bustle of progress. The natural law, revelation, human flourishing, individual virtue, and social morality are thus the proper context for evaluating and appraising Catholic bioethics. Too often the Catholic teaching is reduced to facile political slogans, or it is wedded with a given political ideology or the narrow perspective of some special interest group. It is very easy in our current political climate, particularly with respect to bioethical questions, to approach Catholic ethics from a strictly political vantage point. Hopefully, the preceding chapters may disabuse one from this approach.

One further point and I am done. People who react angrily to Catholic bioethics are sometimes, although not always, animated by a certain rivalry that exists in their minds between science and religion. That is, they think that one must put their trust all in one or the other, and they have put their trust in science and therefore see religion as a threat to "progress" in that regard. However, I think that in the minds of people who hold such a view the rivalry often goes deeper than this; it is in actuality a rivalry between the providence of God and the providence of man. Indeed, this is a common element in every form of sin.

Let us return one last time to the story in Genesis. The serpent begins with a question (which seems innocent enough): "Did God really say, 'You shall not eat of any tree of the garden?'" Eve replies, "We may eat of the fruit of the trees in the garden; it is only about the fruit of the tree in the middle of the garden that God said, 'You shall not eat it or even touch it, or else you will die.'" To this the serpent counters, "You certainly will not die!"[10] There it is. Adam and Eve were faced with the decision of whether to trust God or not. They chose poorly, and the human race is now in the state we find it.

As stated several times already, original sin is better understood as a pattern or prototype than as an isolated occurrence. Understood in this way, we may regard the Fall as something that occurs every day, reiterated down the ages, as it were. Every time we lust after greater control, we reenact the Fall. Every time we strive to drive right praise of God out of the center of our reality, out of our hearts, we reenact the Fall. Every time we prefer ourselves to God, we reenact the Fall. Every time we withhold our trust from the very author of our existence, we reenact the Fall. It really isn't any different with respect to bioethical matters. The specifics of the questions and issues may change, but the fundamental choice seems always to be between trust and doubt. We abandon our moral sense only after a certain internal betrayal of God and self. From this betrayal follows the universe of howling moral confusion in which the modern world currently finds itself.

[10] Genesis 3:1–4.

I must emphasize that the Catholic Church has never rejected the human sciences when these sciences are not sought after as a substitute for God. To the contrary, what Catholic ethics has and must always stand against is the fallen desire to usurp the place of God. More important, however, is what Catholic ethics stands for, which is, put simply, to make us more like Christ. In the final analysis, the Catholic moral tradition is not ultimately ordered to propositions about foundations, individual virtue, social morality, or bioethics. Rather, it is ordered beyond these things to Christ himself. Put briefly, Catholic ethics is ordered to nothing other than drawing people to Christ. If it is not doing that, then it is simply a waste of time.

The Universal Call to Holiness

The Lord Jesus, divine teacher and model of all perfection, preached holiness of life, which he both initiates and brings to perfection, to each and every one of his disciples no matter what their condition of life.

Lumen gentium no. 40

The cornerstone principle of the Catholic moral tradition both before and after the Second Vatican Council is Jesus Christ, the essence of Catholic faith. And the reason why we have a discipline called Catholic moral theology is because Christ calls his followers to holiness: "So be perfect, just as your heavenly Father is perfect."[1] Catholic moral theology is a science ordered to understanding what the achievement of this entails. Holiness, it may be said, is the goal that Christ has placed before us. When Catholic moral theology becomes disconnected from that goal, it ceases to be Catholic moral theology. The topic I wish to address in this epilogue, therefore, is whether this goal of becoming a saint that Christ has given us, and to which Catholic moral theology is ordered, is a worthy one. In order to answer this question, we must ask the larger question of whether Heaven itself is a worthy goal; for Heaven is the proper reward for living a saintly life. It is the consummation and completion of living a holy life, like marriage is the consummation and completion of love.

The first condition of a worthy goal is that it is both difficult and possible to attain. Some people might say that it does not matter if a goal is attainable so long as one is bettered by the pursuit of it. For example, a baseball pitcher may strive to throw a no-hitter, but even if he fails to achieve this, if he approximates it, and comes closer to attaining it than he would have had his goal been only to throw a decent game, then we

[1] Matthew 5:48 *NAB* throughout.

may say that the goal was a good one even though it was not attained. The goal of throwing a no-hitter helped the pitcher to do better than he would have done without it. However, this example does not work, because, of course, throwing a no-hitter is possible. It is rare and difficult, but it can and does happen. It is attainable. In reality, I do not suppose one ever truly aspires for a goal unless one believes it can be attained, even if it is a long shot or if the person is deluded, like so many talentless *American Idol* contestants.

It is not enough for a goal to be difficult and attainable, it must also be worth attaining. In order for a goal to be worth attaining it must bring a true and lasting happiness and sense of satisfaction. We can all think back to goals we have achieved even the memory of which still awakens in us a certain sense of delight. On the other hand, we can also think of past goals that, even though achieved, bring us no delight, or even bring us shame, or possibly just make us feel silly. And then, of course, there is the heavy feeling that still comes when one reflects about goals once pursued but never realized or reluctantly given up on. This is the memory of failure. And this brings me to a further point. In addition to being difficult, attainable, and worth attaining, great goals also entail a real possibility of defeat. A man in love pursues a woman whom he wants to marry. Well, she may not want to marry him. A general fighting for the sake of a just cause pursues a military victory. Well, the battle, indeed the war, may be lost. On a lesser scale, a football team sweats and bleeds in preparation to win a game. Well, they may lose it. And here we come up against something puzzling.

Another thing that great goals share in common is that no one can or does force us to pursue them. It is, in a sense, the very goal that attracts us to itself. We long for it; we hope for it. Sometimes the hope feels oddly similar to pain or fear, but we cannot stop striving after it. The more we try to push away, the more intensely we feel its pull. This is partly because great goals are accompanied by great stakes. The greater the goal, the greater is the chasm between what we hope to achieve by gaining it and what we fear to lose by failing to achieve it. And we recognize the possibility of failure. Without this recognition, there would be no occasion for courage or hope.

Let us sum up briefly what we have arrived at so far. There are all kinds of goals, and we all know what it is like to have them. These goals may be hard or easy or somewhere in between. In addition, they may be good, bad, better, or worse. However, worthy goals seem to possess the following properties:

1. They are both difficult and possible to attain.
2. They are worth pursuing in their own right, and we feel naturally drawn to them. No one forces us or compels us to pursue them.
3. They keep their promises, in the sense of actually providing the true and lasting happiness that inspired us to pursue them in the first place.
4. There is an equal proportion between that which we hope to gain from achieving them and that which we fear to lose by failing to do so, and we recognize both success and failure as real and rival possibilities. The better the goal, the more total the victory or defeat.

The question that confronts us, then, is whether the goal of Heaven possesses these four properties. But, let us first clear away some possible distractions.

The first potential distraction is the question of whether Heaven is real. Obviously, if Heaven does not exist, then it does not qualify as a great goal. It would not possess the four properties just discussed. First, one could not speak of striving toward a possible destination if that destination did not exist. If there were no such place as New York, then any journey to New York would be bound to fail. Second, imaginary things are not worth pursuing in their own right; we are not naturally drawn to them, and if one were, then we might think him or her a lunatic. Third, a thing that did not exist could not make or fulfill any promise to you. The offer and the result would both be hallucinations. And, finally, there could be no proportion between gaining and losing it; no intended results follow from failing to arrive at a place that does not exist. Only the curing of the delusion that the place you have sought after exists could be achieved, and even this would be an unintentional benefit accidentally gained over the course of what was an otherwise useless endeavor.

So how do we know that Heaven is real? Because God revealed it, of course. I know that in the scientific age we are mocked for believing things to be true that cannot be empirically verified, but scientists who are candid with themselves know that there are classes of truth outside of this narrow definition. The honest scientist knows that he or she cannot empirically prove that the universe spontaneously generated or that human beings lack a soul. And where objective knowledge is lacking there can be no such thing as probability. We can speak of probability when it comes to prediction. I can predict that the coin will land on heads or tails, but when it comes to supernatural truths, there is no such thing as probabilistic predictive power. There is no question of whether God probably exists or humans probably have a soul. God exists or does not, and we do or do not have souls. In the absence of objective verification, one is left only with guesswork and subjective preference. Now, if observation, experimentation, and verification were the only path to truth, then that is all belief about the important things would or could ever be. But, happily, reality extends beyond the narrow confines of empiricism.

If the domain of science is the visible, material world, then science could never, except perhaps by accident, tell us anything of the invisible world. It could not tell us whether such a world existed or whether it was even plausible, possible, or probable that there was such a world. All the scientist could really tell us is his or her personal view, and he or she will likely also inform us that the science of invisible things is really quite beyond his or her domain. Again, this is definitional. If the object of science is gaining knowledge through observation of the material world, then it is not interested in gaining knowledge of the immaterial world, if such a world exists, nor does it claim to have access to such knowledge. Asking a physicist or biologist to tell us about Heaven by using the tools of his field, then, would be rather like asking a mathematician to assess a poem through the Pythagorean Theorem. The mathematician has a realm of truth that he is trained to evaluate, and so he naturally employs the proper tools for that evaluation. Applying the Pythagorean Theorem to the beauty of a poem would be as silly as using Darwin's theory of natural selection to contemplate the doctrine of the Trinity. Darwin's theory is as useless to this end as the Pythagorean Theorem is to evaluating Longfellow.

Very well then; science can answer some questions but is and must be utterly silent on others. If there were no other way to arrive at truth, then, as I said before, all questions of the invisible would be reduced to subjective guesses. However, Christians believe that "by divine revelation God wished to manifest and communicate both himself and the eternal decrees of his will concerning the salvation of humankind."[2] It is true that we cannot arrive at these truths through our efforts alone, but that is precisely why God revealed them. We must remember that our limitations are not God's limitations. I do not wish to go deeper into the doctrine of revealed knowledge. Indeed, this would require another book. My only point is that revelation is a fitting way to arrive at certain kinds of truths. The scientists have not disproved this, nor have they disproved any of the content of revelation, nor could they ever, because the tools of their field have

---

[2] *DVer* no. 6.

no recourse to the invisible. Therefore, we need not bother further about whether the existence of Heaven can be empirically proven. It can't. But it can't be disproven either. Christians believe Heaven exists on the authority of their revealed doctrines. This is not an escape into subjectivity. We are not submitting that our doctrines are true merely because we believe them to be. We agree with the materialist that objective truth exists; we disagree as to its scope. And there is an end to the matter.

A second distraction is the question of whether the doctrine of Heaven is good for society. It is such a vague question. When you hear Christians debate with atheists about this what you find is that the Christians point to all the good examples of people acting well in this world through focusing on the next. They speak of figures such as Mother Theresa or Martin Luther King Jr. The atheist, on the other hand, will either point out imperfections in the saints or, as is much more likely, bring up examples of people behaving badly in pursuit of the next world, like medieval crusaders or the 9/11 hijackers. Contrariwise, the Christian will then point out the bad behavior of certain atheists, such as Stalin, and argue that had they believed in an absolute justice that awaited them in the next world, then they would have behaved better in this one. Next, the atheist is very likely to respond that if Mother Theresa or whoever else was only working to better society in pursuit of Heaven, or worse to avoid Hell, then this somehow reduces the merit or honor she is due for having so acted. Wouldn't it be better to behave well or work to better society without any regard for one's own personal gain?

These debates do not really go anywhere. No one does or can win. There are several reasons for this. To begin with, the question of whether Heaven is good for society is far too vague. The atheist and Christian, very understandably, do not agree on what the doctrine of Heaven entails or on what "good for society" means. This is why the conversation always ends up with the Christian pointing to the good examples of Christians who have lived well and the atheist to examples of those who have lived poorly. The dialogue goes nowhere. Just as the scientist cannot disprove the doctrine of Heaven, or even show it to be improbable, so the atheist cannot demonstrate that this doctrine is bad for society. All he can really do is point to particular bad examples and construct totalizing theories based on them.

A third and final distraction that requires a response I refer to as "speculative pluralism." Unlike previous ages, it is highly probable that all of us know people who subscribe to different religions than our own. Therefore, we are very likely to hear people objecting to the idea that Heaven is only for Christians, given that the Church today operates in a global context of religious pluralism. What about Buddhists, Hindus, Jews, Muslims, or ordinary decent people who subscribe to no religion at all? Cannot they, too, enter Heaven?

The purpose of the Christian doctrine of Heaven is not to invite speculation about the eternal fate of some other group. In the Scripture, the disciples learn this when they ask our Lord if only a few will be saved. He responds by exhorting them to "strive to enter through the narrow door." He goes on to say that "many will attempt to enter but not be strong enough."[3] Notice how our Lord wisely does not answer their question. They had asked him if few would be saved. He responds that many will try but fail. This really does not tell us whether a few will be saved. The mind naturally wants to deduce that because many tried and failed, then only a few tried and succeeded. But Jesus does not say that. It is as though he is admonishing the disciples by responding to the real motivation behind their question rather than the question itself. What they are really asking is whether the goal of Heaven is hard or easy, so he responds that it is difficult, which is why you must strive for the narrow door. And this is reinforced when he says that many will try but not be strong enough.

I think the same response is suitable for those who ask speculative questions about whether people of other religions can make it to Heaven.[4] There is certainly nothing wrong with worrying about others and wanting to help them along the way when and where we can. We are obligated to do so. There is certainly nothing wrong with wanting everyone to be treated fairly at the final judgment. However, neither of these things exempts one from striving for the narrow door.

These, then, are the three points I wanted to make. Whether or not Heaven can be proven to exist in the scientific sense, whether or not the doctrine is good for society, and whether or not non-Christians can go there are all important questions, but may also serve as unhelpful distractions that develop into obstacles to the actual pursuit. Jesus did not teach the disciples about Heaven in order to furnish them with speculative debate topics. He was giving them a goal after which to strive. Whether or not this goal was a worthy one, or even the best one, is the question we are examining in this epilogue, so let us now return to that.

---

[3] Luke 13:24.
[4] It would require a different book to adequately treat this topic here. The short answer is that no one can achieve salvation without Christ but it may be possible for someone to receive Christ's grace without being aware of it. See *CCC* no. 605.

Christians believe that Heaven is real and that it is possible to make it there. This belief is common among Christians, but Christians have, at times, disagreed over the question of how to make it there. Anyone who has seriously studied theology or church history knows that it is perhaps this topic more than any other that divides Catholics and Protestants from each other. However, the disagreement is not total. Rather than emphasizing the differences between Catholic and Protestant views of salvation, the aim of what follows is to point out what they have in common. More specifically, my task is to show how each view understands the difficulty involved in striving after Heaven. Difficulty combined with attainability is, after all, the first property of a worthy goal.

Great goals make demands on us. This is where the difficulty comes in. When we are striving after a goal, there are things we must do that, again, are not arbitrary things forced on us from the outside, but rather things we must accomplish because doing so is intrinsically related to striving after the goal in question. The tennis player practices her swing. The football player lifts weights. They do these things because they are intrinsic to the goal of becoming a good tennis or football player. The goal itself makes these demands, and we fulfill them in pursuit of the goal. So what demands does the goal of Heaven make? What must one accomplish in pursuit of it?

Whenever I ask my students what one must do in order to make it to Heaven, there are generally two kinds of responses. Some students emphasize the ethical or moral demands that must be met. They say we have to be kind to others and not hurt people and that sort of thing. Another group of students tends to focus on the relational aspect. In order to enter Heaven, a person must have the right kind of relationship with God through accepting Christ into his or her heart and so forth. Both groups are right, but both groups are also wrong. The truth is that the relational and ethical components of salvation are inseparable. I can't have one without the other. That is, I cannot have the right kind of relationship with God if I do not live as God wants me to live, but I cannot live as I ought to without the right kind of relationship with God.

Now, here someone might ask which comes first. Does the relationship precede the right living, or does the right living precede and even occasion the relationship? But this is really a silly question. If two things are inseparable, then one does not precede the other. Both are either present or not present. At the same time, as I stated in Chapter 6, being in right relationship with God is the cause, not the result, of moral goodness. This is why the relationship and the kind of life proper to that relationship are either present or they are not. The fundamentalist thinks that living well is entirely about one's interior relationship with God. The atheist thinks living well only entails following ethical duties. For the Catholic mind the two cannot be separated.

With that being said, it could be argued that what separates Catholic and Protestant views of salvation is that whereas the Catholics tend to emphasize the difficulties of the ethical and moral demands of Heaven, the Protestants tend to emphasize the relational demands. To the Protestant mind, salvation hinges on whether one realizes his or her total dependence on God. The Protestant thinks that one can do no good on his or her own and that all attempts to do so are mere vainglory. You are saved once you give up all delusions about your own goodness and self-worthiness and learn to rely wholly on God. And that is precisely where the difficulty lies; for we are always falling under the deception that we can set up on our own and rely on our own efforts.

Indeed, one of the factors involved in the difficulty of realizing one's dependence on God is that it is easy to imagine we have accepted it when we really have not. The test is not whether we feel anxiety when the terrible times come. Of course we do. The test is rather about what happens to our relationship with God during and after these times. It is easy to acknowledge God's sovereignty and intrinsic worthiness when the sun is shining and all the cards seem to be falling in your favor, but what about when tragedy strikes? Do we draw closer or pull away? If I doubt God's goodness, then I will come to rely on what I perceive to be my own goodness. I will come to see God as an obstacle to my happiness and flourishing, thinking that I know better than God as to what is best for me. Thus, the relational component of salvation is a great difficulty, for tragedy or even the memory of tragedy mixed with conceit are always whispering to us that God, if God exists at all, is not to be trusted.

Catholics do not deny this difficulty, but the Catholic emphasis tends to be more on the difficulty of sanctification, which means the process of becoming holy. To become holy entails far more than merely acting in a certain kind of way. It means allowing God's grace to transform our whole being from the inside. Recall the discussion from Chapter 6 on interiority. Christ constantly emphasizes that it is not enough to merely act in certain kinds of ways; we must also have interior dispositions by which we do so. Thus, the man who lusts after a woman, even if he does not sleep with her, is just as guilty as the man who does. Becoming holy is not about just acting well; it means becoming good. This entails forming a character marked by the seven great virtues discussed in Part II.

At any rate, the point for the moment is that Catholics and Protestants, whatever their disagreements with respect to how salvation works, agree that Heaven is a difficult goal. It demands both that we have the right kind of relationship with God through love and that we live out this love in every domain of life. This is just another way of saying that we are to love God with our whole heart, mind, and soul, and love our neighbors as ourselves. Protestants tend to focus on the "right kind of relationship" part whereas Catholics focus on the living out of this relationship, but both agree at bottom that the two cannot be separated.

Furthermore, Catholics and Protestants agree that salvation would be impossible if Christ had not died for our sins. But he did. And in so doing, he accomplished far more than the mere paying of a penalty. He ushered in a new kind of life. The new life is given to us through all of the sacraments but in a special way when we receive the Eucharist. Catholics believe that, since Christ is really present in the bread and wine, when we participate in the Eucharistic celebration "we unite ourselves to Christ."[5] And it is from this union that all our good deeds flow.

I am the true vine, and my Father is the vinegrower. He takes away every branch in me that does not bear fruit, and every one that does he prunes so that it bears more fruit. You are already pruned because of the word that I spoke to you. Remain in me, as I remain in you. Just as a branch cannot bear fruit on its own unless it remains on the vine, so neither can you unless you remain in me.[6]

Notice that Christ does not present bearing fruit and remaining in him as two rival options. We must be in the right kind of relationship with God, and we must also bear fruit. And we cannot do one without the other. However, our starting point is the divided self marked by sin. Thus, the demands of Heaven entail overcoming our very selves. Only new life in Christ makes this possible. Heaven, then, possesses the first property of worthy goals. It is difficult and attainable.

The second property of worthy goals is that they are worth pursuing in their own right, and we feel naturally drawn to them. No one forces us or compels us to pursue them. There are at least three features that Heaven, as Christians understand it, possesses that align with the features of what people long for when they long for ultimate fulfillment. First, in the most basic sense, we want to be happy. Second, we want what may, for lack of a better term, be called security. That is, in order to really be happy in

[5] *CCC* no. 1331.
[6] John 15:1–5.

the ultimate sense, we want some assurance that this happiness can be expected to last and won't be snatched away from us when we are least expecting it. And, finally, we want our unshakeable happiness to be shared with others. As Benedict XVI observed, "Our hope is always essentially also hope for others."[7] The ultimate fulfillment we desire is this shared and unshakable happiness. The object of Christian hope is a happiness that both transcends and fulfills this longing: "Eye has not seen, and ear has not heard…what God has prepared for those who love him."[8]

The point, then, is a simple one. If you find in yourself the desire for a shared and unshakable happiness, then you have found in yourself a desire for Heaven. It is a very natural desire. Wouldn't we be concerned about someone who said that what they wanted above all else was a cessation of the vicissitudes of this life and eternal nothingness? Isn't this plainly a sign of depression? Could there be anything more unnatural than a genuine desire for one's own annihilation? Very well then; it is natural to desire shared and unshakeable happiness, and it is this desire we find in ourselves when we look hard enough. Accordingly, the ultimate goal of Heaven is something we find ourselves naturally drawn toward. Thus, Heaven possesses the second property of worthy goals; we are naturally drawn to it.

The next question, then, is whether the Christian understanding of Heaven can actually deliver the kind of unshakable and shared happiness it promises. Such is the third property of worthy goals; they keep their promises. This third property of worthy goals is the easiest to address with respect to Heaven. Indeed, it is often we who determine whether the pursuit of a goal is wise or unwise based on what we hope to attain from it. And the fundamental point here is this: nothing can keep the promise of providing ultimate fulfillment except for God, because God is the only one who has it to give. This is why, as Augustine observed, God created us to enjoy praising God, and "our heart is restless until it rests in Thee."[9] Ultimate fulfillment is God's eternal gift of himself. Worthy goals keep their promises. If nothing in this life can keep the promise of providing shared and unshakable happiness, then the fulfillment of that goal must dwell beyond the present life.

Before advancing, I wish to clarify the point I am trying to make. I am not claiming that there is no happiness to be had on earth. Indeed, there may be previews of the kind of unshakable and shared happiness that Heaven entails even in this life. There may even be continuity between

[7] *SS* no. 48.
[8] 1 Corinthians 2:9.
[9] *CONF* I.i.1.

the happiness here and the happiness there. Rather, my point is that it is unwise to try to make any of the things in this world into a source of the kind of happiness available only in the next world, because none of them can provide it.

Thus far I have tried to demonstrate that Heaven is both difficult and possible to attain, something we naturally pursue, and that it is really the only goal that can keep the promise of providing ultimate fulfillment. We come now to the fourth and final property of worthy goals: there is an equal proportion between that which we hope to gain from achieving them and that which we fear to lose by failing to do so, and we recognize both success and defeat as real possibilities. Thus, we arrive at the doctrine of Hell.

From the outset, it must be noted that the very concept of Hell can only have meaning in the shadow of the pulsating reality of Heaven. When pastors and teachers present Heaven as though it were valuable chiefly as an alternative to Hell, they misrepresent Christian teaching. Consider the following lines from Jonathan Edwards's famous sermon *Sinners in the Hand of an Angry God*:

[Everyone walking the earth] are now the objects of that very same anger and wrath of God that is expressed in the torments of hell: and the reason why they don't go down to hell at each moment, is not because God, in whose power they are, is not then very angry with them; as angry as he is with many of those miserable creatures that he is now tormenting in hell, and do there feel and bear the fierceness of his wrath. Yea, God is a great deal more angry with great numbers that are now on earth, yea doubtless with many that are now in this congregation, that it may be are at ease and quiet, than he is with many of those that are now in the flames of hell.

In the context of such a presentation, escape from a wrathful god becomes Heaven's distinctive feature and essential promise. Puritanical eighteenth-century preachers, however, were not the first to present the afterlife in a very terrible aspect. Indeed, the gods of ancient Greek religion were also regarded as arbitrary and lacking any special concern for the fate of human beings whether in this life or the next. *Tartaros* is replete with torment and suffering of the most gruesome sorts. And this is precisely what gave rise to ancient materialism. This is why the central goal of the philosophy of Epicurus and Lucretius was to discharge people from the fear of punishment after death. The truth is, however, that Hell is not just some arbitrary punishment visited upon us by the whims and caprices of a wrathful deity. Rather, it is merely a description of the non-reality of Heaven's shadow. Recall our earlier discussion of the prodigal son. The point of the parable is not that sinners are dropped into Hell from the hands of an angry god. Rather, they are permitted to remain outside in the dark by a pleading and compassionate father eternally welcoming and inviting them inside. This is because it is God who "wills everyone to be saved and come to knowledge of the truth."[10]

I have said that a property of worthy goals is that there is an equal proportion between that which we hope to gain from achieving them and that which we fear to lose by failing to do so, and we recognize both success and defeat as real possibilities. Such is why we must admit the doctrine of Hell. But surely it is best to keep the focus on the object of our hope rather than the object of our fear. Think about it with respect to the ordinary things of life. If you were helping a friend to prepare a marriage proposal, would you encourage him to focus on how heartbroken and lonely he will be if she says no? If you were encouraging your daughter to take up a sport, would you start by warning her all about the agony of defeat? Moreover, would you present the outcome of their respective endeavors as already predetermined in the negative? Of course not! And neither does God. "Strive to enter through the narrow door," means to keep your focus on what dwells beyond that door. We will have moments in which we reflect on what failing to make it through that door entails, but if that becomes our focus, then we lose sight of the goal. All this being said, when despair begins to creep in, as it sometimes does, then just remind yourself that making Heaven your goal only means partnering with God by sharing in the goal God already has for you. The grace of God creates the goal in us and sustains the pursuit and achievement of it. Surely this is a relief. The same God who created the entire universe out of nothing has something to accomplish in your life. Shall God succeed? God is not an indifferent spectator with respect to our earthly pilgrimage. God has cleared the path for us and walks beside us on our journey down the narrow road, picking us up when we fall, healing our wounds, and renewing our spirits when we become forlorn. The source of this renewal, both of the individual and of society, is the animating spirit of the Catholic moral tradition both before and since Vatican II.

[10] 1 Timothy 2:4.

Appendix

CHAPTER I

Review Questions

1. What do philosophers mean when they use the words "objective" and "subjective" and what relevance does this have for the discipline of ethics? What do ethicists mean when they speak of "the foundations problem," and what are some ways ethicists have attempted to deal with this?

2. What is moral relativism? What does moral relativism assume about the nature of ethical reality? Is there any truth in the various versions of moral relativism? What are some key areas in which moral relativism fails?

3. What does Bentham mean by "the principle of utility" and how does Mill expand this view? Where does Mill agree and disagree with Bentham and what difference does this make for utilitarianism as an ethical theory?

4. How does "act-utilitarianism" differ from "rule-utilitarianism," and in what ways does Kant's categorical imperative inform the latter? How is Kant's ethical theory importantly different from all forms of utilitarianism?

5. Imagine an ethical debate between a slave abolitionist and a slave owner in the United States in, say, 1835. They are debating about whether slavery is morally acceptable or reprehensible. Now imagine that Hobbes, Hume, Hegel, Bentham, Augustine, and Socrates all show up. Based on what you learned in this chapter, who do you think would end up on the side of the slave owners, and who would end up on the side of the abolitionists?

Important Thinkers

Socrates, Plato, Aristotle, St. Augustine, Thomas Hobbes, David Hume, Georg Wilhelm Friedrich Hegel, C.S. Lewis, Jeremy Bentham, Richard Brandt, Immanuel Kant, J.S. Mill.

Terms to Know

Cultural relativism, emotivism, historicism, historical relativism, moral relativism, objective and subjective, the romantic ideal, Ring of Gyges, romanticism, social contract theory, absolute moral norms, act utilitarianism, rule utilitarianism, consequentialism, deontology.

Further Reading

For issues of clarity and scope, I have not dealt with the more contemporary forms of moral relativism. For a contemporary version of emotivism, see A.J. Ayer, *Language, Truth, and Logic* (New York: Dover Publications, 1952). For a defense of the historicism of Hegel, see Richard Rorty, *Philosophy and the Mirror of Nature* (Princeton, NJ: Princeton University Press, 1979). To see how social contract theory has developed in the twentieth century, see John Rawls, *A Theory of Justice* (Cambridge, MA: Belknap Press, 1971). For a modern approach to Kant, see Robert Audi, *The Architecture of Reason* (Oxford: Oxford University Press, 2001). For an excellent and accessible investigation into moral relativism and natural law theory, see Montague Brown, *The Quest for Moral Foundations: An Introduction to Ethics* (Washington, DC: Georgetown University Press, 1996).

CHAPTER 2

Review Questions

1. What does Aquinas mean when he refers to the eternal law? How does the eternal law relate to the natural law? What do the terms "objective, subjective, perception, and reality" have to do with the eternal and natural law respectively?
2. What is the first principle of the natural law? What are the primary precepts? How are specific moral norms formed? What are examples of specific moral norms in accord with natural law morality?

3. What is the theory of basic goods? What are the basic goods according to John Finnis? How can these goods be used as a natural law criterion for moral judgments?
4. What is revealed morality? How do the Beatitudes correspond to the natural law? What is the relationship between revealed morality and the natural law?
5. What is proportionalism? How is authority understood in the Catholic Church? Why does the Pope say that proportionalism is not rooted in the Catholic moral tradition?

Important Thinkers

Aristotle, St. Anselm, St. Thomas Aquinas, St. John Paul II, Richard McCormick, John Finnis, Germain Grisez.

Terms to Know

Basic human goods, Beatitude, faith seeking understanding, *Fides et ratio*, eternal law, natural law, revealed morality, specific moral norms, double effect, evil (ontological, premoral, moral), proportionalism, *Veritatis splendor.*

Further Reading

Servais Pinckaers, O.P., *The Sources of Christian Ethics* (Washington, DC: The Catholic University of America, 1995); Jean Porter, *Nature as Reason: A Thomistic Theory of Natural Law* (London: Eerdman's Publishing Company, 1999); Martin Rhonheimer, *Natural Law and Practical Reason*, tr. Gerald Malsbary (New York: Fordham University Press, 2000); Richard Gula, *Reason Informed by Faith: Foundations of Catholic Morality* (New York: Paulist Press, 1989). For a sampling of the proportionalists' own appraisal and a presentation of their views, see Charles Curran, "Absolute Moral Norms" in *Christian Ethics: An Introduction*, Bernard Hoose, ed. (Collegeville, MN: The Liturgical Press, 1998): 72–83. Also see Bernard Hoose's *Proportionalism: The American Debate and Its European Roots* (Washington, DC: Georgetown University Press, 1987); and Richard McCormick and Paul Ramsey, eds. *Doing Evil to Achieve Good* (Chicago: Loyola University Press, 1978). For more recent treatments that relate proportionalism to natural law theory, see Brian Johnstone, "Objectivism, Basic Human Goods, and Proportionalism," *Studia Moralia*

43 (2005): 97–126; Todd A. Salzman, *What Are They Saying about Catholic Ethical Method* (New York: Paulist Press, 2003); for a concise summary of *Veritatis splendor*, see Servais Pinckaers, O.P., "An Encyclical for the Future: Veritatis splendor" in *Veritatis Splendor and the Renewal of Moral Theology*, J. Augustine DiNoia, O.P., and Romanus Cessario, O.P., eds. (Huntington, IN: Our Sunday Visitor Press, 1999): 11–71.

CHAPTER 3

Review Questions

1. Is moral relativism a suitable foundation for criticizing either the practice of female circumcision or efforts on the part of colonial or missionary forces to prohibit it?
2. Of all the possible foundations for ethical judgments and responsibility considered in the previous chapters, which do you find most applicable to the issue of female circumcision and why?
3. What has been the Catholic response to the practice of female circumcision? Explain how it draws from moral norms derivable both from the natural law and from revelation.
4. Why has Fiona decided that she is not going to believe in an objective moral law? What advice would you give her?

Important Thinkers

Ngũgĩ wa Thiong'o, Bénézet Bujo, Agbonkhianmeghe Orobator, Emmanuel Katongole, Lisa Sowle Cahill, M. Shawn Copeland.

Terms to Know

Catholic Relief Services, Colonial mentality, *Donum veritatis*, FGM.

Further Reading

Ngũgĩ wa Thiong'o, *A River Between* (Johannesburg, South Africa: Heinemann Educational Publishers, 1965); Agbonkhianmeghe E. Orobator, *Theology Brewed in an African Pot* (New York: Orbis, 2008); Bénézet Bujo, *African Theology in Its Social Context*, tr. John O'Donohue,

M. Afr (New York: Orbis, 1992); M. Shawn Copeland, *Enfleshing Freedom: Body, Race, and Being* (Minneapolis, MN: Fortress Press, 2010).

CHAPTER 4

Review Questions

1. What are the cardinal virtues? How are they attained? How do they relate to the powers of the soul as understood by Aristotle?
2. Define prudence. What is its relationship to conscience and the natural law? Is it possible to have an erroneous conscience? What difference does vincible and invincible ignorance make in this respect?
3. What is a just order or harmony with respect to the powers of the soul? How does the idea of right order as found in St. Anselm's treatment of the Incarnation pertain to this?
4. What are the stages in which the virtue of temperance is acquired? What does each stage entail and how does one progress from stage to stage?
5. What are the two parts of the virtue of fortitude? Give examples of each.

Important Thinkers

Socrates, Plato, Aristotle, St. Ambrose, St. Anselm.

Terms to Know

Cardinal virtues, prudence, intemperance, incontinence, continence, temperance, justice, fortitude, erroneous conscience, vincible and invincible ignorance, nutritive soul, appetitive soul, rational soul.

Further Reading

Aristotle, *Nicomachean Ethics*, 2nd ed., tr. Terence Irwin (Indianapolis, IN: Hackett Publishing Company, 1999); Julia Annas, "Virtue and Eudaimonism," in *Virtue and Vice*, Ellen Paul, Fred Miller, and Jeffrey Paul, eds. (Cambridge: Cambridge University Press, 1998); G.E.M. Anscombe, "Modern Moral Philosophy," *Philosophy* 33 (1958): 1–19.

CHAPTER 5

Review Questions

1. What is the relationship of grace and human action? Is human action irrelevant to the virtues of grace? When God infuses the soul with virtues, does it cancel out the cardinal virtues?
2. How is St. Thérèse of Lisieux's life exemplary of the virtues of grace?
3. What is the difference between *fides qua creditur* and *fides quae creditur*? How can it be virtuous to believe in something? What are the stages leading to theological faith?
4. What is the difference between the "disillusioned sensible man" and "the fool's way"? Respond using the terms *ad finem* and *in finem*.
5. What are the four loves? What is the main difference between the divine love and the natural loves? Is the divine love a rival to the natural loves?
6. What factors account for the rise of modern atheism? What are the different kinds of atheism? How does *Gaudium et spes* suggest that modern atheism be countered?

Important Thinkers

St. Augustine, St. Jerome, St. Francis of Assisi, St. Thomas Aquinas, St. Thérèse of Lisieux, C.S. Lewis, Niccolò Machiavelli, Isaac Newton, Ludwig von Feurbach, Sigmund Freud, Karl Marx.

Terms to Know

Ad finem/in finem, *agape*, *storge*, *filia*, *eros*, faith, hope, love, infused cardinal virtues, *Fides qua creditur*, *fides quae creditur*, grace, the fool's way, the way of the disillusioned sensible man, R.E.N.E.W., extra-volitional factors (internal and external), mortal and venial sin, works of mercy.

Further Reading

William C. Mattison III, "Can Christians Possess the Acquired Virtues?," *Theological Studies* 72 (2011): 558–85; R.E. Houser, *The Cardinal Virtues: Aquinas, Albert, and Philip the Chancellor* (Toronto: Pontifical Institute of Mediaeval Studies, 2004); Michael Sherwin O.P., *By Knowledge & By Love: Charity and Knowledge in the Moral Theology of St. Thomas Aquinas* (Washington, DC: CUA Press, 2005); Angela McKay-Knobel, "Two Theories of Christian Virtue," in *America Catholic Philosophical Quarterly* 84/3 (Summer 2010): 599–618.

CHAPTER 6

Review Questions

1. Why do proponents of the isolation thesis reject the unity of the virtues? How might proponents of the unity of thesis respond to these objections? Reply using specific examples.
2. What relevance does the unity of the virtues have for the Catholic moral tradition? What are three takeaways from the high moral standards set by Christ in Matthew 5:17–37?
3. What is the difference between a morality of obligation perspective and a morality of happiness perspective? How do these differing understandings of morality result in differing understandings of freedom?
4. Who is offering Fiona better advice, Glaucon, or Augustine and Aquinas?

Important Thinkers

Socrates, Plato, Aristotle, St. Augustine, St. Thomas Aquinas.

Terms to Know

Isolation thesis, unity of the virtues, unity thesis, morality of obligation, morality of happiness, freedom of indifference, freedom for excellence, transitive, intransitive.

Further Reading

William C. Mattison III, *Introducing Moral Theology: True Happiness and the Virtues* (Grand Rapids, MI: Brazos Press, 2008); Andrew Kim, "Thomas Aquinas on the Connection of the Virtues" (PhD diss., The Catholic University of America, 2013); Andrew Kim, "Progress in the Good: A Defense of the Thomistic Unity Thesis," *Journal of Moral Theology* 3.1 (January 2014): 147–74; Jean Porter, "The Unity of the Virtues and the Ambiguity of Goodness: A Reappraisal of Aquinas's Theory of the Virtues," *The Journal of Religious Ethics* 21:1 (Spring 1993); T. Penner, "The Unity of Virtue," *The Philosophical Review* 82 (1973): 35–68; Daniel McInerny, *The Difficult Good: A Thomistic Approach to Moral Conflict and Human Happiness* (New York: Fordham University Press, 2006); Servais Pinckaers, O.P., *The Sources of Christian Ethics* (Washington, DC: Catholic University of America Press, 1995); Julia Anna, *The Morality of Happiness* (New York: Oxford University Press, 1993).

CHAPTER 7

Review Questions

1. What are "the quartet of themes" found in the Scripture and in the writings of the early fathers? How do these themes relate to each other and in what way are they applicable to the modern world?
2. Are love-mercy-forgiveness and justice incompatible? Is it possible to think about the former independently of the latter? What does the parable of the prodigal son seem to indicate about the relationship of love and justice?
3. In what ways does the New Testament reaffirm the themes of justice of the Old Testament? Specifically, what role does Jesus play according to the worldview of Christians with respect to these themes?

Important Thinkers

Pope Emeritus Benedict XVI, St. Clement of Alexandria, St. Cyprian of Carthage, St. John Chrysostom, Julian of Norwich.

Terms to Know

Ius, justice as rights, justice as right order, the *Magnificat, mishpat*, primary justice, the Prodigal Son, retificatory justice, *suum cuique, tsedeqa*.

Further Reading

Pope Benedict XVI, *Caritas in veritate*, Encyclical Letter addressed by the Supreme Pontiff Pope Benedict XVI to the Bishops, Priests, and Deacons, Men and Women Religious, the Lay Faithful, and All People of Good Will on Integral Human Development in Charity and Truth (Vatican City: Libreria Editrice Vaticana, 2009); Nicholas Wolterstorff,

Justice: Rights and Wrongs (Princeton, NJ: Princeton University Press, 2008); Alasdair MacIntyre, *Whose Justice? Which Rationality?* (Notre Dame, IN: University of Notre Dame Press, 1988); Brian Tierney, *The Idea of Natural Rights: Studies on Natural Rights, Natural Law, and Church Law 1150–1625* (Grand Rapids, MI: Eerdman's Publishing Company, 1997).

CHAPTER 8

Review Questions

1. What are the principles of CST and how do they relate both to each other and to the themes of justice explored in the previous chapter?
2. How does C.S. Lewis's analogy of a fleet of ships help illuminate aspects of CST?
3. What does the preferential option for the poor entail? What does it not entail? Respond with relevant passages from the Scripture.
4. Is CST practical? Does it matter? In what ways do sweatshops violate CST and what can be done about it? What do you make of the actions taken by activists like Jim Keady?

Important Thinkers

Pope Leo XIII, St. John Paul II, Pope Emeritus Benedict XVI, Pope Francis.

Terms to Know

Human dignity, community, the common good, participation, subsidiarity, preferential option for the poor, stewardship, solidarity.

Further Reading

Pontifical Council for Justice and Peace, *Compendium of the Social Doctrine of the Church* (Vatican City: Libreria Editrice Vaticana, 2004); Joe Holland, *Modern Catholic Social Teaching* (New York: Paulist Press, 2003); Kenneth R. Himes O.F.M., *Responses to 101 Questions on Catholic Social Teaching* (New York: Paulist Press, 2001). J. Brian Benestad, *Church, State, and Society: An Introduction to Catholic Social Doctrine* (Washington, DC: CUA Press, 2011); Jozef D. Zalot and Benedict Guevin, O.S.B., *Catholic Ethics in Today's World* (Winona, MN: Anselm Academic, 2008).

CHAPTER 9

Review Questions

1. Are the claims in *The Challenge of Peace* contradictory? Is it possible to consistently hold that war and pacifism are both legitimate moral options?
2. What conditions need to be observed in order to avoid total warfare? Is this realistic? How would you respond to the argument that observing moral injunctions in war gives too much of an advantage to the enemy?
3. Why does Stanley Hauerwas think that being a faithful Christian necessarily entails a pacifist outlook? Do you agree or disagree with this view?
4. Is the use of predator drones intrinsically immoral? Can the use of predator drones in civilian areas pass the conditions of double effect? Does the use of predator drones in civilian areas square with just war theory if collateral damage is foreseeable and unavoidable?

Important Thinkers

St. Augustine, St. Thomas Aquinas, Stanley Hauerwas, John Howard Yoder.

Terms to Know

Ius ad bellum, ius in bello, discrimination, pacifism, proportionality, total war mentality.

Further Reading

Michael Walzer, *Just and Unjust Wars* (New York: Basic Books, 1992); Richard B. Miller, *Interpretation of Conflict Ethics: Pacifism and the Just War Tradition* (Chicago: University of Chicago Press, 1991); Lisa Sowle Cahill, *Love Your Enemies: Discipleship, Pacifism, and Just War Theory* (Minneapolis, MN: Fortress Press, 1994); Kenneth Himes, "Intervention, Just War, and U.S. National Security," *Theological Studies* 65, no. 1 (March 2004): 141–57; Eileen P. Flynn, *How Just Is the War on Terror? A Question of Morality* (New York: Paulist Press, 2007).

CHAPTER 10

Review Questions

1. What is the relation of the capacities approach to the assumption of selective human dignity? According to the capacities approach, what distinguishes a human person from a human nonperson? How does John Finnis reply to the capacities approach?
2. What is the principle of universal human dignity affirmed by the Catholic moral tradition? How does revelation perfect the ordinary understanding of human dignity we can gain through reason alone?
3. What according to Thomas Merton is the "pattern and prototype" of all human sin and how does this relate to the assumption of selective human dignity? How does the parable of the Good Samaritan respond to this assumption and affirm the principle of universal human dignity?

Important Thinkers

Thomas Merton, Ronald Dworkin, John Finnis.

Terms to Know

The principle of universal human dignity, the assumption of selective human dignity, the pattern and prototype of sin, the capacities approach, human person, human nonperson, *Nostra aetate*.

Further Reading

Paul VI, *Humanae vitae*, Encyclical Letter of the Supreme Pontiff Paul VI on the Regulation of Birth (Vatican City: Libreria Editrice Vaticana, 1968); John Paul II, *Evangelium vitae*, Encyclical Letter Addressed by the Supreme Pontiff John Paul II to the Bishops, Priests, Deacons, Men and Women Religious, Lay Faithful, and All People of Good Will on the Value and Inviolability of Human Life (Vatican City: Libreria Editrice Vaticana, 1995); Congregation of the Doctrine of the Faith, *Donum vitae*, Instruction on Respect for Human Life in Its Origin and on the Dignity of Procreation, Replies to Certain Questions of the Day (Vatican City: Libreria Editrice Vaticana, 1987); Congregation of the Doctrine of the Faith. *Dignitas personae*, Instruction on Certain Bioethical Questions

(Vatican City: Libreria Editrice Vaticana, 2008); Anthony Fisher, O.P., *Catholic Bioethics for a New Millennium* (Cambridge: Cambridge University Press, 2012).

CHAPTER 11

Review Questions

1. Why does Catholic teaching not allow for the practice of contraception? How is this teaching grounded in the principle of universal human dignity?
2. What does Catholic teaching say about abortion? Is it possible to advocate for abortion rights without endorsing some version of the assumption of selective human dignity?
3. Are there any activities taking place in the world that both Catholics and pro-choice advocates could agree are grave affronts to women?
4. How can contemplating the Blessed Virgin Mary reframe the conversation about commercial surrogacy? What does it mean to respect the dignity of women?

Important Thinkers

Pope Paul VI, St. John Paul II, Elizabeth Johnson, Debra Satz.

Terms to Know

Abortion, commercial surrogacy, contraception, gendercide, procreative, unitive.

Further Reading

John C. Ford and Germain Grisez, "Contraception and the Infallibility of the Ordinary Magisterium," *Theological Studies* 39 (1978): 258–312; Charles E. Curran, "The Catholic Moral Tradition in Bioethics," in *The Story of Bioethics*, Jennifer K. Walter and Eran P. Klein, eds. (Washington, DC: Georgetown University Press, 2003): 113–130; John R. Connery, S.J., *Abortion: The Development of the Roman Catholic Perspective* (Chicago: Loyola University Press, 1977); William E. May, *Catholic Bioethics and the Gift of Human Life*, 2nd ed. (Huntington, IN: Our Sunday Visitor Press, 2008).

CHAPTER 12

Review Questions

1. What is euthanasia and why is this practice forbidden by Catholic moral teaching? What is the Catholic teaching regarding ANH and when it is and is not morally obligatory to provide this or other ordinary or extraordinary means of preserving life?
2. What is the "peaceful exit pill?" Does the distribution, manufacturing, and prescribing of this pill violate Catholic moral teaching?
3. What is "the problem of suffering?" How does a theology of providence respond to it? How does this help inform the U.S. bishops' directive to help patients appreciate "the Christian understanding of redemptive suffering?" (*ERD* no. 61)

Important Thinkers

C.S. Lewis, Thomas Aquinas, John Finnis.

Terms to Know

ANH, excessive burden, involuntary euthanasia, voluntary euthanasia, the peaceful exit pill, redemptive suffering, dysteological suffering.

Further Reading

Benedict M. Ashley and Kevin D. O'Rourke, *Ethics of Health Care: An Introductory Textbook* (Washington, DC: Georgetown University Press, 2002); Theo Boer, "Recurring Themes in the Debate about Euthanasia and Assisted Suicide," *The Journal of Religious Ethics* 35, no. 3 (2007): 529–55; Arthur Dyck, *Life's Worth: The Case Against Assisted Suicide* (Grand Rapids, MI: William B. Eerdman's Publishing Company, 2002); Neil Gorsuch, *The Future of Assisted Suicide and Euthanasia* (Princeton, NJ: Princeton University Press, 2006); John Keown, ed., *Euthanasia Examined: Ethical, Clinical, and Legal Perspectives* (Cambridge: Cambridge University Press, 1995); Nicanor Pier Giorgio Austriaco, O.P., *Biomedicine and Beatitude: An Introduction to Catholic Bioethics* (Washington, DC: CUA Press, 2011).

Bibliography

Adams, Robert Merrihew. *A Theory of Virtue: Excellence in Being for the Good* (Oxford: Clarendon Press, 2006).

Annas, Julia. *The Morality of Happiness* (New York: Oxford University Press, 1994).

———. "Virtue and Eudaimonism," in *Virtue and Vice*, Ellen Paul, Fred Miller, and Jeffrey Paul, eds. (Cambridge: Cambridge University Press, 1998).

Anscombe, G.E.M. "Modern Moral Philosophy," *Philosophy* 33: 124 (January 1958): 1–19.

Anselm, *Why God Became Man, in Anselm of Canterbury the Major Works*, tr. Janet Fairweather (Oxford: Oxford University Press, 1998).

Aquinas, Thomas. *Summa Theologiae*, trans. Fathers of the English Dominican Province (New York: Benziger, 1948).

———. *Questions on Virtue: Quaestio disputata de virtutibus in communi, Quaestio disputata de virtutibus cardinalibus, de fraterni correctionis*. E.M. Atkins and Thomas Williams, eds., tr. E.M. Atkins (Cambridge: Cambridge University Press, 2005).

———. *On Love and Charity: Readings from the Commentary on the Sentences of Peter Lombard*, tr. Peter A. Kwasniewski (Washington, DC: CUA Press, 2008).

Aristotle. *De Anima* (On the Soul), tr. Hugh Lawson-Tancred (London: Penguin Books, 1986).

———. *Nicomachean Ethics*, tr. Terence Irwin 2nd ed. (Indianapolis, IN: Hackett Publishing Company, 1999).

Ashley, Benedict M., and O'Rourke, Kevin D. *Ethics of Health Care: An Introductory Textbook* (Washington, DC: Georgetown University Press, 2002).

Audi, Robert. *The Architecture of Reason* (Oxford: Oxford University Press, 2001).

Augustine. *Contra Academicos* (Against the Academics), Johannes Quasten and Joseph C. Plumpe, eds., tr. John J. O'Meara (Westminster, MD: The Newman Press, 1950).

———. *De moribus ecclesiae catholicae et de moribus Manichaeorum.* (On the Morals of the Catholic Church Against the Manicheans). CSEL 90. J.B. Bauer, ed. (Vienna, 1992).

———. *De Doctrina Christiana* (On Christian Teaching), tr. R.P.H. Green (Oxford: Oxford University Press, 2008).

———. *Enchiridion* (CCEL 78).

————. Letter 167 to Jerome (CSEL 44): 586–609.

Austriaco, O.P., Nicanor Pier Giorgio. *Biomedicine and Beatitude: An Introduction to Catholic Bioethics* (Washington, DC: CUA Press, 2011).

Ayer, A.J. *Language, Truth, and Logic* (New York: Dover Publications, 1952).

Barron, Robert. *Catholicism: A Journey to the Heart of the Faith* (New York: Image Books, 2011).

Benedict XVI, *Deus caritas est*, Encyclical Letter addressed by the Supreme Pontiff Pope Benedict XVI to the Bishops, Priests, and Deacons, Men and Women Religious, and all the Lay Faithful on Christian Love (Vatican City: Libreria Editrice Vaticana, 2005).

————. *Spe salvi*, Encyclical Letter addressed by the Supreme Pontiff Pope Benedict XVI to the Bishops, Priests, and Deacons, Men and Women Religious, and all the Lay Faithful on Christian Hope (Vatican City: Libreria Editrice Vaticana, 2007).

————. *Caritas in veritate*, Encyclical Letter addressed by the Supreme Pontiff Pope Benedict XVI to all the Bishops of the Catholic Church on Integral Human Development in Charity and Truth (Vatican City: Libreria Editrice Vaticana, 2009).

Benestad, J. Brian. *Church, State, and Society: An Introduction to Catholic Social Doctrine* (Washington, DC: CUA Press, 2011).

Bentham, Jeremy. *The Principles of Morals and Legislation* (New York: Hafner Press, 1948).

Boer, Theo. "Recurring Themes in the Debate about Euthanasia and Assisted Suicide," *The Journal of Religious Ethics* 35, no. 3 (2007): 529–55.

Brody, Baruch. "The Problem of Exceptions in Medical Ethics," in *Doing Evil to Achieve Good*, Paul Ramsey and Richard McCormick, eds. (Lanham, MD: University Press of America, 1985): 54–67.

Brown, Montague. *The Quest for Moral Foundations: An Introduction to Ethics* (Washington, DC: Georgetown University Press, 1996).

Bujo, Bénézet. *African Theology in its Social Context*, tr. John O'Donohue, M. Afr (New York: Orbis, 1992).

Cahill, Lisa Sowle. *Love Your Enemies: Discipleship, Pacifism, and Just War Theory* (Minneapolis, MN: Fortress Press, 1994).

————. *Sex, Gender & Christian Ethics* (Cambridge: Cambridge University Press, 1996).

Camosy, Charles. *Abortion: Beyond Polarization* (Grand Rapids, MI: Eerdman's, Forthcoming 2015).

The Catechism of the Catholic Church, 2nd ed. (Vatican City: Libreria Editrice Vaticana, 1997).

The Catholic Bible New American Bible Revised Edition (Oxford: Oxford University Press, 2007).

Cavanaugh, William. *The Myth of Religious Violence* (Oxford: Oxford University Press, 2009).

Chang, M. "Wombs for Rent: India's Commercial Surrogacy," *Harvard International Review* 31.1 (2009): 11–13.

Compendium to the Catechism of the Catholic Church (Washington, DC: Libreria Editrice Vaticana, 2006).

Congregation of the Doctrine of the Faith. *Instruction on Certain Aspects of the "Theology of Liberation"* (Vatican City: Libreria Editrice Vaticana, 1984).

———. *Donum vitae*, Instruction on Respect for Human Life in its Origin and on the Dignity of Procreation, Replies to Certain Questions of the Day (Vatican City: Libreria Editrice Vaticana, 1987).

———. *Donum veritatis* (Vatican City: Libreria Editrice Vaticana, 1990).

———. *Dignitas personae*, Instruction on Certain Bioethical Questions (Vatican City: Libreria Editrice Vaticana, 2008).

Connery, S.J., John R. *Abortion: The Development of the Roman Catholic Perspective* (Chicago: Loyola University Press, 1977).

Copeland, M. Shawn. *Enfleshing Freedom: Body, Race, and Being* (Minneapolis, MN: Fortress Press, 2010).

Curran, Charles. "Absolute Moral Norms," in Bernard Hoose, ed. *Christian Ethics: An Introduction* (Collegeville, MN: The Liturgical Press, 1998).

———. "The Catholic Moral Tradition in Bioethics," in *The Story of Bioethics*, Jennifer K. Walter and Eran P. Klein, eds. (Washington, DC: Georgetown University Press, 2003).

Deonandan, Raywat. "The Ethics of Surrogacy," *India Currents* (February 3, 2012). https://www.indiacurrents.com/articles/2012/02/03/ethics-surrogacy.

Dickenson, Donna. *Property, Women, and Politics: Subjects as Objects* (Cambridge: Polity Press, 1997).

Dyck, Arthur. *Life's Worth: The Case Against Assisted Suicide* (Grand Rapids, MI: William B. Eerdman's Publishing Company, 2002).

Elshtain, Jean Bethke. "Citizenship and Armed Civic Virtue: Some Questions on the Commitment to Public Life," in *Community in America: The Challenge of Habits of the Heart*, Charles H. Reynolds and Ralph Norman, eds. (Berkeley: University of California Press, 1988).

Farley, Margaret A. *Just Love: A Framework for Christian Sexual Ethics* (New York: Continuum, 2006).

Finnis, John. *Natural Law and Natural Rights* (Oxford: Clarendon Press, 1980).

Fisher, O.P., Anthony. *Catholic Bioethics for a New Millennium* (Cambridge: Cambridge University Press, 2012).

Flynn, Eileen P. *How Just Is the War on Terror? A Question of Morality* (New York: Paulist Press, 2007).

Ford, S.J., John. "The Morality of Obliteration Bombing," *Theological Studies* 5 (1944): 259–309.

Ford, John C. and Grisez, Germain. "Contraception and the Infallibility of the Ordinary Magisterium," *Theological Studies* 39 (1978): 258–312.

Francis, *Evangelii gaudium*, Apostolic Exhortation of the Holy Father Francis to the Bishops, Clergy, Consecrated Persons, and the Lay Faithful on the Proclamation of the Gospel in Today's Word (Vatican City: Libreria Editrice Vaticana, 2013).

————. *Lumen fidei*, Encyclical Letter addressed by the Supreme Pontiff Pope Francis to all the Bishops, Priests, and Deacons, Consecrated Persons, and the Lay Faithful on Faith (Vatican City: Libreria Editrice Vaticana, 2013).

Gaillardetz, Richard R. *By What Authority?: A Primer on Scripture, the Magisterium, and the Sense of the Faithful* (Collegeville, MN: Liturgical Press, 2003).

Gilbert, S.F. "Ecological Developmental Biology: Developmental Biology Meets the Real World," *Developmental Biology* 233 (2001): 1–12.

Gorsuch, Neil. *The Future of Assisted Suicide and Euthanasia* (Princeton, NJ: Princeton University Press, 2006).

Grisez, Germain. *The Way of the Lord Jesus: Christian Moral Principles* (Chicago: Franciscan Herald Press, 1983).

Gula, Richard. *Reason Informed by Faith: Foundations of Catholic Morality* (New York: Paulist Press, 1989).

Hamlin, J. Kiley, Wynn, Karen, and Bloom, Paul. "Social Evaluation by Preverbal Infants," *Nature* 450 (2007): 557–9.

Hauerwas, Stanley. "Courage Exemplified," in *The Hauerwas Reader*, John Berkman and Michael Cartwright, eds. (Durham, NC: Duke University Press, 2001).

————. "Should War Be Eliminated: A Thought Experiment," in *The Hauerwas Reader*, John Berkman and Michael Cartwright, eds. (Durham, NC: Duke University Press, 2001).

Hauerwas, Stanley and Pinches, Charles. *Christians among the Virtues: Theological Conversations with Ancient and Modern Ethics* (Notre Dame, IN: University of Notre Dame Press, 1997).

Hegel, G.W.F. Philosophy of Right, Preface, in *Hegel's Philosophy of Right*, tr. T.M. Knox (Oxford: Clarendon Press, 1952).

Himes, O.F.M., Kenneth R. *Responses to 101 Questions on Catholic Social Teaching* (New York: Paulist Press, 2001).

————"Intervention, Just War, and U.S. National Security," *Theological Studies* 65, no. 1 (March 2004): 141–57.

Holland, Joe. *Modern Catholic Social Teaching* (New York: Paulist Press, 2003).

Hoose, Bernard. *Proportionalism: The American Debate and Its European Roots* (Washington, DC: Georgetown University Press, 1987).

Houser, R.E. *The Cardinal Virtues: Aquinas, Albert, and Philip the Chancellor* (Toronto: Pontifical Institute of Mediaeval Studies, 2004).

Hume, David. An Enquiry Concerning the Principles of Morals, Section IX, Part I, in *Enquiries*, L.A. Selby-Bigge, ed. (Oxford: Clarendon Press, 1975).

————. *An Enquiry Concerning Human Understanding*, Section IV, Part I.

John Paul I. *Angelus September 10* (Vatican City: Libreria Editrice Vaticana, 1978).

John Paul II. *Love and Responsibility*, tr. H.T. Willets (New York: Farar, Straus and Giroux, Inc., 1981).

————. *Centesimus annus*, Encyclical Letter addressed by the Supreme Pontiff Pope John Paul II to all the Bishops of the Catholic Church Regarding the 100th anniversary of *Rerum novarum* (Vatican City: Libreria Editrice Vaticana, 1991).

———. *Veritatis splendor*, Encyclical Letter addressed by the Supreme Pontiff Pope John Paul II to all the Bishops of the Catholic Church Regarding Certain Fundamental Questions of the Church's Moral Teaching (Vatican City: Libreria Editrice Vaticana, 1993).

———. *Evangelium vitae*, Encyclical Letter Addressed by the Supreme Pontiff John Paul II to the Bishops, Priests, Deacons, Men and Women Religious, Lay Faithful, and All People of Good Will on the Value and Inviolability of Human Life (Vatican City: Libreria Editrice Vaticana, 1995).

———. *Sollicitudo rei socialis*, in *Catholic Social Thought: The Documentary Heritage*, David O'Brien and Thomas Shannon, eds. (Maryknoll, NY: Orbis, 1995), no. 38.

———. *Fides et ratio*, Encyclical Letter of the Supreme Pontiff John Paul II to the Bishops of the Catholic Church on the Relationship between Faith and Reason (Vatican City: Libreria Editrice Vaticana, 1998).

———. *Mulieris dignitatem*, Apostolic Letter of the Supreme Pontiff on the Dignity and Vocation of Women on the Occasion of the Marian Year (Vatican City: Libreria Editrice Vaticana, 1998).

———. *Man and Woman He Created Them: A Theology of the Body* (Boston: Pauline Books and Media, 2006).

Johnson, Elizabeth. *Truly Our Sister: A Theology of Mary in the Communion of the Saints* (New York: Continuum International Publishing, 2003).

Johnstone, Brian. "Objectivism, Basic Human Goods, and Proportionalism," *Studia Moralia* 43 (2005): 97–126.

Kant, Immanuel. Grounding for the Metaphysics of Morals, in *Kant's Ethical Philosophy* tr. James W. Ellington (Indianapolis, IN: Hackett Publishing Company, 1983).

Katongole, Emmanuel and Rice, Chris. *Reconciling All Things: A Christian Vision for Justice, Peace, and Healing* (Downers Grove, IL: IVP Books, 2008).

Keenan, S.J., James F. *Catholic Theological Ethics in the World Church: The Plenary Papers from the First Cross-cultural Conference on Catholic Theological Ethics* (New York: Continuum, 2007).

Keown, John, ed., *Euthanasia Examined: Ethical, Clinical, and Legal Perspectives*, John Keown, ed. (Cambridge: Cambridge University Press, 1995).

Kim, Andrew. "Thomas Aquinas on the Connection of the Virtues" (PhD diss., The Catholic University of America, 2013).

———. "Have the Manicheans Returned? An Augustinian Alternative to Situationist Psychology," *Studies in Christian Ethics* 26.4 (November 2013): 451–72.

———. "Progress in the Good: A Defense of the Thomistic Unity Thesis," *The Journal of Moral Theology* 3.1 (January 2014): 147–74.

———. "The Mother of God and Commercial Surrogacy," The Catholic Moral Theology Blog, entry posted September 27, 2013, http://catholicmoraltheology .com/the-mother-of-god-and-commercial-surrogacy/ [accessed April 7, 2014].

———. "A Catholic Appeal to the Pro-Choice Movement in the U.S.," The Catholic Moral Theology Blog, entry posted February 13, 2014, http://catholicmoraltheology.com/a-catholic-appeal-to-the-pro-choice-movement-in-the-u-s/ [accessed April 7, 2014].

Leo XIII. *Rerum novarum*, Encyclical Letter of the Supreme Pontiff Leo XIII on Labor and Capital (Vatican City: Libreria Editrice Vaticana, 1891).

Lewis, C.S. *The Problem of Pain* (San Francisco: Harper Collins, 1940).

———. *Mere Christianity* (San Francisco: Harper Collins, 1952).

———. *The Four Loves* (New York: Harvest, 1960).

———. *A Grief Observed* (San Francisco: Harper Collins, 1961).

Lyotard, Jean-François. *The Postmodern Condition: A Report on Knowledge* (Minneapolis: University of Minnesota Press, 1984).

MacIntyre, Alasdair. *Whose Justice? Which Rationality?* (Notre Dame, IN: University of Notre Dame Press, 1988).

Massingale, Bryan N. "A Parallel that Limps: The Rhetoric of Slavery in Pro-Life Discourse of the U.S. Bishops" in *Voting and Holiness: Catholic Perspectives on Political Participation*, Nicholas P. Cafardi, ed. (New York: Paulist Press, 2012): 158–77.

Mattison III, William C. *Introducing Moral Theology: True Happiness and the Virtues* (Grand Rapids, MI: Brazos Press, 2008).

———. "The Changing Face of Natural Law: The Necessity of Belief for Natural Law Norm Specification," *Journal of the Society of Christian Ethics* 27, no. 1 (2007): 251–77.

———. "Can Christians Possess the Acquired Virtues?," *Theological Studies* 72 (2011): 558–85.

May, William E. *Catholic Bioethics and the Gift of Human Life*, 2nd ed. (Huntington, IN: Our Sunday Visitor Press, 2008).

McCormick, Richard A. "The New Medicine and Morality," *Theology Digest* 21 (Winter 1973).

McCormick, Richard and Ramsey, Paul, eds. *Doing Evil to Achieve Good* (Chicago: Loyola University Press, 1978).

McInerny, Daniel. *The Difficult Good: A Thomistic Approach to Moral Conflict and Human Happiness* (New York: Fordham University Press, 2006).

McKay-Knobel, Angela. "Two Theories of Christian Virtue," in *America Catholic Philosophical Quarterly* 84/3 (Summer 2010): 599–618.

Merton, Thomas. *The Seven Storey Mountain: An Autobiography of Faith* (New York: Harvest Books, 1948).

Mesle, Robert C. "The Problem of Genuine Evil: A Critique of John Hick's Theodicy," *Journal of Religion* 66 (1986): 412–430.

Mill, J.S. *Utilitarianism*, Ch. 2, Oskar Piest, ed. (Indianapolis, IN: Bobbs-Merrill, 1957).

Miller, Richard B. *Interpretation of Conflict Ethics: Pacifism and the Just War Tradition* (Chicago: University of Chicago Press, 1991).

O'Brien, David and Shannon, Thomas, eds., *Catholic Social Thought: The Documentary Heritage* (Maryknoll, NY: Orbis Books, 1995).

Odozor, C.S.Sp., Paulinus Ikechukwu. *Moral Theology in an Age of Renewal: A Study of the Catholic Tradition since Vatican II* (Notre Dame, IN: University of Notre Dame Press, 2003).

Orobator, Agbonkhianmeghe E. *Theology Brewed in an African Pot* (New York: Orbis, 2008).

Palattiyl, G., et al. "Globalization and Cross-border Reproductive Services: Ethical Implications of Surrogacy in India for Social Work," *International Social Work* 53.5 (2010): 686–700.

Paul VI. *Humanae vitae*, Encyclical Letter of the Supreme Pontiff Paul VI on the Regulation of Birth (Vatican City: Libreria Editrice Vaticana, 1968).

———. *Marialis cultus*, Apostolic Exhortation of the Holy Father Paul VI to the Bishops, Clergy, Consecrated Persons, and the Lay Faithful on the Right Ordering and Development of Devotion to the Blessed Virgin Mary (Vatican City: Libreria Editrice Vaticana, 1974).

Penner, T. "The Unity of Virtue," *The Philosophical Review* 82 (1973): 35–68.

Pinckaers, O.P., Servais. *The Sources of Christian Ethics* (Washington, DC: The Catholic University of America, 1995).

———. "An Encyclical for the Future: *Veritatis splendor*," in *Veritatis Splendor and the Renewal of Moral Theology*, J. Augustine DiNoia, O.P., and Romanus Cessario, O.P., eds. (Huntington, IN.: Our Sunday Visitor Press, 1999): 11–71.

Plato, Gorgias, in *Plato: Complete Works*, John Cooper, ed. (Indianapolis, IN: Hackett Publishing Company, 1997).

———. Theaetetus, in *Plato: Complete Works*, John Cooper, ed. (Indianapolis, IN: Hackett Publishing Company, 1997).

———. The Republic, in *Plato: Complete Works*, John Cooper, ed. (Indianapolis, IN: Hackett Publishing Company, 1997).

Pontifical Council for Justice and Peace, *Compendium of the Social Doctrine of the Church* (Vatican City: Libreria Editrice Vaticana, 2004).

Porter, Jean. "The Unity of the Virtues and the Ambiguity of Goodness: A Reappraisal of Aquinas's Theory of the Virtues," *The Journal of Religious Ethics* 21: 1 (1993): 137–63.

Rawls, John. *A Theory of Justice* (Cambridge, MA: Belknap Press, 1971).

Rhonheimer, Martin. *Natural Law and Practical Reason*, tr. Gerald Malsbary (New York: Fordham University Press, 2000).

Rist, J.M. *Stoic Philosophy* (Cambridge: Cambridge University Press, 1969).

Salzman, Todd A. *What Are They Saying about Catholic Ethical Method* (New York: Paulist Press, 2003).

Satz, Debra. *Why Some Things Should Not Be for Sale: The Moral Limits of Markets* (Oxford: Oxford University Press, 2010).

Shah, N. "Race, Class, Gender and Economics: A Discussion about the Indian Commercial Surrogacy Boom" *Fem* 2 (2012).

Shalev, C. *Birth Power: The Case for Surrogacy* (New Haven, CT: Yale University Press, 1989).

Sherwin O.P., Michael. *By Knowledge & By Love: Charity and Knowledge in the Moral Theology of St. Thomas Aquinas* (Washington, DC: CUA Press, 2005).

Taylor, Charles. *A Secular Age* (Cambridge, MA: Harvard University Press, 2007).

Tierney, Brian. *The Idea of Natural Rights: Studies on Natural Rights, Natural Law, and Church Law 1150–1625* (Grand Rapids, MI: Eerdman's Publishing Company, 1997).

United States Conference of Catholic Bishops, *Ethical and Religious Directives for Catholic Health Care Services*, 5th ed. (Washington, DC: United States Conference of Catholic Bishops, 2009).

Vatican. "Pope's Discourse to South African Bishops," *Zenit.com*, April 25, 2014, http://www.zenit.org/en/articles/pope-s-discourse-to-south-african-bishops [accessed April 27, 2014].

Vatican II. *Dei Verbum*, Dogmatic Constitution on Divine Revelation, tr. Austin Flannery (Dublin, Ireland: Dominican Publications, 1996).

———. *Lumen gentium*, Dogmatic Constitution on the Church, tr. Austin Flannery (Dublin, Ireland: Dominican Publications, 1996).

———. *Nostra aetate*, Declaration on the Relation of the Church to non-Christian Religions, tr. Austin Flannery (Dublin, Ireland: Dominican Publications, 1996).

———. *Gaudium et spes*, Pastoral Constitution on the Church in the Modern World, Austin Flannery, O.P., ed. (Dublin, Ireland: Dominican Publications, 2007).

Walsh, William, S.J., and Langan, John, S.J. "Patristic Social Consciousness—The Church and the Poor," in *The Faith That Does Justice*, John C. Haughey, ed. (New York: Paulist Press, 1977).

Walzer, Michael. *Just and Unjust Wars* (New York: Basic Books, 1992).

Wolf, Susan. "Moral Psychology and the Unity of the Virtues," *Ratio* XX (June 2007).

Wolterstorff, Nicholas. *Justice: Rights and Wrongs* (Princeton, NJ: Princeton University Press, 2008).

Yoder, John Howard. *The Original Revolution* (Scottdale, PA: Herald Press, 1971).

———. *The Politics of Jesus*, 2nd ed. (Grand Rapids, MI: Eerdman's Publishing Company, 1994), 1–59.

Zalot, Jozef D., and Guevin, O.S.B., Benedict. *Catholic Ethics in Today's World* (Winona, MN: Anselm Academic, 2008).

Index

Made in United States
Troutdale, OR
01/12/2024

16899158R10136